THROUGH
HER
Opera Glasses

THROUGH
HER
Opera Glasses

The Collected Letters of Betty Harbert's
1930–1931 European Tour
with Fictionalized Narrative by Her Daughter

Betty Harbert and Pat Butler

IGUANA

Publisher: Meghan Behse
Editor: Holly Warren
Front cover design: Meghan Behse

ISBN 978-1-77180-549-0 (paperback)
ISBN 978-1-77180-550-6 (epub)

This is an original print edition of *Through Her Opera Glasses*.

To my beloved mother

Table of Contents

Note to the Reader

Interspersed with letters written by my mother, Betty Harbert, I have included a fictional narrative. Even though the letters describe true places, people, and events, I have elaborated on them in the service of the story, and I assure you, the added narrative is entirely made up.

The letters, however, have been copied almost verbatim, with the spelling errors and inconsistencies inherent in letters handwritten in ink. To avoid boring the reader, I have omitted a few comments about Betty's distant relatives' well-being, believing that no one is all that concerned about Aunt May's bunion. As well, instead of including Betty's nickname for her cousin, "Babe," I have decided to insert "Win," short for Winifred, in its place. That's how she would announce herself whenever I answered the telephone, and I want to honour what I believe would be Win's preference.

Pat Butler

This sample, written on May 4, 1931, illustrates Betty's handwriting:

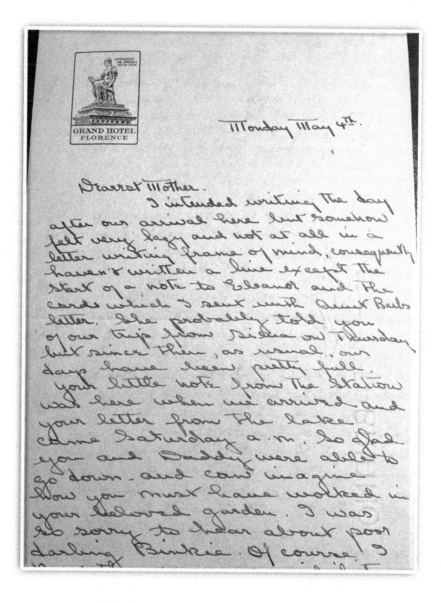

A Lady's Accessory

I inherited these little mother-of-pearl opera glasses from my mother. If the glasses could speak, they would describe sophisticated cultural events, like the time they helped Betty get a closer look at Sergei Rachmaninoff as he played his *Prelude in G minor.*

Purchased in Switzerland in 1930, they look useful, but they don't *really* accomplish much. Present-day binoculars do a much better job of magnifying faces, birds, pianists.

When she used the glasses, Betty's field of vision must have been restricted, which would have been fine when she was zeroing in on Rachmaninoff — she didn't need to see anything but him. But when she was at the opera and she wanted to see the actors' faces or their costumes or sets, the glasses were limiting. Betty knew that using these glasses to see a performer up close made her appear refined, but she couldn't discern facial expressions the way she'd hoped to. She couldn't see what was happening on either side of the stage. In fact, perhaps their actual purpose was to prevent her from being distracted by others on stage. Regardless, she did so love to use them, and while she waited for performances to begin, she was able to better peruse the audience to check out fashion choices.

Thanks to the generosity of her wealthy Aunt Barbie, Betty lived in Europe from August 1930 to June 1931. On Christmas morning, Aunt Barbie gave her the opera glasses in their Swiss hotel. With her focus on the exciting life of theatre, restaurants, and travel, Betty missed what else was on the European stage at the time: the adjacent political tensions that were gradually building around her.

Living in a bubble of luxury and thrilling experiences, her gaze was like sun shining on a wildflower while the tornado was forming just a mile away.

CHAPTER 1

Several Sets of Deck Tennis

As the uniformed chauffeur opened the car door for her to climb into the black Stutz sedan, Betty Harbert glanced down and noticed something on the sidewalk that made her heart drop: masses of small dark circles. Each was about the size of the pinky fingernail she painted with nail polish just an hour ago, but the circles were multiplying by the second.

It was suddenly raining in Montreal, in the middle of a glorious August day in 1930. *Of course, it will rain in Europe too*, she thought. She'd been so fixated on a glamorous, sunny tour, she'd packed only one raincoat somewhere deep in her luggage and left her umbrella in her parents' coat closet.

"Darn it," she said to herself, glancing at the chauffeur to see if he'd heard. "Could you please just wait while I go back for my brolly?"

"Sorry, mademoiselle," he said, still holding the door. He pointed at the huge black cloud overhead. "I'm afraid we're rather tight for time now. I still need to pick up the others."

She looked up at the sky, surprised to see it had darkened in the west as rolls of thunder crashed like bowling pins. *How very annoying*, she thought, *I'll just have to buy a new one once I get there*. Her luggage was already in the car and the ship sailed at 5:00 p.m.

Instead of travelling with a few carefully coordinated outfits the way she usually did, Betty had packed to excess. Moving to France for a whole year meant taking all her favourite clothes for every season and including outfits for every occasion: casual, dressy, and formal. A freight company had already picked up her huge steamer trunk with stuffed drawers and compartments, so today she was taking only a hat box and two suitcases.

Everything had gone smoothly a few years earlier. In the summer of 1927, when Betty was twenty-one, Aunt Barbie first took her to Europe. Betty was invited to travel in order to keep an eye on her two fourteen-year-old cousins — Barbie's daughter, Winifred, and niece, Grace. Her widowed aunt travelled with a lady companion and expected Betty to make sure the girls didn't get into trouble or sticky situations in any foreign locale.

Betty had found the girls' immaturities more charming than bothersome, and because the younger girls shared a room, she had had a luxurious suite all to herself. The whole trip was perfection and she'd been fascinated by the glories of European culture and cuisine.

Several months earlier, Aunt Barbie had dreamt up the extravagant idea of sending Betty to Paris for a year to accompany her only child. At seventeen, Win was a painfully shy introvert who was far too young to go by herself. That spring she'd graduated from Miss Edgar's and Miss Cramp's School and decided to postpone going to university. She still had no idea what she wanted to study. When Barbie had asked her if she wanted to join Win this time around, Betty had leapt at the chance to go back.

Although Betty usually wore her dark-brown hair loose in a shoulder-length bob, today she had rolled it into a bun at the nape of her neck. She was slightly nervous about meeting other passengers for the first time that day, and she was hoping to look sophisticated. Betty was a strong believer that first impressions mattered. To that end, she'd also decided to wear a fashionable floral yellow-and-white day dress. Before heading out to meet her aunt's chauffeur, she'd taken a good look at herself in the full-length mirror in her parents' bedroom and decided she looked mature and approachable.

She hadn't said a proper goodbye to her family yet. Her younger brother, Dick, still didn't have his driver's licence at seventeen years old, so Daddy would drive him and Mother in the Hupmobile to the Montreal dock. Passengers Betty, Barbie, and Win would board the

SS *Duchess of York* on the early side, and Betty's family would come aboard to look around a bit before the ship set sail.

That morning, as her family gathered at the breakfast table, Betty suddenly realized how much she was going to miss everyone. She knew from experience that poignant farewells on the day of parting could provoke tears, which she was not having, so she chatted away about inconsequential topics, like the delicious tomatoes from the late-summer garden. When they were finished eating, Betty lingered over the mundane task of washing the breakfast dishes. *I won't be doing this again until next summer,* she thought glumly. *Snap out of it, Betty. It's just sudsy dishwater.*

Dick would be entering first-year pre-med science at McGill next month and was the only one of her three siblings still living at home. Her mother, Nell, had painful, deforming arthritis in her hands and knees; her father, John, was losing his eyesight from glaucoma. Her guilt nagged at her as she got ready to go. She knew it was quite possible something awful would happen while she was off flitting around Europe. *No point in picturing disaster today,* she told herself.

At the dock, her misgivings about leaving Montreal faded and excitement took over. A steward transferred Win's and Betty's luggage on a wheeled trolley to their luxurious cabin. Betty had studied the brochure in the weeks leading up to their departure and knew it by heart: Launched in 1928, the SS *Duchess of York* had 580 cabin-class beds, 480 tourist-class beds, and 510 third-class beds. She hadn't quite understood what *cabin-class* meant but assumed it was the highest standard as it appeared first in the list. *Whenever I travel with Aunt Barbie, we're always in first class,* she reflected. *I am so very lucky.* Betty fully appreciated being treated to luxury by others. She looked all around the vessel as she walked toward her cabin, thrilled to see the two-year-old furnishings and wood panelling for herself. *No signs of wear anywhere,* she thought.

Betty and Win arrived at Cabin 366 and immediately started to unpack, placing their clothes in the built-in drawers and closets. Betty finished unpacking first but she decided to linger in the cabin to keep

Win company and so that her family didn't have any trouble finding her on the enormous vessel when they arrived.

She didn't have to wait long before she heard a knock on the door and a familiar voice loudly declare, "Room service!" Betty opened the door to see her brother's sly smile. Her family walked in and began admiring the cabin's décor. Her father pointed out, "Aren't you lucky to be on the top level of cabins on the starboard side? You'll have plenty of sunshine sailing east."

Without even trying to hide his envy, Dick pleaded, "Couldn't I just sleep in your closet?" She wished he could and wasn't looking forward to their final departure. She'd never been away from her brother and parents for longer than a few months.

Win carried on getting settled while Betty and her family toured the elegant dining rooms, lounges, ballrooms, and fitted-out sports facilities. They all found the deck-tennis court most intriguing.

On their tour, the Harberts stopped by Aunt Barbie's grand cabin. She was by herself on the crossing because her travel companion, Miss Armstrong, would be meeting them in London. They wished her bon voyage and made sure to check that the yellow roses they'd ordered for her had been delivered. Betty spotted them and gave them a sniff, but their delicate scent was barely noticeable as they were so fresh.

The loudspeaker blared, "All visitors must leave the ship within thirty minutes. All ashore that are going ashore!" Betty's heart sank and tears stung her eyes. *Don't go*, she thought, as the four of them started to walk toward the exit. The reality of not seeing her family for almost a year descended like a shroud, but she kept smiling. *No tears*, she reminded herself.

"I'm planning to write to you a couple of times a week, to tell you about our doings. I've packed plenty of stationery and pens," she said. "Only a small bottle of ink, though. I'm worried about leaking blue ink everywhere!"

"It will be a real joy to hear what you're up to. We'll write to the addresses Barbara gave me," her mother answered. "If there's an emergency, we'll send a cable."

"Mother, please just save my letters in a pile instead of chucking them out. It will be a hoot to read them when I'm home again!"

"Don't worry about us at all, Bet. The whole point is for you to have fun and keep Win company. She'd be awfully bored without you."

They exchanged final longer-than-usual hugs and warm kisses, and then Betty watched as her family, along with the rest of the ship's visitors, ambled down the gangplank.

Just before departure, stewards handed out rolls of brightly coloured paper streamers. Betty looked around to see what she was meant to do. In imitation of the other passengers, she tightly held one end of her streamer and tossed the roll down to the wharf below. Arms reached out from the crowd as the passengers' families and friends valiantly caught the rolls. The lovely coloured paper blew in the breeze and sparkled in the afternoon sun. Betty saw the ship's crew lift the gangplank and shortly after, she felt the ship begin to move. Her eyes stung as the ship's movement away from the dock broke the paper strands, and she could hear people on the dock call out, "Bon voyage!"

The travellers were off. The storm clouds that had dripped rain back at the house had blown over and the evening shadows lengthened. *This is pure heaven*, she thought as she gazed down at the ship's wake. *I'm so lucky.* As their speed increased, so did the expanse of white froth against the dark-blue water. Betty was mesmerized by the waves. She lingered on deck for about twenty minutes, only heading to the cabin when she realized it was time to dress for dinner. She'd already decided to wear her floor-length pale-blue silk dress on this first sensational night.

Both her older siblings lived outside Montreal. Ted was a mechanical engineer in Sherbrooke and her sister Eleanor taught English at Bishop Strachan School in Toronto. The only job Betty did was a volunteer position. She taught four-year-old orphans two days a week. She was glad that, without any real job or school commitment, she was free to travel with Win — with no fixed return date. Aunt Barbie made all the arrangements and paid all the bills. *Invisible strings are attached, of course*, Betty considered as she prepared for dinner.

As she got dressed, Betty looked over at her cousin. Win was ready to go. She wore her wavy light-brown hair parted on one side, cut in a bob, and she preferred to dress as conservatively as someone twice her age.

"Do you think this dress is okay?" asked Win, peering down at the brown chiffon she'd chosen.

"It's just fine," answered Betty, wishing her young cousin were at least wearing a more youthful modern necklace.

Thanks to her mother's wealth, all Win's clothes were high quality, but she had no interest in fashion. She was also incredibly shy. In many social settings, it took real effort for her to join in the group's conversation. Win only fully relaxed when alone with Betty or close girlfriends, then her quick wit and wry sense of humour would emerge. She struggled to make even casual chit-chat with boys, so Betty made a point of including her in group conversations whenever boys were present, hoping to build her confidence. In Montreal they would occasionally frequent the same gatherings, and Betty would invariably say something like, "Win, come and meet Freddy," after noticing her hovering alone in a corner. The two treated each other as sisters, and the seven-year age gap seemed to shrink a little every year.

In Paris they'd be living in a residence for young ladies, and Betty would study singing and French, with some lectures at the Sorbonne. Before classes began in October, Aunt Barbie was going to take them on a grand tour of Europe, and she'd visit them again for the Christmas holidays. Uncle Henry had died nine years ago, so now her aunt spent her considerable wealth any way she pleased.

Canadian Pacific S.S. Duchess of York
Aug. 29, 1930

Dearest Family,

I intended to start this yesterday and keep a daily log of our doings, but somehow didn't get at it. We had a gorgeous day yesterday, a little cooler but quite sunny. Today is still lovely, though we are beginning to feel the roll a bit as we passed through the straits about two hours ago. We could just see Newfoundland in the hazy distance but passed quite close to Belle Isle — such a huge, barren island with the white surf dashing on the rocks and the only sign of life being the red and white lighthouses.

Yesterday we walked and read in the morning, after lunch played several sets of deck-tennis, and in the evening, we walked and danced. We are beginning to know a few people on board. Compared to the last crossing, there seem to be very few Americans. I guess people are feeling the effects of the Great Depression and can't afford to travel much.

We have been talking to some very nice people from London, Ontario — an elderly couple, their married son and daughter-in-law and the dearest little old aunt. It is their first trip across, and they are all enjoying it so much. Then we've chatted with Mr. and Mrs. Weaver from Galt and two men from Toronto.

Win and I played deck-tennis with the men this morning. You play with the same rules as tennis on land only on a much smaller court and with a rubber ring about eight inches across which you toss instead of hitting a ball with a racquet. The men later invited us to the card room for cocktails, where we politely had ginger ale. There have been no organized games or horse racing yet. I suppose they think the crowd too small. We were talking of getting up a deck-tennis tournament on our own and may do so yet. Hist! The lunch bugle, I must away.

XX Aug. 30. Today started cold and foggy but by noon the sun was out and we enjoyed six sets of tennis after lunch. Then we had tea with a Mrs. Francis from Montreal, a friend of Mrs. Ramsden of North Hatley. Tonight, walking and dancing as usual.

XX Aug. 31. Today has been quite busy. We finished breakfast about 10, then were taken up to the bridge by the third officer, who showed us the gyrocompass, let me look through his sextant, etc. and invited us to tea in his cabin. Then we went to church service in the dining saloon, followed by a walk until dinner.

I went up and played some tennis and stayed to watch some of the Men's Doubles tournament being played off. The last game was most exciting: 4-6, 6-4, 6-5 and almost every game going to deuce several times. That finished just in time to keep our tea date. Aunt Barbie and Win didn't want to go (of course) but it was really quite fun. The other guest was a former purser on the Empress of France — most interesting to talk to. Now it is just time to dress for dinner so I must stop. I'm so glad to say Aunt Barbie seems to feel much better already and is eating quite good meals. More tomorrow.

XX Sept. 2. As you see I didn't get time for "more tomorrow" yesterday being such a busy day. It was rather foggy in the morning but soon cleared and we spent most of the day playing in and watching the tennis tournament. In the evening we attended the concert — really rather clever in spots - put on by members of the crew.

As Betty and Win arrived at the cabin-class dining room, the maître d' escorted them to their assigned table, Table 13. That evening, the older Jewish couple at their table, whom they'd gotten to know during their meals throughout the crossing, had already been seated, and they cordially greeted the new arrivals.

Mrs. Schwartz wore a lovely black velvet dress with long sleeves and an interesting white lace collar. "What did you two do today?" she asked. While the girls were answering her, a married couple and their teenage son appeared. *A little late as usual*, Betty observed.

That night, Betty was uncharacteristically quiet. She knew the trip was coming to an end. She looked around, savouring her surroundings: glowing mahogany panelling, huge mirrors, crystal chandeliers, white tablecloths set with blue-and-gold-trimmed fine china, silverware, stemmed glasses. *So many delightful touches of elegance*, she thought. She took in the string quartet playing a Strauss waltz in one corner of the large room and the waitstaff gliding among the tables.

After dinner, all eight tablemates wandered into the ballroom to enjoy a concert. The Schwartzes chose seats directly behind Betty and Win. Betty relaxed into the atmosphere and continued observing her surroundings in a type of melancholy reverie. Suddenly, loud German voices crashed through her silent observations. The voices were coming from directly behind her.

Doing her best to block out the heated argument, Betty said to Win, "What do you think we'll do after the concert? As we dock soon, I suggest we join whichever party we can find tonight." It took genuine effort to stop herself turning around and asking them, "What on earth is the trouble?" Thankfully, as soon as the orchestra conductor took to the little podium, the Schwartzes fell silent.

After the performance, the two young ladies returned to their cabin to fetch sweaters before heading up to the deck. Betty freshened her red lipstick and applied a light spritz of perfume. Win turned to Betty. "Why would they yell at each other in public?" Win asked. "It was appalling. So rude!"

"Who knows?" Betty replied. For Betty, such jarring behaviour within the ship's serene atmosphere didn't bear thinking about.

The girls headed off to find a party.

(Letter continued)

When the concert was over, we danced until the music went to bed at 11:30. We achieved a portable gramophone and danced on deck until about 1.

We find we are getting in tonight instead of tomorrow morning having made a record run, due to no fog and good winds. This morning when we came on deck we were quite close to Ireland and within easy distance of various islands off Scotland. The Irish coast is not nearly as green as one is led to expect, but quite rocky and barren covered with numerous small farms.

Now we have just been packing and expect to land in two or three hours. I'm sorry to say this part is over...it has been so pleasant. We were thinking of you yesterday with your Labour Day party. Hope you had nice weather for it. Now I must stop.

Best love,

Betty

Stafford Hotel,
London (Green Park)
Sept. 3, 1930

Dearest Mother,

I was awakened out of a sound sleep this morning by a sound so much like the one which greeted us every morning the two days before we left, that for a moment, I thought I was back at Marlowe Avenue. Then I realized I was in bed in this large and spacious room at the Old Stafford, and the noise merely workmen doing something across the street. It is nearly noon but Aunt Barbie and Win are still asleep due to our late arrival last night — 3 a.m. Doesn't that sound rash? I'll tell you how it happened.

On Sunday they told us we would dock about 6:30 p.m. Monday night, get clear of the customs by 7:30 or 8:00 p.m. and be down in London by midnight. Yesterday morning was really quite amusing. One person was sure we would get in — had been told so by the deck steward or the second engineer — the next person you spoke to was equally sure we would not make it — his steward said the customs wouldn't look at us unless we were in by 7:00 p.m. and that was impossible — however, we packed up and waited to see what would happen.

About 3 o'clock several of the men went to the captain to protest at being landed so late in the day, but it didn't do any good and we docked at exactly 9 p.m. by the clock in the city hall. Of course, the immigration officers had to come on board, inspect our passports, etc. so by the time we were landed, through the customs and the train started, it was 10:30 p.m. We made a non-stop run down to London arriving here about 3:00 a.m., where were met by our Dean & Dawson's man and convoyed here in one small taxi — accompanied by our two trunks and five pieces of hand luggage. Of course, the streets were almost deserted at that time and when we arrived here had to ring loud and long to wake the night porter who brought us up to our rooms and bed which certainly looked mighty nice at that time — 3:45 a.m.!! A unique time to reach staid old London.

XX Must stop and dress for lunch. The others are awake.

XX Have just come up from lunch, during which Miss A arrived. It was very nice to see her, but nicer still to find two letters waiting for me. It was darling of you and Eleanor to think of writing and hard to realize they were written just two weeks ago today, just about the time we were setting out for the Regatta.

I will try to describe how perfectly beautiful it was coming into Liverpool last night. We had dinner early so about 7:00 p.m. I went up on deck just as we were drawing near the mouth of the Mersey. The sun went down just like a ball of fire slipping into the water and leaving such a gorgeous pink glow which lasted until dark. There were numerous other boats coming and going from two big liners which steamed past us and dropped over the edge of the world, to several small freighters and fussy, smoky little tugs, puffing about. Then the big gulls soaring and darting about us — such strong graceful things — all rosy in the sunlight. Then, as it grew darker, though the pink still lingered in the sky, we could see the silver path of the moon on the water, first few tiny lights blinking and winking on the shore and then finally the lights of Liverpool itself, dominated by the city hall with its illuminated clock tower, whose chimes pealed out nine just as we bumped the dock.

We are going out now so this must go too, though I fear my attempt at description is very faulty perhaps you can imagine what a lovely sight it was. I'll write later, with my first impressions of "London Revisited."

Best love,

Betty

Stafford Hotel,
London (Green Park)
Sept. 5, 1930

Dear Daddy,

It is your turn for a letter, I think, and I'm writing it in your favourite position — sitting in the park in the sun. I only wish you were here too, puffing your pipe on the next little green chair. Miss Finley came to lunch today, so while she and Aunt Barbie and Miss A are discussing the YWCA, Win and I came through the little archway to get fresh air, read, write, and amuse ourselves with glances at the big red buses and funny little cars dashing up and down Piccadilly.

We certainly have been lucky in our London weather, so far at least, three lovely sunny days. Let me see what we have done since our arrival. Wednesday afternoon we went for a short walk, returning in time for dinner and to bed early — as we still had some lost sleep to catch up. Yesterday we went to see Archie and were shown around his studio and had a long talk. He inquired after you and Mum.

Then we had lunch at Lyons Corner House on the Strand. Very nice. Aunt Barbie then went back for her afternoon rest and Win and I spent the afternoon at the National Gallery, enjoying it immensely, though it was pretty tiring standing about. We walked home, stopping on the way to buy a tea cloth as a present for Miss Green. Tell Mother I wrote a card for her as she forgot to give me one of hers.

We dined early and went to the Hippodrome to see an awfully amusing musical play called "Sons o' Guns." Do go if by any chance it's in Montreal this winter. It really was splendid.

Our plans for the rest of our time here are rather vague, probably another theatre tonight and I think a bus drive tomorrow to see the Tait Gallery and St. Paul's. Sunday we plan to go to Westminster Abbey in the morning, then to drive with Miss Finley to spend the afternoon and tea with her sister at Marlowe on Thames.

Best love,

Betty

Betty was delighted to be back in Central London after a three-year hiatus. Not only did she know her way around on the Underground system and on foot, she recognized many of its principal sites, like Trafalgar Square and Westminster Abbey. She was also accustomed to cars driving on the left-hand side of the road — opposite of cars in North America — so whenever she and

Win were about to enter a pedestrian crosswalk, she made a point of noticing which direction her cousin was looking. If her head was turned to the left, Betty extended her arm to stop Win, yelling "Watch out!" She did what she could to keep Win safe.

One day as they were wandering around Piccadilly Circus, Betty observed, "I'm so glad I'm not expected to drive a car in this country. Much as I love driving, I'd mow somebody down for sure! Which, I'm quite sure, would rather dampen our spirits." The girls laughed as they continued their promenade.

Stafford Hotel,
London (Green Park)
Sept. 7, 1930

Dearest Mother,

All packed up and ready for the next stage of our journey, as we leave for Ostend at 10:30 a.m. tomorrow morning. Our stay in London has seemed so short, though it feels like a month since we left home instead of only ten days! By this time Eleanor will be in Toronto. I wonder if you drove up with her.

This morning we woke to a typical London day of sun and showers. It was fine at church time so we walked down through the park to the Abbey to the 10:15 a.m. service. We managed to arrive in good time and sat near the front of the north transept, facing the big window and able to see into the choir and round the edge of the pulpit to the altar. It was a very impressive service as usual, though I wasn't so keen on the music. All in a very minor setting, even the anthem, and it sounded rather thin and strained. I don't think it was a full choir. During the service the sun came out brightly, sending shafts of coloured lights down through the grayness — very beautiful.

We walked home again through the Park, full of people enjoying the sunshine and feeding the birds. There are still masses of gorgeous flowers but in places the grass is covered with yellow leaves looking quite autumnal.

This afternoon was very enjoyable. Miss Finley called for us at 2:00 p.m. and with Miss A we drove out to the summer home of Miss Finley's sister. Such a charming house and garden, at Marlow right on the Thames. They have a son and daughter, both very nice and both doctors practicing in Harrow and in Kensington. After tea, four of us walked along the river for quite a little way, seeing numerous summer places, people fishing, swimming and punting. We were going to punt too, but it started to rain. We stayed until after 6:00 p.m. and arrived home about 8 p.m., had dinner, and now have just finished packing.

I find my bags so convenient. Just the right size and the rack in the big one keeps my dresses so neatly. I am going to carry my smaller one, to avoid having to paste on labels and have it all knocked about. We are travelling very lightly on this trip — wearing my suit and carrying my brown coat, taking a sweater and skirt, red evening dress, black silk tweedy one, and brown chiffon and coat for informal dinner.

The Dean and Dawson people seem very good — they had a man in Liverpool to take us from the boat to the train, one here to bring us from the station, one to take us to the train tomorrow. So glad because Aunt Barbie does get rather hot and bothered!

Yesterday morning we went down to St. Paul's by bus, arriving just at the end of the morning service. We stayed until it was finished, then wandered about. Such a difference since we were there before, when so much of it was boarded up. Isn't it awe-inspiring to stand in the centre of that huge dome?

XX Later — I must go to bed as we will be up early. Last night we went to the Haymarket Theatre and saw Marie Tempest in "The First Mrs. Fraser." Awfully clever and so well done.

Very best love to you all,

Betty

As they were leaving the Haymarket Theatre, Betty and Win did their best to ignore the two tramps sprawled on the pavement, caps in grubby outstretched hands. Betty found it most repulsive to see them begging for handouts right in the centre of London's marvellous theatre district. She felt that having dirty beggars nearby ruined the luxurious theatre-going experience, where most patrons were resplendent in evening dress. *I've put in all this effort to dress up for the occasion and they're here tarnishing this beautiful atmosphere. Why couldn't they beg somewhere more common?* she wondered.

Betty turned her back on the beggars in disgust and regally raised her right hand to hail a black London taxicab. *In Montreal, I never had a reason to hail a cab*, she thought. She felt rather classy knowing how to do this and was happy when one pulled in right away.

"You get in first," she said to Win. Then, as Betty got in, she told the cabbie, "Take us to the Stafford Hotel, please."

"Right away, miss," the cabbie responded, and off they sped.

During the ride, Betty and Win discussed some of Marie Tempest's best moments on stage and decided to order cupcakes from room service as a bedtime snack. They exchanged zero words about the dirty vagrants.

CHAPTER 2

A State of Decaying Grandeur

Hotel Kursaal & Beau-site,
Ostende
Sept. 8, 1930

Dearest Mother,

Well, we've slept our last night and eaten our last meal on British soil for many a long day. We had such a lovely day to start and the countryside looked beautiful from the train, all the pretty little gardens and field after field of hops. We embarked on the "Ville de Liege" at 12:15 and arrived here at 4:05 after a very smooth and sunny crossing. The boat, a Belgian one, not nearly as clean and neat as the English line, was very crowded - so much so there was no room for walking about. Luckily we achieved deck-chairs and were quite comfy. There was a large Cooks tour on board, en route to Oberammergau, also several other Dean and Dawson people.

After our arrival here, we taxied up from the docks, past ever so many small fishing boats moored together — with the sailors and fishermen very dirty but quite picturesque sitting in the sun making and mending nets.

This hotel is facing the sea, divided from it by a long promenade. It seems to be a city of hotels. We walked along past dozens this afternoon, ranging from large imposing ones to tiny pensions. I believe "the season" is over and some of the biggest places are closed, though this seems quite well filled — a great many English people. The beach is lovely, such fine clean sand with rows and rows of gaily painted bathing houses. There were hundreds of kiddies wading and building sandcastles, bigger boys flying bright-coloured kites, small girls and ever so many women chatting and knitting.

I seem to be awfully sleepy tonight so think I will retire early. We are leaving by motor for Brussels about 9:00 a.m. tomorrow.

Best love to you all,

Betty

Hotel Astoria & Claridge,
Bruxelles
Sept. 9, 1930

Dear Dick,

Today has been such a busy and interesting one, I must tell you all about it. To begin with, we left Ostend at 9:30 a.m. in a huge Minerva car, a perfect beauty with a long narrow hood. The chauffeur sat out in front and the back part of the hood let down - you know the kind. It ran wonderfully, we travelled at 60-70 kilometres per hour all day.

Our chauffeur was a burly, red-faced Englishman, very good, though he seemed to have the usual habit over here of tooting at every corner. It's terribly amusing to see how casual they are — passing standing cars on either side and parking on whichever side of the road they feel inclined. The traffic cops are very smart and important looking in dark blue uniforms, white helmet and gloves, and a short blue cape slung over their shoulders.

From Ostend we drove a few miles along the shore to Zeebrugge. The country there is low rolling sand dunes covered with scraggy grass. We saw various cement foundations where the Germans had had their guns, then went on to the canal which was the submarine base and the actual place where the boats were sunk to block the exit. It all looked so calm and peaceful it was hard to imagine it was the scene of such terrible fighting about 15 years ago. It was dull and misty, but we could see the outline of the mole curving out into the sea.

Then we drove to a small museum which has been constructed as an exact copy of the German officers' headquarters there, decorated with cartoons and various articles captured from sunken Allied vessels. There were also very good maps and photographs showing how it was all planned and carried out. From Zeebrugge we drove to Bruges and finally on through Ghent arriving here about 6.

Best love and I do hope you like college. You'll be home to register when you get this, I think.

Betty

In the Bruxelles letter to her brother Dick, Betty mentioned the Great War for the first time. She knew that the fighting had ended only twelve years earlier, but, like many of her contemporaries, she knew little else, paying almost no attention to politics or current events.

Betty was only eight years old when the war started. She remembered overhearing adults around her discussing it, and, picking up on their distress, especially when Canada joined the conflict, she knew that things were pretty bad and scary. Her older sister, Eleanor, who was fifteen years old in 1914, had told Betty about the boys she knew who lied about their ages in order to enlist. Although Betty felt the pall that settled over the house for days every time a Harbert acquaintance was killed or badly wounded in battle and she heard the many names of the dead or missing announced at their Anglican church every Sunday, she never got a clear understanding of the events of the war. She didn't grasp the real horror, being so young and so far away from the fighting.

Betty grew up fairly content and unconcerned about the state of the world, really. Still living at Marlowe Avenue meant that she'd always been taken care of, even at twenty-four years old.

Her older brother, Ted, would tease her about being interested only in wearing pretty clothes, going to parties, and dating young men. After recently hugging her goodbye, he declared, "Well, I'm sure living in Europe will be good for you. I expect you to grow up a bit and be more realistic about how life actually works. There are some nasty, dishonest types out there, so be careful, Bet dear."

Hotel Astoria & Claridge,
Bruxelles
Sept. 10, 1930

Dearest Mother,

Winifred and I have just been going over our diaries trying to bring them up to date with our various doings of the summer. Looking back, it certainly was a happy summer, with lots of picnics and outings. It's hard to picture you still at Lake Memphremagog. It seems such ages since we left, I will send this to Montreal as you may be back at Marlowe Avenue by the time it arrives. I will continue with our doings, which I'm afraid sound rather like a guidebook.

After we left Zeebrugge we drove to Bruges, such a quaint old place with narrow winding streets lined with tall houses, and crisscrossed with rather grubby, though very picturesque, canals. They are not used much now except for sightseers. We took a very chuggy old launch and went for a 40- minute trip under numerous bridges, covered with moss and toad-flax. Then we drove about the town visiting a very ancient church, started in 800 and finished in the 13th century. Unfortunately, like so many of the churches here, it was terribly ornate inside, cluttered up with pictures and gilt images which ruined the effect.

The Cathedral (1100 and something) was really lovely with marvelous windows and some good carving. Then we saw a rather unique place — a small museum of Memline pictures inside the Old Hospital of St. Jean - about 12th century. After lunch, which we ate on the sidewalk facing a big square opposite the famous old belfry and within sound of the chimes, we visited the Basilica of the Holy Blood, a beautiful old church with a marvelous chapel underneath it — very dark and gloomy, illuminated by light from three lovely windows. After a view of the Aldermeus Hall, in the Town Hall, we left and drove on to Ghent, pausing just to see the outside of the Cloth Hall and Corporation

Houses and arriving here at 6:00 p.m. The country throughout is very flat and not very beautiful though it is made interesting by the windmills, canals and tall narrow houses of red brick or whitewash with red tile roofs. Just this side of Bruges we passed a great many wholesale florists, field after field of tuberous begonias of the most gorgeous colours.

The country people are mostly fair, short and sturdy-looking — the children with bare legs and little black pinafores. No one wears a hat but almost every girl or woman had a small fringed shawl over their shoulders ready to use as a hat in case of rain. In the country a great many wear sabots. We saw several men riding bicycles with them on, it looked so odd. If they don't have wooden shoes, they wear what looked like ordinary felt bedroom slippers — all sorts of violent purples and reds. We saw them on kiddies going to school and girls and boys coming from factories.

XX Bedtime arrived so this must be continued. Yesterday morning we took a bus trip around the city, seeing the Palace, Hotel de Ville, Cathedral, Wiertz Gallery and numerous statues, parks and public buildings. It is rather depressing going through Brussels - in fact, through any of the cities we've seen. They all seem in a state of decaying grandeur, living in memories of a former state. There are so few people on the streets and they are all rather shabby and down-at-heel. Then there are heaps of lovely old houses all shuttered up and so many with "To Let" or "For Sale" signs.

In the afternoon we drove out through some lovely beech woods to the field of Waterloo. We were taken into a huge round building to see a panoramic view. It is very cleverly done. You mount stairs to a platform in the centre of the round and right below is real grass and earth, strewn with dummy horses and men and guns, and swords. Then this merges into the base of the wall on which is painted scenes from the battle. We had the quaintest old woman who explained everything in terrible English. We climbed up 226 steps to the top of a huge mound of earth topped by a bronze lion, put up as a memorial. They told us it took 400 women 4 years to build the mound, carrying baskets of earth. From the top we had a splendid view of the neat countryside, dotted with white farmhouses, poplar trees and windmills.

I'm afraid Brussels would never do for you and Daddy to visit because it's so fiendishly noisy. Every bit of the roads is built of cobblestones, both here and in the country and you can imagine the noise of the autos and numerous wagons. In spite of the small amount of traffic, they toot their horns at every corner!

I didn't sleep very well last night. It was as noisy as ever when I finally got to sleep after midnight. When I woke at 3:30 a.m. I could absolutely feel the silence. But it didn't last long! In the distance I heard an ominous rumble which grew louder and finally reached a crescendo under my window. I looked out and saw a row of market carts, piled high with vegetables, lit by feeble old lamps and drawn by sleepy-looking horses whose feet clip-clopped on the cobblestones.

This morning is dull and cool. The others have gone out to stroll but I decided to catch up on my correspondence. I have written to the Junior League Secretary, telling her I will be away and asking her to send the Jack for my fees to you. Will you keep track of that, also my Jack from Dr. Wather? You might have my bank book made up and let me know the bad news! I must stop — you'll be worn out trying to decipher this.

Best love,

Betty

Thinking about her Junior League membership reminded Betty of the social life she'd left behind in Montreal. Now that she was approaching her midtwenties, she was getting anxious to fall in love, marry, and settle down. Although she'd had plenty of invitations to tea dances, the theatre, and other glittering parties, the highlight of her year was always the St. Andrew's Ball. Her girlfriend had told her that the ball was first held in 1848 and had been "steadily increasing in cachet." Betty sighed as she recalled all the men in kilts; *they looked simply dashing.* Then, as she lay in bed trying to fall asleep, she relived some of her favourite balls, her dates' names, and what she'd worn that year.

Although Betty had been invited to attend St. Andrew's by some attractive young man every year since turning seventeen, her parents were not wealthy enough for her to be a debutante. Over the years, she'd watched four of her girlfriends come out, and she tried awfully hard to suppress her feelings of envy. In a way, missing this year's glamourous spectacle was a welcome change. As she finally closed her eyes, she thought, *Well, at least this year I don't have to worry about whose invitation to accept or whether I should have a new ball gown made.*

Dom-Hotel,
Germany
Sept. 13, 1930

Dearest Mother,

Here we are in Cologne and are liking it so much. Somehow it was a great relief to get away from Brussels. There was not much to do there, everything seemed so quiet and the second day so dull and rainy it quite gave me the blues. In fact, I think we were all glad to get on board the train yesterday morning and arrive here about noon. We were met by the Dean and Dawson man and convoyed to our hotel - just about a block from the station. And as soon as we got here we were handed mail! It seemed such a long time without letters and I was so glad to hear from you and Eleanor all about the Labour Day weekend, your plans for driving to Toronto and especially of Dick's starting at McGill.

From where I am writing I can look across the square and see the south transept of the Cathedral, such a beautiful building with its graceful flying buttresses and tall spire. The interior is perfect, tremendously high nave with a double row of aisles, and single aisles on the transepts. There are several very lovely 16th century windows though some of the later ones are crude in colouring. It was started in 1238, but about 1550 they had to stop work through lack of money and did not do any more for 300 years. It was finally completed in 1880. In spite of this, the whole thing is wonderfully symmetrical and in keeping. We noticed the absence of the rather tawdry shrines and images seen in the Belgian churches.

Yesterday after lunch, Aunt Barbie went to sleep while Win and I went into the Cathedral, then with aid of our map discovered the Wallraf Richartz Museum of pictures and sculptures. They have quite a large collection, but most of them are rather mediocre works by obscure Flemish and German artists. There were some very good Franz Hals, two Rembrandts, one or two fine Van Dykes and quite a few Reubens, which personally I don't care for at all. We stayed until closing time then walked around a bit and came back and slept until dinner.

This morning we left at 9 a.m. for a bus tour of the city, leaving from in front of the Cathedral and more or less following the route shown on this little map. The city is really lovely — so clean and tidy with beautiful public buildings and such nice-looking stores.

After our tour ended, we walked to the old Rathus or town hall, a fascinating old place. We were taken through it by a very nice guide who only spoke a few words of English, but he led us to the various rooms then showed us where to read about them on our guide sheets.

On our way back to lunch we bought some gloves and Aunt Barbie got a dainty little pair of opera glasses. This afternoon we went to the Cathedral again, hoping to go into the choir and up the spire but could not see anything as Saturday afternoon is the time for confession and no visitors are allowed. Then we walked along finally discovering St. Maria im Capitol, one of the oldest churches in Cologne founded in the 7th century. Such a quaint old place tucked in between two great buildings. It was closed to visitors too, so we just peeked in the door.

On our way back we had tea, with the most marvelous little cakes. You order your tea or coffee then go and pick out your own cakes. I had a porcupine — most beautifully made of sponge cake — the quills made of slivers of almonds and the whole coated with chocolate, while Win had a chicken, similarly made.

XX I have just washed my hair and had a lovely hot bath scented with the delicious salts and soaps you gave me. The soap is proving most useful as we are not supplied with it anywhere.

We have the most palatial rooms here, adjoining though not connected. They are on the first floor in the front and are big enough to contain two beds, dressing table, small chest of drawers, two huge wardrobes, desk, two tables, a chesterfield, four stuffed and three ordinary chairs and still not be crowded. The bathroom is done in bright blue tiles.

The beds are most intriguing. They are made with an ordinary sheet on the bottom, but the top sheet turns down about 18 inches and buttons on to the huge eiderdown comforter which is all there is on the bed. It is beautifully warm and cozy for this time of year but would be rather awkward in warmer weather. Then there is a bolster, of course, and a huge square pillow buttoned into a pillowcase, the edges of which (like the sheet) are neatly scalloped! The bath towels are as big and soft as blankets so you see how luxurious we are here.

The meals are awfully nice too, and all the waiters and porters are so pleasant and cheerful. The head waiter is a dear old fellow and insisted on our trying sauerkraut at lunch today, edible but not very nice.

XX Excuse interruptions but we have just had dinner and must now pack up as we are due to leave at 7:45 a.m. tomorrow for the next stop. I do hope it is fine for our trip down the Rhine.

Very best love to you all

Your loving Betty

On their second-last day in Cologne, while Betty, Win, and Aunt Barbie were enjoying their breakfast on the hotel's patio under their table's umbrella — Betty thought it was quite clever of the hotel to have an umbrella at every table to shade guests from the morning sun — a noisy German family nearby began yelling at each other. Betty looked over as the teenage son suddenly tore up a newspaper, spat on the ground, and left.

"How rude!" Betty said, because someone had to say something.

"What do you think they are arguing about, Mother?" asked Win, her nose still deep in yesterday's *Times* crossword.

"The election results, I imagine," said Aunt Barbie, stopping the waiter. "This milk is warm," she said. "I asked for cold, please."

A sudden gust of wind blew across the patio. Betty felt something brush her ankle and looked down to find part of the torn newspaper. She bent over to pick it up, then she looked across at the German family. She noticed that the father, with one of those huge Prussian moustaches, looked delighted with life; his tiny wife, less so. They were toasting their younger children — two boys, perhaps nine and eleven years old — with mugs of hot chocolate.

Betty crumpled up the annoying newspaper, got up from the table, and tossed the paper into a nearby bin.

> Hotel Europaisher Hof,
> Heidelberg, Germany
> Sept. 16, 1930

Dearest Mother,

It will be hard to write a coherent letter as Miss A is pounding away at her typewriter beside me and most beguiling jazz is sounding from below. There seems to be a supper dance going on tonight, but as Aunt Barbie wouldn't get us a "gigolo," we had to come meekly up and write letters in bed! Sad state of affairs for 9:30 on a gorgeous evening!

Today has been lovely. We left Weisbaden this morning and drove first to Frankfurt — stopping there for a while, then on to lunch at a quaint little place called Reinheim. We arrived here about 3:00 p.m. and just left our luggage. We drove up to the castle, a huge and fascinating ruin dating from 1214 and used as a residence and fortress by the Electors of Palatine. It was captured and destroyed by the French in 1689 and since has been left as a ruin. It is built high above the city, of red sandstone and covered with ivy now tinged with red. It is a beautiful sight. I took quite a few pictures and hope they turn out well. There is not much else to see here. The town is lovely — built on both sides of the winding Neckar but it is much more modern than I expected. We will see the university when we start tomorrow for Rothenberg.

XX Sept. 17. I am writing this in my room in a 700 year-old building in the quaintest old town imaginable. Rothenberg was once a flourishing and prosperous city but at the end of the Thirty Years War all progress came to a standstill. Now the city, with red tiled gabled houses and an almost complete wall around it with 33 gates and towers, is a perfect example of a medieval town. Of course, now it is kept as a show place and no one is allowed to build a new house inside the walls. The town was founded somewhere around 1100 (most of the houses built in the 13th and 14th centuries) so that a portion of the town hall burnt and rebuilt in 1572 is considered "quite modern."

The hotel where we are staying was formerly two houses, converted into an inn 45 years ago. Downstairs it is attractively decorated with modern reproductions. Upstairs it is much like the place you described in Oxford — very uneven floors and steps up and down. Our rooms are very comfy with electric light, running water and — wonder of wonders — a beautifully tiled bathroom! Our beds — very high and narrow- are made with one blanket and a huge puff made simply of a bag filled with feathers — like a miniature feather bed.

This morning we left Heidelberg in a misty rain which kept up until about noon. The first part of our drive was along the banks of the Neckar — a narrow sluggish river with low tree-covered hills on either side, with here and there a cluster of red-roofed houses. Here everyone seems to live in villages and go out to their farms. We saw ever so many people working in the fields - many women and children, sometimes whole families. The women always with a scarf over their heads and the children with gaily colored pinafores. All the little girls have their hair in braids. Just now they seem to be getting up potatoes, though we saw some fall ploughing being done. They use oxen a great deal and ...

Hotel Eisenhut,
Rothenberg
Sept. 17, 1930

...several times we saw a horse and an ox harnessed together. We drove through a great many small towns — one narrow twisting street of cobble stones, tall narrow houses on either side, almost everyone with some kind of window box or pots of bright flowers. They all seem very damp with moss growing on the tiles and stones — very picturesque and seemingly quite healthy. All the people look sturdy and even the children go around in all weathers very lightly clad and without hats. There seemed to be dozens playing about in every village, making driving rather nerve-wracking as we met numerous geese, ducks, chickens, and even pigs at every turn. Several times we had to stop short to wait for a slow-moving oxen team to pull out of the way.

After lunch we had an old man take us through the town, walking part of the way around it on the wall. It was too dark for pictures, but if it is fine tomorrow I will go out early and get some. I'll continue this tomorrow and post it at Nuremberg.

Best love,

Betty

Savoy Hotel,
Merano, Italy
Sept. 23, 1930

[Written at the very top of the page] Dear Mother, Excuse the peculiar place to start but we have to buy our note paper here, so must conserve it. This is a perfectly lovely place. We arrived just at dark last night and will be here until Thursday — sleeping three nights in one bed makes us feel quite settled down. We enjoyed our drive from Oberammergau so much — leaving there at 8:20 a.m. in a bus. It was very cold and rainy the first part of the morning, but we stopped about 11 and had hot chocolate and the sun came out, so we were quite comfy the rest of the way. Even in the rain the country looked beautiful with low clouds covering the mountain tops and drifting up and down the valleys.

From 10 a.m. until about 3:30 p.m. we were driving through the Austrian Tyrol — so had breakfast in Germany, lunch in Austria and dinner in Italy. Quite an international day! So far any of the customs we've passed have been very casual, just opening one or two bags as a matter of form, but at the Italian border we were stopped by very smartly dressed soldiers who took our passports while all our baggage was opened and peered into. There were eight English, two Americans and one German in our bus and everyone got through except the German girl, whose passport was not in order and she had to go back.

Betty was inspired by all the languages she heard around her as their tour took them into the heart of Europe. She was keen to learn a new language and thought learning German and Italian would be most interesting, as well as useful. She'd taken French in high school, so she had a rough idea of how to approach a new language. *Of course, once classes start in Paris, my French will take off,* she thought excitedly.

In Brussels, she bought a phrasebook that was small enough to carry in her purse. Columns in English, French, German, and Italian listed equivalent words. She demonstrated its use to Win.

"Just locate the word you want to translate in the English alphabetical list," she said, "then follow the row to the corresponding word in the language you want to use."

"Fine, but if you overhear something in German, how do you translate that?"

"I have absolutely no idea!" Betty answered with a laugh.

Betty made it a habit to pull out her phrasebook while she was bored waiting for a meal to be served. She would work on learning German words for ordinary things. She'd always tell Win what she learned, but her cousin wasn't remotely interested and just kept ploughing through one Agatha Christie novel after another. Sometimes the disparity in age between Betty and her young cousin felt gigantic. *Win is so clever,* she thought as she pulled out her phrasebook, *she could at least try to learn more languages. I bet she'd be so good at it if she put in a bit of effort.*

(Letter continued)

And as soon as we arrived at the Hotel, they demanded our passports again and filled out lengthy forms about us! After the border we were changed into an Italian bus with a very rash driver. The roads all seem to be under repair and are terribly bumpy, so we were tired and glad to arrive. We had dinner, baths and "so to bed." This morning we were all lazy, had breakfast in bed. Then unpacked and did our washing. Now I am sitting on the balcony in front of our room looking up the valley to a little village of red-roofed houses right at the base of a mountain, with its head in a mass of fluffy white clouds. Merano is in a hollow surrounded by mountains — the Dolomites, I suppose. We are taking a drive this afternoon so must go to lunch now.

XX 8:45 p.m. Have just come up from dinner and retired to bed as the best light for writing is beside it. Had a gorgeous drive this afternoon to a place called Mendola, about two hours from here and a climb of about 3000 feet up a wonderfully graded road. The view from the top was lovely — first the green valley with fields of grapevines and several small villages, each clustered around a tiny church, then the wooded foothills, and finally the rugged gray mountain tops. They are a lovely grayish red stone and turn rosy pink during sunset. Of course, we couldn't wait for that, but drove down and had tea in Bolzano and as we left there we could look back and see all the peaks growing quite rosy. It would be wonderful to see the sunrise from Mendola. We'll do it next time we say!

I don't think I've written since the letter I posted in Nuremberg. From there we went to Munich and on Saturday to Oberammergau, a most attractive town of white-washed and pale pastel-coloured stucco houses nestling in the hills. The card I am enclosing gives you an idea of it. We stayed in a house on the left-hand side of the town — a small one painted pale orange with green shutters and trimmings, all decorated with painted flowers and animals — very gay and so clean and tidy. Our rooms and meals were very simple but quite comfortable. The family consisted of Joseph Mayr who took the part of a Rabbi, his wife, and three darling red-haired kiddies. There was also a party of three men, two German girls and a German priest, his mother and sister. I don't know where they put them all, the house seemed so tiny.

The Passion Play was — I don't really know what to say — certainly very beautifully and wonderfully done. It followed the lines of a Greek play with a chorus who came out and gave a prologue before each tableau and scene. The prologue was spoken by Auton Lang, then the chorus of men and girls sang while the tableau was shown. Then the next act continued. The singing was lovely, especially the soprano and bass soloists. Of course, all the people taking part do other things in the village and it was really funny to see the men and boys in ordinary clothes with long hair and beards carrying luggage, serving in stores and driving motor cars. Even the little boys who take part have long hair and it was hard to tell them from girls sometimes when they had it neatly fastened back with bobby pins! A great many of the men wear the native costume too.

The morning we left we had the most unusual and picturesque chauffeur drive us down to the bus. He was quite young with long curly dark hair and beard. On his head he had a green felt mountaineer's hat with a feather, a white shirt, short coat, gray doeskin shorts, bare knees and white golf socks and sandals! Unluckily it was raining, so I wasn't able to get a snap of him. Really words are inadequate. Today being the 23rd I can imagine you driving into Montreal and Dick going down bright and early to register at McGill.

Best love,

Betty

On many Italian streets, Betty noticed newsboys selling papers, but she knew there was no point buying one. Betty knew how to say things in Italian like *"per favore"* (please), *"grazie"* (thank you), *"quanto costa…"* (how much is…), and *"dov'è…"* (where is…) but that was really all. She found her new phrasebook was especially helpful for urgent situations, like locating a toilet or ordering food from a menu, but it didn't prepare her to read the news in another language.

Lorenzo, the good-looking waiter serving their breakfast, had a twinkle in his eye and openly flirted with Betty. She did her best to hide her glee from the others but, drawn to his broad smile and dark curly hair, she couldn't help meeting his gaze as he carried their food all the way from the kitchen.

Aunt Barbie usually maintained a formal distance with waitstaff, but this one was friendly and spoke clear English. She asked, "Is there any news we should know about? We're feeling rather out of touch."

He replied, "Prime Minister Mussolini recently spent half an hour parading around a square on a horse to show how healthy he is — in front of journalists. Our fascist dictator needs to always appear strong and in control." Betty had no idea what "fascist" meant and wondered if Lorenzo was confusing his English and Italian words. "He'd been out of sight for weeks. More tea for anyone?"

"Yes, please," said Aunt Barbie.

"There have been rumours about him being very ill, so I guess he was showing he's very much in charge."

Betty smiled and said, "That sounds good." Then she turned to Win and asked, "Please pass the apricot jam, Win. It's my absolute favourite with these lovely warm rolls."

When Lorenzo offered to pour her more coffee with frothed hot milk, she smiled and nodded yes, feeling giddy from his attentions.

Grand Hotel,
Lago di Garda, Italia
Sept. 26, 1930

Dearest Mother,

Such a nice big budget of letters arrived this morning, brought up while Miss A and I were breakfasting on our balcony overlooking the beautiful lake. And such interesting news about Ted and Kay being engaged. Of course, we were not really very surprised, but I am glad to hear it is settled and Ted has "cinched the candlesticks" as he said. I had such a nice letter from him, which I have just answered and I will write to Kay soon. Aunt Barbie also had letters from Ted, Eleanor and Auntie May so we are pretty well up on news. As you say, it did seem funny to keep writing without answers — even though our letters have crossed we really haven't had answers to our first ones. It makes you realize what a long way there is between us.

Miss A, of course, has no desire to go home and talks of a lengthy trip to Spain in the spring taking five or six weeks for it, then spending three or four weeks in England. Aunt Barbie seems to want to do it too, so you may see me arriving home alone. I could go to Emsworth and see Aunt Mary and then leave from Liverpool.

By this time, the four travellers had become aware of each other's idiosyncrasies. Betty noticed that although Miss A was merely Aunt Barbie's travel companion, she often acted like she was steering the ship. Betty was surprised by how demanding Miss A could be, given that she wasn't paying for anything herself. This tall, angular spinster dreamt up expensive things, like a trip to Spain, and for some reason felt comfortable enough to complain loudly about the service or the food. Betty thought that Miss A expected too much and should be happier than she was.

Betty knew that she had only been included in the travelling party to accompany Win, so she was in no position to criticize. Plus, she'd been brought up to respect her elders. Miss A could make it hard sometimes, though, and Betty would catch herself, having to bite her tongue to stop from confronting the older woman aloud.

The issue of payment for their luxurious hotel rooms, multi-course meals, and tour guides was resolved before the trip began, so none of the travellers had to think about the expense of it all. Aunt Barbie had surreptitiously paid everyone's expenses, without comment.

At about the age of fourteen, Betty had first become aware of the Munderloh family's extravagant lifestyle: huge mansion partway up Westmount Mountain, enormous compound on Lake Memphremagog, servants, limousine, expensive wardrobes. So Betty the teenager had asked her mother where all that money had come from.

Her mother had told her that Win's paternal grandfather, Wilhelm Munderloh, immigrated to Canada in 1857 and later became the German consul in Montreal. At some point he founded Munderloh & Company — importer of German and Belgian goods — which his son Henry (Win's father) ran after Wilhelm's sudden death. It was a hugely successful business, which continued to support their elaborate lifestyle.

It struck Betty that it might be difficult for Barbie and Win to reconcile their German ancestry with what Germany had done in the Great War. Ever since her tour of German officers' headquarters in Belgium, Betty had been paying closer attention to the consequences of the war. Appalled at the unspeakable destruction Germany caused in other countries, she found herself disapproving of many of the German adults she observed. Plus, it was difficult not to notice that many German tourists were loud and obnoxious. *Some German tourists are so overbearing. They act as if they won the war!* she thought. Betty tried to be nice to them despite this, but she noticed how Aunt Barbie and Win treated any Germans they encountered — usually with neutral formality, but occasionally with barely concealed contempt. She empathized with Italian hotel and restaurant employees as she watched them provide polite service to the German guests.

When alone in their hotel room, she commented to Win, "It must be horrible to have to stand around hoping for tips from German tourists. The havoc and death the Germans caused must make them really angry. I resent their attitude and I'm only another tourist!"

Only silence. *Perhaps Win didn't respond because she's embarrassed about her heritage*, Betty considered. *It must be so awkward for her, being half-German.*

Despite their rude behaviour, many of the German boys about her age were strikingly handsome, with blond hair, blue eyes, slim build, and erect posture. She tried to avoid making eye contact, although some were almost aggressive in trying to catch her attention.

(Letter continued)

I can't remember if I told you about our all-day drive in Merano on Wednesday. It was the most heavenly day. The sky so blue and white, the mountains seemed to stand right out from it. We left about 10 in the same car we had the day before, taking a picnic lunch with us of which we ate about two-thirds on the way up, sitting in the sun and getting coffee from a little refreshment stand. The fifth person in the car was a rather nice lad, a Czecho-Slovak, though originally Austrian. He lives in Cairo and was in Merano recuperating from a motor accident which happened seven weeks ago. He was really very interesting, speaking fairly good English as well as Italian, German, French and Arabic.

Yesterday morning I woke up about 6 a.m. (you'll be very surprised to hear that, or earlier, is my usual time for waking nowadays) and about 7 a.m. it was such a gorgeous day I couldn't resist any longer so got up and went for a walk along the river before breakfast. After breakfast, Miss A, Aunt Barb, and I walked along the promenade — stopping to indulge in glasses of grape juice and thin wafer biscuits, the proper thing to do in Merano. Then they went back to the hotel and I continued a little further with Hugo, the Czecho-Slovak lad, hearing great details of life in Egypt.

We left at 12:30 p.m. on an ordinary Italian train, changing from it at Roverto to the funniest, dirtiest little puff-puff train, which wended its way, with many stops, to Riva where we embarked on an almost equally dirty steamer. We had dinner on board, up on deck, and by the time we were half-way through it was so dark we had to light matches to see what we were eating. There were few people on board until about half an hour before we arrived when about 50 Italian girls came on, in the charge of several nuns, evidently returning from a picnic. They sang all the way, really very well. One girl with a lovely contralto voice sang the solo part and the rest joined in choruses.

We docked about 9 o'clock and soon went to bed. At least, I had a bath and then sat on my balcony in my coolie coat looking at the lake and the stars and a tiny sliver of a new moon and listening to some music in the distance — very lovely but rather lonely!

Lonely indeed. The tight controls on Betty's social life were beginning to chafe. Whenever any boy spoke to her in her aunt's vicinity, Betty would have to decide whether Barbie would approve before engaging with him. Her benefactor was staid and old-fashioned, and Betty learned early in life that Aunt Barbie's opinions overruled her childish desires. Barbie wasn't unusual in this regard, as many adults of her social class were excruciatingly judgmental. Betty had to content herself with only snippets of male company when rare opportunities presented themselves — like strolling along the Merano promenade with Hugo, the Czechoslovakian.

Sitting on her balcony by herself, while looking at *Lago di Garda* with moon and stars overhead, Betty wished for some company. She felt dreadfully isolated. *What a waste*, she thought. *The night sky is so beautiful and it's so peaceful by the lake with the music in the distance, and here I am with my dull cousin who only wants to read books and go to bed early.* Eventually, Betty headed back into their room and into bed. The gorgeously romantic atmosphere made falling asleep beside her young cousin not an easy thing to do. *It's ridiculous to be in bed this early*, she pouted. Betty spent the next while repeatedly shifting her bedclothes before she eventually dozed off on that warm autumn evening.

(Letter continued)

This morning we had breakfast outside, also in our pajamas. Almost every room has a balcony and everyone breakfasts there. There is an artificial beach in front of the hotel, with chairs and tables and gay red and orange umbrellas, also a place with diving board. A little while ago we saw a man go past on water skis, long red rubber things with fins underneath to keep them steady. His legs seemed to be laced into rubber leggings fastened into the sockets of the skis and he propelled himself with a double paddle. It looked most intriguing.

It started to sprinkle about 10 a.m. and now has settled down to a steady rain. If it keeps up we may have to resort to bridge. We actually haven't played bridge yet, just a few games of solitaire. Miss A and Aunt Barbie always seem so worn out at the end of the day that we go to bed right after dinner and read and write until about 11 p.m. Lunch is ready now so I'll leave this.

XX Sept. 27. Have just been reading this over and I'm shocked to find that I had not finished telling you about Wednesday. The object of our trip on Wednesday was the summit of the Stelvio Pass (9052 ft.) with a gorgeous view of the Ortler Glacier. Merano has an altitude of about 1000 ft. so we had a pretty high climb, but the road was marvelously graded and the exciting places bordered with stone — much to Miss A's and Aunt Barbie's relief.

From the end of the road we climbed 300 ft. on foot to a monument which formerly marked the meeting of three boundaries (Italy, Switzerland, and Austria) though that part of Austria is Italian now. There was quite a lot of fresh snow, but the sun was so hot we were quite comfy. It rained until tea-time yesterday, after which we went for a short walk - thinking it had cleared - but it was pouring again at bedtime. At 12:30 p.m. we had a terrific thunderstorm with bright flashes of sheet lightning illuminating the whole lake. This morning is sunny and cloudy by turn. We had intended taking a drive but are postponing it until we see how the weather behaves.

Please excuse all the scraps of paper. Paper is very precious in Italy and though we don't have to buy it, it is doled out very sparingly by the hall porter.

I will picture Dick going to McGill next week. I do hope he likes it. And next month the football games! The first time I've missed them for years.

Best love,

Betty

Hotel Commodore,
Paris
Oct. 1, 1930

Dearest Mother,

Just wakened from the soundest sleep I've had for ages, strange to have to come to noisy Paris for it! Although we arrived at 11 o'clock last night, so did not really see much of this hotel, it seems very nice. Our rooms are on a side street still within earshot of the tooting horns!

We have come to the end of a very enjoyable month of dashing about and it will be odd to settle down again. I haven't written since Gardone. We left there at 1:30 p.m. on Sunday taking a boat to Desenzano and then a train to Milan. We had rather a hectic time. To begin with the boat was over half an hour late, so we missed our train connection and had to wait nearly two hours for the next. Then it was pouring rain and the water was quite rough, so we all huddled down in the cabin with the second and third classers feeling rather like emigrants sitting on our luggage, surrounded by people talking French, German and Italian, smelling of garlic and eating grapes! Not the most pleasant spot but frightfully interesting. From the dock we were driven up to the station in a most picturesque old cab with a piratical-looking old driver. Here we boarded the train and arrived in Milan just in time for dinner.

The next morning, we got a car and guide and "did" the city. The Cathedral is lovely- a huge place, but very wide, which takes away from its length and height. I think I liked the outside best — covered with the most wonderful carvings, giving a lace-like impression and with beautifully done statues everywhere. The guide said there were over 4000 inside and out. Then we went to see "The Last Supper" by Da Vinci. It is in an old monastery which was used as a barracks by Napoleon and the room with the picture was used as the officers' mess. A door cut through the wall to connect it with the kitchens took a large piece out of the centre of the picture.

That last page is very involved but it was interrupted by breakfast and a long discussion in French with the porters who wanted to bring our trunks in, instead of sending them on to the school.

Very best love to you all,

Betty

CHAPTER 3

All Rather Shabby Genteel

Having been travelling in the company of her fifty-seven-year-old widowed aunt for five long weeks, Betty was eager for a change. Fond as she was of her mother's sister, she rarely felt light-hearted around this chronically dour lady. One day while they were all having an amusing conversation, Betty looked over to see Barbie's stern face. *Does Barbie ever laugh?* she wondered. *She rarely even smiles.*

Here they were in Paris at last and the concept of spending the winter with Win — as her sole family-member companion — was exciting indeed.

Betty so missed the company of her elder sister, Eleanor, but now that it was September, Eleanor wouldn't be at Marlowe Avenue now even if Betty still were at home. For the previous two years, Eleanor had left right after Labour Day to teach at a swanky private school in Toronto.

After all this tripping about Europe, Betty longed to be in control of her own daily schedule again, although to what degree this would be possible remained to be seen. They were living at a finishing school, after all. *Golly,* she thought, *I hope they don't knock on our doors to wake us in the morning like at boarding school!*

Breakfast was delivered to their hotel room and consisted of café au lait, sliced oranges, and croissants with butter and peach jam. *Nobody makes croissants like the French,* she thought contentedly. *I expect we'll be treated to these delicious pastries several times a week while we're in Paris.*

After polishing off the last delicious crumb, she carefully chose a suitable outfit for their meeting at the bank. *My dark-green wool day dress with matching cloche hat feels businesslike*, she decided.

38 Rue de L'Yvette,
Paris 16e
Oct. 2, 1930

Dearest Mother,

(Please note the address of our school on this page. I will just add this to the letter I wrote in the hotel.)

Well, here we are pretty well unpacked and settled down. Yesterday morning we went to the bank and arranged things while meeting Mr. Benson, the manager, who seemed very nice. Then we wandered about a bit — along the Rue de Rivoli to Rue St. Roch, past our old hotel then back to lunch. About 2:30 p.m. we departed in a taxi along with all our touring suitcases — really the amount they can carry is marvelous — arriving here about 3 p.m.

From the outside Le Gui looks very jail-like with a high iron fence, a rather scraggy garden, and a large square building very much in need of paint. Inside it is all rather shabby genteel, but our room is large with two windows facing west. It has three beds but Win and I are to be alone. There are nine others — three of them still to arrive. Of those here there are two rather snippy English girls, a Swedish girl, a Yugoslav and who do you think — the plump Hackett girl we met at Mrs. Atkins' that day and her sister! They seem rather nice and at least they seem a bit familiar.

The De Broin family consist of Madame La Contesse — very "grande dame" and not speaking any English. La Conte is very ordinary, rather overwhelmed by all the rest. The eldest daughter is sweet and really seems in charge of the whole thing. Then there are two other daughters (one teaches), a little one about ten, and a son of 14 who leaves today for boarding school. Then, just as we were at tea a married daughter, her husband and parents-in-law arrived — all very noisy and French. The married daughter and son-in-law were here to dinner too, so I don't know whether they live here or not. I hope not. He's the most objectionable-looking little thing with atrocious table manners!

Dinner last night was terribly funny. Everyone making feeble attempts in French. We had soup, fried eggs and bacon on toast, creamed spinach and fritters — all served by one very harassed-looking man servant. We had only one black-handled knife, with a little glass rest to put it on to keep it for the next course. I may have all sorts of "foreign ways" when I get home. This morning we have just come in from a walk in the "bois," about 10 minutes from here. Then we had to go and have additional photos made for our "Carte d'identitié" which we have to apply for at the Police Station. This afternoon we are meeting Aunt Barbie to shop and have dinner with her at the hotel. She leaves tomorrow morning for Montreux again.

Lovely to find your letters waiting here, also a long one from Eleanor. You say you will write on Sunday. I probably will too and Thursday which is a free day instead of Saturday. I'm afraid Sundays will be pretty awful, church in the morning then nothing else, not even a walk, and you know how long a Sunday afternoon and evening can be?! Lunch, so must stop. Will write again tomorrow.

Best love,

Betty

> 38 Rue de L'Yvette,
> Paris 16e
> Oct. 5, 1930

Dearest Mother,

We are beginning to feel quite settled down. I wrote you on Thursday, I think, and since then have quite a lot to write about. Thursday afternoon we went to the hotel right after lunch, met Aunt Barbie and did some shopping. Nothing very exciting, only stamps, letter paper, and two very heavy comforters as we're supposed to have our own, then back to the hotel for tea and dinner. We were called for again by Henriette, one of the daughters, at 9 o'clock. Friday morning the classes started. From 9:30 till 10:15 a.m. Conversation with Madame, then 10:30 to 11:15 a.m. French History and 11:30 to 12:15 p.m. Composition. In addition, we have one lecture a week on each subject — Literature, Painting and Architecture — all by outside professors. We had our first one on Painting yesterday given by such a funny, but rather nice, old Frenchman. He talked awfully fast, but we were able to follow fairly well.

On Friday afternoon, a beautifully warm day, we took the streetcar in to see the outside of the Louvre and the gardens, reserving visits to the interior for wet days which they say we will have plenty of later on. Then yesterday we went to see a small museum of old furniture, paintings, tapestries and miniatures — a private collection given to the city.

Aunt Barbie and Win and I talked things over before Aunt Barbie left. Win and I both think, except for the French, this is really too elementary for us — especially Win who had such wonderful courses in History of Painting and Architecture at Miss Edgar's and Miss Cramp's School. So we are determined to study French awfully hard, stay until Christmas holidays which start on Dec. 16th, then leave. Aunt Barbie will come here for January and we will live "en pension" or at a hotel, and attend lectures, theatre, and opera. Then take a trip to Spain ending up with Holy Week in Seville instead of starting there, a few weeks in England, and head home earlier than expected. Of course, all this depends on how well we do and if we become so in love with Le Gui we can't bear to leave it, so perhaps you had better not say too much about it.

This morning we went to the British Embassy church — a rather hideous place. A very nice service except that we were sitting in the gallery and could only hear, or at least follow, the portions of the service we knew. Excuse this awful ink. My pen has run dry and I'm too lazy to go up for more. Win invested in a large bottle of Parker's ink as this is the only sort they supply us with.

Win and Betty sat chatting in the gallery of the British Embassy church before the service started. They stood up when a young man came to join them in their pew. He said, "Excuse me, please," as he moved by them to an empty space beside Win. Betty detected a British accent when the dark-haired man spoke. He was — Betty guessed — in his late twenties and he wore an expensive navy-blue suit with a vest, white dress shirt, and a bright-red tie. When the service started, Betty turned *most* of her attention to the sermon, but from time to time, she would catch her mind wandering back to the handsome man next to them.

After the service, Betty realized she'd misplaced a glove. The man noticed her searching for it. "What have you lost?" he asked her.

"My glove," Betty replied. "It's so silly, really. I just had it a second ago."

He crouched down so he could look beneath the surrounding pews, trying to help her find it. "Oh, here it is," he smiled, kindly passing it to her, then followed up with an introduction. "Allow me to introduce myself. I'm David McKay. I don't believe I've seen you here before."

"Oh, you wouldn't have! This is our very first time attending this church. We're just settling into Paris." Betty felt her cheeks turn red as she met his friendly brown eyes. "We'll be here all winter," she added.

Win and Betty took turns shaking David McKay's hand and offering their names, then Betty explained they were from Montreal and they'd be spending time in Paris for at least a season. The girls felt fairly comfortable and natural chatting with him, especially because they were meeting at church. He was the first complete stranger — who wasn't serving them a meal — either of them had spoken to in ages, and it was a treat to talk with him while they all carefully descended a narrow stairway to the church vestibule and then out to the sunny sidewalk. They stood together outside the church for a while, exchanging stories. The organist's Mozart postlude wafting through the open door completed the scene.

They learned that David worked in the British Embassy as a junior clerk and lived in a flat on the Rive Gauche. They described their studies and vaguely explained where they were living, purposely omitting the exact address. Both made a habit of remaining aloof with strangers.

Then David invited the two girls to join him for lunch at a nearby restaurant. Win declined by saying, "Thank you, but I must get home to write my usual Sunday letters."

The rash idea of having lunch alone with a complete stranger in the City of Light was incredibly appealing to Betty. *I am twenty-four, after all*, she reasoned in an instant, *and it's broad daylight. Plus, we met in an Anglican church! I can simply take a taxi home after lunch.* She answered, "That would be lovely, David!" while grinning from ear to ear.

The two strolled to a sweet little café nearby. Right away they were shown to a table in the corner. As David helped her off with her coat and they perused the menu, Betty felt rather giddy. He explained that he studied political science at the University of Oxford and had lived in Paris for just over a year.

Dressed in the crisp white shirt, black vest and trousers, and long white apron typical in Parisian restaurants, a waiter arrived to take their order. Speaking French quite fluently, David ordered a croque monsieur for Betty and salad niçoise for himself, with a half-bottle of white wine. *Wine at lunch? What a rare treat*, she thought. *First time since I left home. How glorious!*

An important part of David's job at the British Embassy was staying informed about current events. "A copy of *The Times* appears on my desk every day," David explained. "The day after its publication as it has to be shipped across the Channel."

When describing their respective backgrounds, Betty said, "I'm a little embarrassed to admit how undereducated I am. You are so lucky to have gone to Oxford."

"Yes, it was quite a challenge to get accepted, but once you enter Oxford, you don't have to work all that hard," David explained. "I had a fabulous time on the rowing team. Not Oxford's, just my college's team."

"I visited the university when I was over here three years ago. Which college were you in?"

"Christ Church," David replied. Then he continued, "And look, the reason you're living here now is to upgrade your education, so there's nothing to be embarrassed about." He gently brushed her forearm with his fingers. "Perhaps we can meet some weekend afternoon and I can take you to some out-of-the-way art galleries and cafés. Most tourists just go to famous places like the Louvre, but there's a lot more to see in this city."

"I would love that," she said, blushing and holding his gaze. Meeting David added a whole new layer of fun to her life. It was far too early to say whether this would be a friendship or a romance, but the idea of seeing him for another outing made her heart skip. She ate slowly, purposely trying to make their lunch last as long as possible.

But eventually, lunch ended, and David paid the bill. He then asked for Betty's mailing address, which he wrote into a little address book. When they stepped outside, David flagged a taxi for her and off she went. *I won't mention David to Mother unless we get together again*, she thought. *I don't want her to be shocked or to think I'm ignoring Win.*

Back in her room at Le Gui by about 3:20 p.m., Betty nonchalantly responded to Win's queries about her lunch with the handsome Brit, tamping down her utter glee.

Keeping her tone casual, she said, "I expect we'll see him again. You really should come along as he's friendly and knows his way around Paris," knowing darn well that her shy teenage cousin would never join them. Having a friend for private outings would be ideal. In a way, she felt a page being turned in her life story. There would be no going "back to normal" after chancing upon such a noteworthy male friend.

(Letter continued)

I am finding my clothes quite all right both with regard to quality and quantity. We don't wear evening dress for dinner but will probably do so the nights we go out. The black and white sports silk I got at Holt Renfrew is proving most useful — another proof of your good judgement! On our trip I took it, my brown chiffon with coat (which I wore nearly every night) and my red chiffon. Oh yes, and my mauve sweater and skirt which I found useful with my big coat for the short motor excursions.

For once in our lives we have plenty of time for letters! We finished lunch about 1:15 p.m. and have nothing more except tea and dinner until 10 p.m. The only other thing to do is to go to the movies which the Catholics seem to do every Sunday. I do wish we knew someone in the city to visit. We have our weekly holiday on Thursday, instead of Saturday, so I don't mind but Win is disgusted after having looked forward to Saturday as a special day of enjoyment for so long. I wonder if there was a football game yesterday and if you went? Of course, Dick will be able to go with the rooters this year.

The sad looking photo enclosed is one of the six we had to have taken for the police. The reason I look so weird is that my hair was in need of waving and I had several mosquito bites, including one on my left eyelid. Mosquitoes are quite bad here and they say they last all year. Terrible thought!

Best love,

Betty

38 Rue de L'Yvette,
Paris 16e
Oct. 6, 1930

Dearest Mother,

The end of another day! Really, I can imagine myself writing absolutely reams as it is the only thing to do at night, except for reading French books or playing rummy. This morning we woke to lovely bright sunshine, so welcome after yesterday's rain. We went for a walk after breakfast in the "bois," then had a very interesting lecture on modern French history. We are to have one every Monday on the period from Napoleon up to today.

This afternoon I went with Win and Henriette (one of the daughters) to assist Win in ordering a dress. It is most intriguing. You go to a couturier and sit in state while a mannequin shows you different dresses. Then you choose your material and have your measurements taken. It is not more expensive than the shops and they say it is very difficult to get nice things ready-made. Win ordered a plain but very pretty dark green wool for wearing in the mornings here. We certainly need warm clothes as it is very chilly and damp and will be even colder later on. We didn't get back from our shopping until nearly 7 p.m. and were thrilled to find two nice hot baths ready for us. Monday, Wednesday and Friday are bath nights so they are greeted with joy! We are lucky having ours at night as two others have them at 7:30 a.m. We don't get up until 8 as we have breakfast at 8:20 a.m. It is quite companionable having baths by twos as they are only divided by a partition so you can luxuriate in the warmth and converse!

(Letter continued)
Oct. 7, 1930

We have just finished lunch and are waiting for a lecturer to come and talk to us on "Paris Artistique" after which we are to go to a display of Modern Furnishings and "Art Moderne." Today started off with brilliant sunshine when I woke at 6 a.m., but it soon clouded over and has rained on and off ever since. We went for a walk, in spite of it, in our berets, big coats, and brogues. Last night the two American girls arrived — one from Virginia and one from Georgia. They are both about 18, marvelously dressed and awfully sophisticated. The Virginian is quite ordinary but the other one, Violet, is terribly amusing. Speaks fluent and frightful French and has all sorts of poise and "nerve." She and Eldred Plaxton, the girl from Toronto, will considerably liven up our quiet existences, I think.

There were times when Betty felt aggravated with having to always share a room with her shy young cousin of only seventeen. *We're together all the time — even at bath time!* The recent arrival of the two new American girls, together with Eldred from Toronto, pleased Betty and brightened her spirits.

She decided to broach the subject of pursuing a life outside of Win, as tactfully as possible. "You know, Win," she said carefully after dinner one evening, "once in a while, it would be fun for us to go our separate ways, for part of the day. Then we'll each have news and hilarious stories to share when we're back together. There's no question that we're amused by similar anecdotes."

"Sounds like a good plan," said Win as she picked up the book she was reading.

Betty decided to implement this occasional distancing immediately. She headed off to knock on Eldred's door. The new arrival from Toronto opened it with a flourish and a grin.

"Why, Betty, what a treat to see you! Come right in and stay a while," said Eldred.

After delighted sounds of a social gathering echoed down the hallway, it wasn't long before Violet arrived to join in. Win was asleep by the time Betty got back to their room.

Well, that worked out beautifully! Betty thought as she brushed her teeth. *I must visit with Eldred again soon.*

(Letter continued)
Oct. 8, 1930

I was so glad to get your long letter this morning, written on September 28th. I'm afraid you've had a busy time getting moved and having the house cleaned. Too bad Celia was such a broken reed. I hope you can get someone really good if you get another maid, or else a woman several times a week. Do take care of yourself dear, don't get all worn out. I will be interested to hear of Dick's first days at McGill. Not having heard anything I conclude he did not get down to the Lake. This is being written while we wait for lunch.

The meals here are really awfully nice, but we are not so keen on the breakfasts. Win and I have fruit, specially ordered for us by Aunt Barbie, then frightfully tough rolls, tea, coffee or cocoa and marmalade. At noon we have hors d'oeuvres or soup, then meat and potatoes, dessert pudding or stewed fruit and always fresh fruit afterwards — generally grapes. Tea is at 4:30 p.m. Bread with peach jam and tea, and cake on Sunday. Dinner isn't really dinner. We have soup then cold meat or eggs, then a vegetable of some sort served as a separate course and dessert.

As Betty wrote to her mum and dad about the daily meals being served to her in grand style, she was reminded of her spectacular good fortune. She felt a stab of guilt at being luxuriously waited on while poor Mother had to cook and keep house while she suffered such awful pain in her arthritic knees. *Broken-reed Celia must be replaced right away*, she thought. *If I were at home now, I could help find someone.*

Earlier that summer at the lake, she'd noticed that her mum tried to limit her trips up and down the stairs to only once a day by carefully planning exactly what she would be needing on the ground floor before she left the bedroom. Mother took her afternoon rest in the downstairs bedroom too.

Every night before bed, Eleanor would massage Mother's sore knees with a liniment called Absorbine Jr. to help her sleep. Its strong smell lingered in the upstairs hallway and reminded the family of the chronic pain she kept to herself.

(Letter continued)

XX Wednesday evening. I think I will finish this now as we are going out early tomorrow and can post it. This afternoon while Win had her first lesson in Italian, I went with two Hacketts to see the Motor Show — very interesting with all sorts of marvellous cars — Italian, French, Spanish, English, German and American — but it was so crowded it was hard to see properly. Tomorrow morning Win and I have our first lessons in Dramatic Art, which we take outside from an actress in the Comédie-Française. Then I am to have two singing lessons a week (Tuesday and Friday) from a man who sings in Opéra-Comique.

Diane, one of the English girls, is taking lessons too so we are to go together — half an hour each while the other one listens.

We are having most disagreeable weather — rain and wind all the time and they say it is even worse next month. Brrr! Wasn't that a terrible accident in England when the R 101 crashed? It will shake people's faith in the R 100. We saw a French paper on Sunday night, giving all the details. Win and I think we will buy an English paper every Saturday to read on Sunday so we won't get too far behind the times.

Oh, I forgot to tell you on Tuesday afternoon we went up the Eiffel tower. Such a wonderful piece of construction and actually room for a tearoom on the first floor, and a tearoom and bar on the top! These people simply must eat all the time. They were even serving eats at the Motor Show! Unfortunately, Tuesday was cloudy so we couldn't get much of a view, though we were able to pick out Notre Dame and the Louvre.

Best love,

Betty

Betty knew that, to the other residents of Le Gui, she and Win appeared to be affectionate, close relatives who shared a room. Being constantly in each other's company, dressing in similar style, going to the theatre together, they appeared to outsiders to be socioeconomic equals. In truth, there was a definite disparity.

John Harbert's bookkeeping practice was adversely affected by the previous year's stock market crash, but he never said anything about family finances. Talking openly about money was considered common. Betty, who was raised to always be frugal, made a habit of prolonging the life of her wardrobe with expert mending and often could remake an outfit for a whole new look.

Having no source of personal income, Betty relied on the spending money that Aunt Barbie paid her every three months, whether in Montreal or Paris. During their meeting with the bank manager, Mr. Benson, a special account had been set up for Betty's private use, and she surreptitiously made periodic withdrawals, to minimize her embarrassment. Win was so used to spending money being plentiful that her older cousin's financial habits barely registered.

Inside her purse, Betty carried a black leather wallet, which she used when paying for Barbie-sponsored joint expenses, like lunches or teas. Her own funds were in a little maroon wallet, chosen because the colour maroon stood for desire and passion. Betty reserved that money for things she longed for.

> 38 Rue de L'Yvette,
> Paris 16e
> Le 9 oct., 1930

Dearest Mother,

What do you think of my new writing paper? I achieved it this morning and think it is nicer than Win's onion skin and yet not too heavy to put several sheets in one envelope. We discovered, to our joy, that the postage to Canada is not 1F,50 (6 cents) as the man at the hotel had told us, but only 75 centimes so we will be able to write twice as many letters!

Today has been quite busy and interesting and for a wonder it hasn't rained. This morning Win and I left with Mlle. Jeanne about 9:30 a.m. and went "en ville." First to a huge store "Au Louvre" on the Rue de Rivoli where we bought paper, soap, and lisle stockings for Win. Then we went for our first lesson in Diction and Dramatic Art, which we are taking from a Mlle. Nizan, an actress in the Comédie-Française — such a charming person, quite young and so vivacious. She has a fascinating apartment on the Rue de Rivoli, four flights up and very tiny but so attractively furnished. She possesses a large, fluffy black cat, still young enough to play very amusingly. We are starting off by learning ordinary short poems, but after our vocabularies and pronunciation have improved, we will have dialogues.

This afternoon we went to a most amusing place — a small Madame Tussaud's containing modern politicians, movie stars, etc. as well as models of all the important revolutionary characters and various scenes such as Marie Antoinette's trial, Marat being assassinated by Charlotte Corday and other cheerful subjects! In addition, they had a short sleight-of-hand performance and various other side attractions. To complete our frivolity, we had the most delicious tea at a small tearoom, instead of returning to bread and jam! A welcome change.

(Letter continued)
Oct. 10, 1930

This morning we had a lecture on literature (the Romantic Revival Period) from an instructress who I think will be very interesting. Then we departed in two taxis, armed with our passports and lengthy applications, and went to the "Prefecture de Police" for our cards of identity. Such a lot of red tape. They paste one picture on your card and keep three — in their rogues' gallery I suppose! Then at 5 p.m. Diane and I went for our first lesson in singing. We have to go right to the other side of Paris for it, to the studio of a man who sings in the Opéra-Comique — over half an hour in a taxi and up four flights of stairs! But I think it will be well worth it as he seems awfully nice and so enthusiastic.

"How glorious is this!" Betty said to Win. "Concerts, operas, the theatre, and sitting in a box, no less. Aren't we having a lovely time going to all these performances? We're flitting around like butterflies and soaking up lots of culture." She spoke with an exaggerated, plummy English accent.

"True," answered Win. "Although, because you are so much more musically talented than I am, you probably get more pleasure from the soloists than tone-deaf me. You can tell whether their singing is ordinary or superior. Though it is fun getting dressed up, isn't it? Tell me what you're wearing to the opera on Saturday so we don't look like twins."

"I'll wear my floor-length red chiffon," Betty said.

"Then," Win decided, "I'll wear my long black one!"

Last night we were very frivolous — going out to a concert which started at 9 p.m. and not getting home until nearly midnight! Think of such rashness!! But oh, it was lovely — a choir of Russians — about 40 male voices. They sang absolutely marvelously, without any accompaniment, conducted by such a funny, jerky little man. They sang all Russian songs, of course, some very rousing and hearty ones and several weird minor things. Part of the time just a soloist with the rest humming, exactly like an orchestra or an organ. They are leaving for the States next week, but I don't suppose they'll reach Montreal, but if they do — go by all means. They are called the "Cossacks du Don."

I had a letter from Aunt Barbie on Thursday. She seems to be enjoying Montreux but not having very good weather. They say it is raining everywhere in Europe, so that is some consolation. I hope you are having our usual nice crisp October weather.

Tonight we are going to the opera to hear "Faust" and tomorrow afternoon some of the others are going to the Opéra-Comique as guests of the Duchess of Something, a cousin of Madame's. She has a box and has offered it to Madame for tomorrow and Friday night, the 24th. As it holds twelve, we are going in two parties. We were divided into five Canadians and six others and drew to see when we would go and luckily we drew Friday.

XX Sunday. Have just come down from an hour in Eldred's room, knitting on one of my baby bonnets, playing the gramophone and reading the Montreal Star and Toronto Sunday papers which arrived just after dinner. So nice to see some home news even though it is nearly three weeks old. The others are all at the theatre so we have the place pretty much to ourselves. We did enjoy the opera so much last night. Six of us went with Mlle. Jeanne — all dressed in our best, and with a huge limousine to take us and bring us home again. Mephistopheles was marvellous, a gorgeous voice and very convincing acting. Marguerite had a lovely voice but was rather fat, and we didn't like Faust at all — very short and stumpy — not at all suited to his character.

In Aunt Barbie's letter she said she was arranging for accommodation in Wengen, near Interlaken, from the 18th of December for about three weeks. Win and I will go to Switzerland from here by night and meet them there. It will certainly be nice to have some dry cold. It is so damp here. All the trees in the garden are covered with green mold, and if you wash out gloves or stockings they take about three days to dry. It's a wonder everyone isn't crippled with rheumatism.

Best love,

Betty

38 Rue de L'Yvette,
Paris 16e
Le 15 oct., 1930

Dearest Mother,

I was so glad to get your letter of the 2nd, enclosing Ted's interesting note. So Pittsie is officially engaged! Isn't it just like the twins to even get engaged at the same time, and even to buy the rings at the same place on the same day! I was awfully interested to hear of Dick's doings, especially that he received an A in his physical exam. It's too funny to think of him being rushed for a fraternity. I'm awfully glad as I think it would do him good to belong to one.

We are actually having some decent weather at last. This is our first sunshiny day and it certainly does make a big difference in one's outlook on life. Aunt Barbie writes that their weather has improved too. They are leaving Montreux Friday, going to Geneva for a few days, then to Locarno.

Last night I went to hear Madame Lottie Lehmann, the German singer, and enjoyed her so much. She has a gorgeous voice with an astounding range. Of course, she sang only in German but I imagine her diction is marvelous, as even I, who knows very little German, could make out a great many words. We had French translations of all the songs. The program was chiefly Schubert and Schumann with five little songs by Brahms and two by Strauss. I liked Schubert's serenade and a berceuse by Strauss best. I'm going to see if I can get a translation of the latter. In the afternoon I had my lesson and he gave me "La Prière de la Tosca." Imagine me warbling grand opera! And all in French!

Yesterday afternoon Win and I had our hair washed and waved. We have to go out for it as we can't very well do it ourselves without running water or facilities for drying it. Monday afternoon Win and I, one of the American girls and Mlle. Jeanne went to Montmartre, where we saw the "Basilique du Sacré Coeur," a huge oriental-looking church of white stone built as a national thank-offering after the war of 1870. It contains some beautiful mosaics but otherwise I didn't care for its Roman-Byzantine style. We then went next door to a very dilapidated and bare little church, the second earliest church in Paris, 12th century erected to commemorate the martyrdom of St. Denis. We wandered about a bit and finally went to the most intriguing little store selling etchings and things. I actually ordered my Christmas cards — awfully attractive little scenes, at about 80 cents a dozen! A marvelous bargain and imagine getting them in October!

XX Thursday. Today is our free day so I have spent the morning doing odds and ends, helping Win fix over a blouse, and tidying my desk drawer. Then I practiced for an hour and am now seated in a sunny spot in the garden, waiting for lunch. It is such a lovely day though not warm enough to be without a coat. For company I have Bimbo, the married-daughter's cat. Such a cute wee thing, a pale beige colour with brown paws, ears and tail. I've never seen one like it before. And the chef's dog, Mistuiguette, a brown and white spaniel, is playing madly about with a tennis ball.

Yesterday afternoon we went to the Louvre for just about an hour to see the early Flemish paintings which we heard about at our lecture on Tuesday. It really is the best way, just to see a few at a time — of one school, so that there is some possibility of remembering. This afternoon I have a dentist's appointment or as they say a "rendez-vous chez le dentist" for 2:15 p.m. and Win has a fitting for her dress at 5 p.m., so we don't know what we'll do in the interval. We've made up our minds about one thing we're going to have — nice hot buttered toast for tea! That sounds terribly greedy but when one lives on the most awful coarse tough bread, and once a week we have the opportunity of ordering our own tea — it's best to make the most of it.

Best love,

Betty

Thrills and cheer! Betty returned from her dentist appointment, tea, and Win's fitting to find a letter from David McKay inviting her out for lunch. *I had a feeling he'd take me out again. How fabulous!* she thought.

Please call me at this number, he'd written, *then we can find a date and time that works for both of us.* She did as requested, and they planned to meet the following Saturday, October 18.

Seven years earlier Betty had begun stepping out with men, and without fail, by the third date her escort would tell her how beautiful she was. She'd heard words like *stunning, gorgeous, striking,* and *dazzling* and she'd gradually learned to not let her head be turned by such compliments. *How a man treats me is much more important than words of flattery,* she believed.

The day was crisp and cloudless when David appeared at 9:30 a.m. He'd planned a tour of several art galleries on the Rive Gauche and had made a reservation at another bistro for luncheon.

Betty wore a beige sweater with a plaid skirt and a touch of lipstick. Other than having her hair done regularly, Betty didn't expend much effort on her appearance. She often heard her friends complain about needing to diet. She felt lucky to stay slender without denying herself rich food or desserts. She simply didn't have a sweet tooth. She also enjoyed being active, which helped. It took real effort for her to sit still long enough to read five consecutive pages of a book. When going out in the evening, she applied mascara with a little brush, rouge, and lipstick to highlight her features and then forgot about her appearance altogether. During the daytime, she applied only lipstick.

While David hailed a taxi, Betty took in his smart outfit. He wore a navy blazer, grey flannels, and a pale-blue shirt with a navy-and-white striped tie. The taxi arrived and they headed off toward the first art gallery.

After a morning walking around several galleries, Betty was pleased to sit down for lunch. David led her to a small bistro, where they were quickly seated. Their table by the window was covered with a red-and-white checked tablecloth. The pair chatted easily over steaming bowls of hearty vegetable soup with baguettes.

Betty talked about life at Le Gui. "The de Broin family consists of Madame la Comtesse. She's lovely, but she can't speak a word of English. Le Comte is a very ordinary little man. He seems rather overwhelmed by having all these young women living in his house."

"I imagine he has to take in boarders to make ends meet," David said. "The stock market crash has wiped out plenty of fortunes."

"The house is rather shabby genteel," Betty continued. "At one time there was lots of money for expensive furnishings, but it's getting rather the worse for wear. Worn places on the stair carpet, for example, and threadbare upholstery on the dining chairs."

Betty paused for a sip of sparkling water. "We all dine at the same time at one long table, with madame and monsieur seated opposite each other in the middle. Our first few dinners were terribly funny with everyone feebly trying to speak French. The many courses are all served by a very harassed-looking manservant hurrying back and forth from the kitchen. Each resident has only one black-handled knife, with a little glass rest to put it on to keep it for the next course."

"I wonder if those are cost-cutting measures," David remarked, then, after a small pause, he veered the conversation to his own work life. "Two new embassy staff arrived from London last week," he said, "which will make my life easier. One speaks fluent Italian and the other can read Spanish, so they can properly follow developments abroad."

Because British Embassy staff received a daily briefing on world events, David was consistently better informed than most English-speaking expatriates living in Paris.

Betty said, "I must admit to living a bit of a sheltered existence at Le Gui. I never listen to newscasts on Parisian radio or peruse the daily French newspapers available in the drawing room. Win and I at least glance at an English paper every Sunday, but by the time we read about events, the information is a bit stale."

The waiter paused at their table to refill their water glasses with Perrier.

"So, tell me, David. What's happening out there?" Betty asked.

The most recent news was about the German election. "The Nazi Party did surprisingly well," he said. "The German *Reichstag* is similar to the British and Canadian houses of parliament. They held only twelve seats before the vote and came away with a hundred and seven."

"So, what does that mean for England?" Betty wanted to know. "Is your work affected?"

"I don't really know. But I'm a little nervous about the power of the Nazi leader. Have you heard of him?" David asked. Betty shook her head, so David filled her in. "His name is Adolf Hitler and, apparently, he delivers very long, rousing speeches that whip listeners up into a frenzy. And he describes a rosy, prosperous future for Germany, which is crazy.

"Right now, the economy is in terrible shape because the country has to pay reparations for the war. In fact, starting in 1921, Germany has had to annually pay two or three billion gold marks to other countries to cover all the civilian damage it caused." Betty had no idea of the value of a gold mark in French francs or Canadian dollars but didn't say so. "I'm not sure if Herr Hitler is loony or simply overly optimistic."

Their waiter delivered demitasse coffee and tartes aux citron. David continued, "Hitler's promised rosy future is in stark contrast to the country's reality, yet somehow ordinary Germans are just enthralled with this guy."

"Hmm, I find Adolf rather an unusual name," Betty commented. "My friend's black Labrador retriever is named Adolf, but I've never met anyone else with that name. The Adolf I know is all warm and sloppy and loves having his ears rubbed. He flops down to the floor the minute I start. I wonder what Adolf the Nazi likes!" They both laughed.

38 Rue de L'Yvette,
Paris 16e
Le 19 oct., 1930

Dear Dick,

Awfully glad to get your letter and to hear of your doings at McGill and the rushing for Psi U. (Thanks so much for the explanation for my "ignorant brain"!) But what on earth is the matter with the football team, losing to R.M.C.! Terrible state of affairs. This is being written in bed, so I fear is not very legible.

I did a very stupid thing last night. As I was dressing, I dashed merrily across the room, skidded on a small rug on a newly waxed floor, described a parabola in the air and landed in a heap, slightly wrecking my shoulder on the way down. I managed to go out, however, but this morning I felt awfully stiff so here I am. Breakfasted in state. Then had a professional visit from Madame La Contesse who tied me up in yards of bandage and doused me with liniment. Fortunately, it is my left side so I write letters in comfort while all the others have departed to church in the pouring rain!

You would be very amused to see our beds, swathed in yards of mosquito netting as if we were living in the tropics. The mosquitoes have been terrible and of course window screens are unknown, so Win and I got desperate and on Thursday bought 16 yards of netting which we made into two tents and have had peaceful sleep ever since. We have started the fashion and now everyone is wanting it! We had such fun trying to find the stuff in the store and no one knew what we wanted, however we poked around and finally discovered a kind of netting — not the real thing, but it serves the purpose splendidly. It's very difficult shopping on Thursday afternoon as it is a general holiday here instead of Saturday and the stores are jammed.

I'm enclosing a pamphlet which I got at the Motor Show and forgot to send you. The little bicycle-cars it describes are really most amusing. I've seen two or three of them in the city. Good practice for your French reading it!

Today being Sunday we all speak English as hard as we can go, though at times you find yourself speaking French, after doing so all week.

Really this is just ruining my spelling (such as it was). It's awfully tricky trying to spell words which are almost the same in both languages.

Best love,

Betty

During Thursday's shopping trip, the girls found themselves in an unfamiliar part of the city. At the main entrance of le Bon Marché, a man wearing a filthy oversized jacket was opening one of the three doors for shoppers, clearly hoping they'd drop coins into his tin cup for this service. Win and Betty paused, glanced at each other, and wordlessly agreed to avoid his door. As she passed by, Betty looked closely at the unshaven fellow. His left leg had been amputated below the knee, his pantleg folded up and tied with cord, and he used a crutch to keep his balance. Skinny and decrepit, he appeared to be only in his midthirties.

When they were out of his earshot, Betty asked Win, "What do you think happened to that poor man?"

"He was probably injured in the war," Win replied. "It's horrible the way vets are not taken care of by the government. They've risked their lives for France, after all."

The image of this emaciated, wounded soldier came to Betty's mind as they were being served their evening meal. The next few evenings, as she tried to fall asleep, there it was again. His sacrifice and suffering made her life of privilege feel distressingly hollow. *Somebody has to help these men!* she decided. *I will always keep a couple of francs in the outside pocket of my purse so I can give them away at a moment's notice. Rummaging around is so awkward.*

38 Rue de L'Yvette,
Paris 16e
Oct. 21, 1930

Dearest Mother,

Three weeks tomorrow since we arrived and though each day passed quite quickly, it really seems much longer than that! Fortunately, our good weather is continuing, with rain very often during the night. Yesterday I didn't go out until my singing lesson which was not until 6 p.m., as M. Pavisnant is very liberal with his time, we were there until 7:40 p.m. and found the others halfway through dinner. After this I am to go at 5:30 p.m. Monday and Friday, which means that I'll have to make some change about my bath, which I now have at 7 p.m. on Monday, Wednesday, and Friday. Big nights! I hope I'll be able to change with someone for other nights as I would hate to have to get up for it in the morning and the water is never really hot then.

XX Wed. 22nd. Thrills and cheer. When we came out from breakfast, I found six letters waiting: yours, Daddy's and one each from Eleanor, Isabel, Marjie and Aunt Barbie. Win suggested just reading a couple and saving the others for mornings when I don't receive any, but I wasn't strong-minded enough for that. Jean's wedding sounded lovely, though the colour combination seemed odd. They also gave me a lengthy description and enclosed clippings so I'm well informed on the subject.

I have a baby jacket nearly finished which I'll give to you for the club next year. You'd be very amused to see us all sitting around like grannies, each with our knitting or tapestry work. The two American girls are most amusing. Neither of them knew how to knit, but they went ahead, bought needles and quantities of wool and started in. They are both making bed jackets, but they have about twice too many stitches so they are going to be simply huge, if they ever get done, which I doubt as they spend so much time picking up stitches! It's rather nice to have something on hand as we have 15 minutes between classes, and generally a few minutes after the bells ring for meals, as it takes some time for 20 people to assemble. A great event happened last week. They actually bought some American cereals for breakfast: puffed wheat, corn flakes and my favorite, grape nuts! A welcome change from the bread rolls.

Win and I really don't often take anything but fruit as there are always two kinds — stewed and fresh — and bread and bitter chocolate at about 10:30 a.m.

I have really no news as I didn't go out yesterday and am staying home again this afternoon as my shoulder is quite sore still. It really isn't serious at all, just a bit uncomfy — and I'm being well looked after. They even had a doctor, much to my disgust! I was in my room Monday afternoon when Mlle. Jeanne appeared with a very nice middle-aged French doctor who said it was only muscular — no ribs or anything — as I already knew.

Do you remember in the little booklet about the school it said parties were sometimes given when we would have the opportunity of meeting "best French society"? Rumor has it that such an event is to happen on the 31st. A regular Hallowe'en party! So, you can picture us bobbing for apples, etc. in the approved and customary fashion.

Very best love to you all,

Betty

38 Rue de L'Yvette,
Paris 16e
Oct. 23, 1930

Dearest Daddy,

So very glad to get your letter written while you (and Binx) were bossing the establishment. I hope Dick and Mother go to the movies together again if being alone inspires you to write your daughter in "furrin parts." So, you are imitating some of the European customs we've told you about! Alas, we don't even have paper napkins at breakfast or teatime. Win and I very often have grapefruit for breakfast and as they are simply cut in half, not stoned or prepared in any way, it is very nerve-wracking trying to eat them without a napkin and endeavoring not to cover yourself and your neighbours with juice! The meals here are really very nice as a rule though now and then we strike one which we don't like. Last night for instance we had soup, a sort of pureé of peas, cold sausage and lettuce, and a gooey milk pudding. But tonight, we fared sumptuously on soup, young roast chicken, vegetables, salad and French pastries! We keep a supply of biscuits in our room for eating after skimpy meals, so never go to bed hungry.

This morning we woke up to pouring rain and though it slackened about 10 a.m. it has been dull and raw all day. When we went out for our lesson in Diction at 10:30 a.m., we even wore our rubbers, the only people in Paris doing so, I think. They seem to have as much rain here as in England and people seem to take very little notice of the weather.

At 2 p.m. I went to the dentist, to be finished up. He is very nice, his office absolutely modern in every respect. But he struck me as being rather fussy and pernickety — such as putting in a temporary filling last week in a very tiny hole and having me go back again. Then I met Win and three of the others and we went to our first French movie. Not a real talkie, only music and singing with titles in French and English. It was supposed to be in Russia at the time of Catherine the Great, very dramatic and hair-raising. Also, a cartoon and Fox-Movietone News. Then we went out and indulged in a schoolgirl tea, hot chocolate, toast and cakes! They make a great fuss over American ice cream sodas, but they really aren't very nice.

It is most amusing here with about six different kinds of music going on at once. There are two pianos and four portable gramophones and Anne Hackett plays the violin. So, you can imagine the noise! Harmony?

It was lovely getting such a nice budget of letters yesterday, now however I must get busy and answer them.

Best love,

Betty

38 Rue de L'Yvette,
Paris 16e
Oct. 26, 1930

Dearest Mother,

This was the afternoon I intended to write so many letters but it's 5:30 p.m. and I'm just starting, so I must hurry and make up for lost time. You see, Win is still in bed and we have had visitors on and off all afternoon. The last one was Mlle. Jeanne who brought her knitting and stayed a long while showing us photographs of all sorts of wonderful chateaux belonging to cousins, uncles, etc. Evidently quite a downfall for the De Broins to descend to keeping a school! Also we bought some magazines (Good Housekeeping and Red Book) and it's such a treat to have something to read.

Oh! I guess I hadn't told you about Win as my last letter was Thursday. Well, that night she wakened up at 1 a.m. and was awake till nearly 5 a.m. with a bad bilious attack.

The next day she had a bit of a temp so they had the doctor, who thought she might be going to have appendicitis, but decided it was an intestinal germ. She has been in bed three days — not feeling sick but not allowed to eat anything solid. She is to get up tomorrow. They have really looked after her as well as possible, but their methods are so different from ours.

This afternoon, being extra chilly, we have even had a fire in our grate — a tiny one but very cozy and cheering all the same! Today was lovely bright sunshine and a nice nip in the air. We went to church by the stuffy old Metro with only about two blocks walk at the other end so really didn't get much advantage of the nice day. Win and I are thinking of asking Aunt Barbie to write Madame and give us permission to go out alone — just in the neighbourhood, for walks in the "bois" and to the hairdresser's, etc. just around the corner. We went to the American church this a.m. — a really lovely building, quite modern. The service is Episcopalian — practically the same as ours only with different settings to the Te Deum, etc. and not very familiar hymns. I hope we always go there because the other one (exactly the same as our service) made me feel so homesick.

Yesterday was quite eventful. In the morning Mlle. Jeanne announced they had six tickets to a meeting at the Academie Française and that the two Hacketts, one of the American girls, and I could go with M. and Mme. De Broin. It was a combined meeting of the five Academies — Beaux Arts,

Belles Lettres, Science, and Politics attended by the elite of Paris and quite a privilege to have an opportunity to go.

So at 1:30 p.m., dressed in our best, we departed in a taxi with Madame. It was held in what was an old chapel in an ancient palace. We went in and sat near the back but it is only a small building and the seats are raised we could see and hear all right. We sat on terribly hard and narrow benches, without backs! Rather a strain to sit for nearly three hours. At 2 o'clock with a rattle of drums and a guard the members came in — about 90 of them, ranging in age from about 50 up to one doddering old fellow of at least 95! Practically everyone with a mustache, and a great many with beards of every variety and colour — from long fuzzy ones, to nicely trimmed Imperials, and from inky black, pepper and salt to pure white. Daddy better come over here, if he wants any pointers on how to grow his! The officers and speakers of the day were in uniform, black trimmed with green braid, cocked hats, some with swords and a great many with decorations.

After lengthy remarks by the president, we heard four addresses — the third and best by M. Func Brutano, the dear old lad who gives us our lectures on painting and is apparently quite celebrated. I wasn't able to understand everything, but except for the two who spoke so quickly, I could understand enough to follow.

After that we took a taxi to a certain corner where we waited hoping to see Coste and Bellonte, who were making a triumphal entry into Paris, but after twenty minutes to half an hour of standing in the wet, being jostled by a garlicky crowd and kept in order by such nice jovial "gendarmes," their motor car — a huge open one with a crest painted on the side came along and we found they had gone to the Aeroplane Club by another route and we had missed them.

Friday night was the time of our "Invitation Attendance" at the Opera — six of us went and sat in state at the Duchess Box. The Opéra-Comique is much the same plan as the Opera House, of course, not nearly so large. Imagine, there are five tiers of boxes! The top ones are not divided but are just ordinary balconies. We were in the second tier, but sad to say, the box was right next to the stage, really too close. The opera was "Pelléas et M'elisande" - very well sung but quite tragic. The music by Debussy, I really didn't care for. Very modern — no melody — all sorts of weird discords, etc. It's very amusing when we all go out and promenade during the "Entr'Actes" (intermissions). It's quite the thing to do — to see and be seen. Sometimes one sees very beautiful and exotic evening dresses, but on the whole, I don't think the people are so awfully well dressed. My writing has about six different slants because I am holding my pad on my lap as I huddle over my precious fire!

Less than a week of October left! And soon time to be thinking of Christmas presents. I don't think I'll try to send much from here but I'll bring people things when we come home. We received a most attractive booklet of the hotel at Wengen (the Regina) where Aunt B has reserved our rooms from Dec.17th — Jan 7th. It looks perfectly lovely — skiing, skating and tobogganing — and the most marvellous scenery. We are going to see about buying breeks early next month. I think I'll get dark green to match my leather coat. Also, I'm thinking of having my brown chiffon dress altered by having the coat cut up and used to lengthen the skirt as it is really too short for evening, but if longer, with my satin slippers would do quite well. Dressing bell has just rung so I must stop this rambling epistle.

Best love,

Betty

Betty was ecstatic that she and Win would be taking the train to Wengen, Switzerland, to spend the Christmas holidays. During her summer trip in 1927, she had stayed in three Swiss cities: Geneva, Montreux, and Interlaken. At the time, she'd found it frustrating to see the magnificent Jungfrau only through a large telescope. The tantalizing snow-covered-in-summer Alps were way off in the distance then, and the concept of now staying partway up a mountain thrilled her.

She studied the Hotel Regina's brochure after writing the letter to her mother. She couldn't wait to "drink in the village's glorious isolation, natural beauty, and spectacular views." December's snowdrifts would be a welcome contrast to grey, damp Paris.

Although Betty had found European cities certainly worth visiting, she was excited to be going to a Swiss alpine village without any cars. *It's unlikely there will be any beggars around*, she thought. *Skiing is a rich person's sport, especially in an expensive country like Switzerland.*

The thought, *Am I becoming a spoiled brat?* puffed through her head briefly like a ring of smoke.

Then she turned to her cousin. "Win, do you know where we should go to see about buying breeks for skiing?" she asked.

"Well, Henriette took us to that super place for dresses. Let's just ask her where we should go."

Betty usually avoided physically risky pursuits like downhill skiing, but the hotel brochure mentioned "small-group ski instruction." She would just go slowly and not advertise the fact that she had been on skis only a few times. *Win is always timid. I'll just act the way she does*, she thought.

38 Rue de L'Yvette,
Paris 16e
Oct. 29, 1930

Dearest Mother,

Very glad to receive your letter of the 16th and to know you had my first Sunday letter from here, I must admit the last two Sundays have been considerably better than the first. Win being in bed on the 26th and me on the 19th, the afternoons really became "salons" with music (gramophone) and talking (lots of it) and refreshments (candy and nuts).

About the smoking, we are allowed to smoke here — much to our amazement, but rest assured I'm not like Cecilia and turning into a smoke fiend to soothe my home sickness! I only have one very, very occasionally. You say I would probably laugh with Kay and Ted at your lecture in the evils of smoking. I really quite agree with you on smoking but maintain that the odd one doesn't hurt. Very good of Mrs. Hackett to call you up. Anne and Florence are really very nice — "young, innocent, convent girls" — a pleasing contrast to the two awfully sophisticated Americans. Don't I sound old and snippy? It's rather amusing: we five Canadians and Cecilia, the Swede, chum together, and the two English and two Americans, more or less keep to themselves.

You ask me if I love Paris? I know you do and I agree with you about its magnificence. It is so wonderfully laid out with great open spaces and though I admire it and like it better than I did, I don't think I'll ever feel at home here as I do in London.

Win got up yesterday for the first time and feels quite okay except awfully weak from lack of food. Really — they have the craziest ideas here — imagine giving soup for breakfast and macaroni and soup with spaghetti for lunch, to anyone in her condition! We are all taking extra precautions against colds and we certainly don't fancy being sick here.

It's too amusing the way they proudly say they have central heating. It's such a huge old place with so many windows that the little bit of heat from the radiators doesn't make the slightest impression. The room Win and I are in has beds, washstands, etc. for three so you can imagine how big it is, with two long French windows and our heater consists of a little hole in the floor, about 4" X 8" which at times exhales a damp gloomy odor, but never any heat — so we keep it closed!

Monday afternoon I had my singing lesson and was given two new songs — one by Greig, a very pretty minor thing, and one by Schumann. Then yesterday I went out and had my hair shampooed and a Marcel wave. We go to a place just around the corner, Monsieur Charles, very nice, clean and modern. It's rather odd because they have a men's hairdressing place downstairs and men kept rushing through all the time. Also, they have three male operators and I had one do me yesterday — a Serbian, quite young but with a black beard! However, he gave me an awfully nice wave so I guess I can stand his hirsute (is there such a word?) adornment.

Then we had our lecture on "Paris Artistique." It's really quite interesting to trace the architecture and symbolism of statues from early times and to see that what were formerly pagan symbols have become embodied in the Christian religion.

This afternoon we are going to a museum and I must go and get ready. Opera tonight — "Le Chevalier et La Rose" by Richard Strauss.

Very best love to you all,

Betty

I must admit, thought Betty, *the cachet of regularly attending the theatre and the opera is becoming quite second nature to me. Here I am — just a bookkeeper's daughter from NDG — hanging around with the upper classes. Am I becoming an elitist? Will my family find me changed?*

Notre-Dame-de-Grâce was a middle-class neighbourhood of Montreal without the prestige and wealth of Westmount, where Barbie and Win lived. The enormous Munderloh mansion on The Boulevard also accommodated their two maids, and René, the chauffeur, lived with his family above the garage.

Finding the Parisian social scene most stimulating, Betty was reluctant to disrupt her current routine in any way. Her previous Montreal existence now seemed drab in comparison. Earlier concern about her mother's struggles without a maid had evaporated because the efficient Annette had been hired to keep everything shipshape.

Now Betty could genuinely move on from her former responsibilities of running the household at Marlowe Avenue. Here she had no groceries to buy, meals to prepare, or dishes to wash. Even her laundry was done by staff, delivered neatly ironed, folded, and exuding a subtle lavender scent. Her only chore was to wash out her stockings every night.

38 Rue de L'Yvette,
Paris 16e
Nov. 1, 1930

Dearest Mother,

We've really been quite frivolous this week with two holidays, a party last night and a tea date for tomorrow! Thursday morning we went into the city for our lesson as usual. Then, as it was a raw damp day, Win and I decided to stay home in the afternoon — do odd jobs, write letters and read. Luckily we were in, because about 4 o'clock we were very surprised and thrilled to be told there was someone to see us in the "salon."

We went in to find Madame Ravel, Mrs. Rinfret's friend, with her little four-year-old girl. Unfortunately, she doesn't speak any English, but she seems so kind and nice and has invited us to spend the afternoon tomorrow from just after lunch until dinner time and spoke of future Thursday afternoons. She has two little boys of seven and ten and one of 14 away at school, but says her niece of 19 or 20 speaks English and will be there. You can't imagine how nice it is to think of going out — even to a friend of a friend and French at that!

The party last night was really most amusing, it was supposed to be in celebration of our North American Hallowe'en (an unknown event in France) and consisted of the usual games, ducking for apples etc. From somewhere they inveigled seven young men to come to the party, but they were not much of a success as they didn't even try to talk or dance with anyone except those who spoke fluent French — the daughters, Vera, the Serbian girl, and two other French girls who were former pupils. So, we sat around like wall flowers and amused ourselves by watching. We all came to the conclusion we don't like Frenchmen, at least if they were a fair sample. We hear tales of a dance near the end of November of about 50 or 60 — horrors!

Today being All Saints' Day we had an all-day holiday. This afternoon Win and I, the Hacketts, and the Swedish girl went in to try and see the movie Byrd at the South Pole which just started last week. Although we arrived quite early, we found a huge line-up and so went to another cinema. Luckily it was a very good picture — a French talkie. A highly improbable plot but laid in the Alps, with perfectly lovely scenery and some awfully good skiing and ski-jumping. They have the Fox-Movietone News here — a local edition in French and a cartoon on the same lines as the animated ones with music, but not nearly as clever.

When returning from the movie, Betty bought herself a copy of *The Daily Mirror* as a little English-language treat. She loved reading about the new baby Princess Margaret, born just before their August crossing on the SS *Duchess of York*, the ship named after the baby's mum. Her older sister, Elizabeth, was pictured gazing happily into the baby pram. *Someday I'd love to have a proper English perambulator,* she thought, *navy blue and white with enormous wheels. They are so elegant.*

The photo's caption stated that Princess Elizabeth was four years old. The child's dark hair and sweet smile reminded Betty of her sister Mary at that age.

(Letter continued)

We have met another one of the De Broin family (there are nine of them). The middle son, who I believe is studying at some university, is just home for the holiday. The other son is a chemist living in Ottawa and engaged to a French-Canadian.

XX Sunday. This is a real autumn day — gray skies and a strong wind, which is rapidly removing the last of the leaves. There is one tree here which has been perfectly lovely the last ten days. A huge horse chestnut with brilliant yellow leaves and shiny black bark — the whole silhouetted against the gray stone wall or occasionally bathed in sunshine. It has really been beautiful. It is visible from one of the upstairs windows and I always take a look as I go by.

Best love,

Betty

38 Rue de L'Yvette,
Paris 16e
Nov. 3, 1930

Dearest Mother,

We've just finished dinner and before settling down to work I'll start this. Tonight we had a chocolate pudding, much like the one we make except thin as a thick soup and served on perfectly flat plates — eaten by the French with much noise and scrapings. Really their table manners are terrible. They all make a noise, eat very rapidly, and mop up their plates with bread! And as they are supposed to be cultured, well-educated people, one shudders to think what the other classes must be like. Excuse this dissertation on food and manners. I sat opposite the son-in-law tonight and I guess that inspired it.

It's rather nice we don't sit in the same place all the time. Monsieur and Madame sit opposite each other at the middle of the table and the son-in-law and his wife at Madame's right — moving down a place whenever there is another guest of honor. Mlle. De la Margine sits at Monsieur's right and the oldest daughter at his left. Then we sit wherever our napkins (with labelled napkin rings) happen to be put, except at noon on Sunday when we get clean ones and we can sit anywhere we like! We only have napkins for lunch and dinner and use the same one all week — a great saving in laundry.

Had a very good singing lesson this afternoon though I still find it difficult to think of pronunciation, breathing, expression, and the music all at the same time. It is so different singing in French, you run your words together in a way which would be terrible in English.

XX Tuesday. This afternoon Winifred and I went "hatting." We were taken to a very small place, really just a room in an apartment, and Win succeeded in getting a very nice brown felt to match her coat, but I couldn't find anything to suit me. I need a new black one as my "Betty's hat shop" one is becoming shabby after two months of almost constant use. I also need a new afternoon dress and a hat to match. I haven't decided on a colour yet. I think probably green, or a dark Royal blue. We are beginning to plan clothes for Christmas. It seems a long time ahead, but we can only get out occasionally and don't want to be rushed. The hotel we are going to in Wengen is quite "swish" and if we will be there three weeks we'll need quite a lot. On a road trip you can do with so little because you frequently change locales.

I must tell you about our very enjoyable Sunday afternoon. We left here about 2:45 p.m. and walked (alone) as it's just about three blocks away. The family lives in a very nice apartment, with a separate entrance. It is very comfortable, though a trifle over-furnished. Madame Ravel is a youngish middle-age and very charming. Monsieur seemed rather silent and unprepossessing at first but we discovered it is because he is quite deaf. Before the afternoon was over (we stayed until 6:30 p.m.!) we became quite chummy as he was the only one who spoke English.

We had tea seated around the table in the dining room. The children came in, too. The two politest little boys of seven and nine I've ever seen, but very pale and unhealthy looking. The little girl is awfully sick-looking too, she had diphtheria a year ago and is still not very strong.

We are invited to lunch on Thursday and in the afternoon Madame Ravel is going to take us to a place to buy ready-made dresses which she says has very good things and is not expensive. We really got along quite well for our first experience with French hosts. Win and I said to each other, "Imagine how we would have felt at the idea of going out for an afternoon with a French family a month ago!"

Betty and her meek young cousin were justly proud of themselves for venturing alone into a French home where virtually no English was spoken. The introduction to Madame Ravel had come by way of Mrs. Rinfret, a Montreal friend of Aunt Barbie's.

The fact that Betty considered it an accomplishment for them to walk three blocks in broad daylight — *unaccompanied* — underscored for her the sheltered existence in which she now found herself.

Betty estimated that Madame Ravel could be only about twelve years her senior. *She's only a bit older than me — maybe thirty-six — and yet she's firmly settled in life with a husband and four kiddies,* Betty thought. *Quite a contrast to my current footloose situation.*

Despite their different life circumstances, Betty was thrilled to have made a new friend and was excited to see Madame Ravel again in just a few days when they would go shopping for ready-made dresses. *How lovely it is to have found a possible real friend here!*

(Letter continued)

XX Wednesday a.m. This morning is beautifully bright but very cold. We seem to have given up our morning walks — I don't know why. It's rather a pity not to get out when the weather is fine! Still no letters this week. I wonder what has happened to the Canadian mails; no one seems to be getting any except the English girls. I think I told you knitting was all the rage here. About the second day Madame suggested it would be a good idea for everyone to have some kind of handiwork. I already had some wool and everyone else bought some, or a tapestry or embroidery project. Yesterday Win bought some red and I some pale orange to make sleeveless sweaters for wearing under our leather coats at Christmas. I've decided to have my ski breeks made dark green and think my wool will look very nice with them.

Joy! Jean, the waiter, "valet de chamber" and handyman, has just built a fire in what is called "la grande piéce" where we have our classes and use as a sitting room. I'm not a very good architect but it's something like this [floor plan of room]. The wallpaper is very vivid, covered with parrots and baskets of flowers in reds and blues! And with flowered chintz on the furniture, long plain yellow curtains at the windows (which by the way all have leaded glass) with a border of blue, yellow and mauve — you can imagine the hectic appearance.

Oh! While I think of it, I must tell you one of their favourite deserts here is roasted chestnuts — served hot. I didn't like them at first, but we have them once or twice a week so I'm cultivating quite a taste for them.

By the way what would you think of sending me "Good Housekeeping"? We bought the November issue but they are so frightfully expensive — about 80 cents and not worth it. But cutting out the advertising pages in the front and back would make it much lighter. Don't do it if the postage is really too high. Also, we'd be awfully glad of any interesting clippings from the "Montreal Star." We feel we're rather behind the times in world happenings.

Best love,

Betty

Before Thursday's trip to the dress shop, Madame Ravel had offered to take the girls to a small jewellery shop in the same block.

Speaking French, Madame Ravel told the girls, "They have a wide selection of genuine gold and silver. And costume pieces. The prices are most agreeable."

"Oooh," Betty replied. "That sounds wonderful."

"The place is run by a Jewish family," Madame Ravel added. "You'll be sure to find something pretty and modern."

Betty was planning to buy a couple of bracelets or necklaces to go with the new clothes she'd bought for the Wengen holiday.

As the group approached *le magasin de bijoux* Goldman, they all stopped dead in their tracks. The front window of the shop had been smashed and all the merchandise was gone. Betty noticed an ugly black spidery shape that was crudely painted on the front door.

"How appalling! What a horrible thing for someone to do to a tiny shop," Win moaned.

The place was deserted. Two other jewellery shops in the same block were open for business. In French, Betty asked Madame Ravel, "Do you think one of those other stores would have good deals too? I was really excited about getting something for our trip. I even brought along a sweater to coordinate with."

"No, those others are rather exclusive with very high prices, unfortunately," Madame Ravel replied.

Without saying anything further on the subject, the three women continued walking toward the dress shop.

38 Rue de L'Yvette,
Paris 16e
Nov.7, 1930

Dearest Mother,

Excuse this being started in pencil but I am writing in bed. Having slept very badly last night I stayed in for breakfast and a nice long sleep and am so warm and comfy I hate to get up even to cross the room for my pen. There seem to be a great many cats in the neighbourhood. There are two here, and last night about 2 a.m. they held a concert or a fight underneath our window making blood-curdling howls — which woke us both and for some reason I didn't get to sleep again until dawn!

It was so nice to get your long letter yesterday morning and also one from Eleanor. We have had two letters from Aunt Barbie since she reached Florence and she seems to be very comfortably settled. I do hope they have good weather. Everyone says Florence is very rainy and foggy in the winter. We have just had two days and two nights of almost steady rain, but this morning is bright and cold — just the sort of day for a nice long drive in the country with plenty of rugs and a bag of crisp red apples!

Yesterday we had intended to go and order our ski costumes, but the rain was so bad we just taxied straight to Mlle. Nizan's for our lesson. We are starting a short dialogue, supposed to be two girls talking during a ball sometime in the 1890's, I think, and quite amusing.

Then we went to lunch at Madame Ravel's and met her niece, awfully sweet, about my age, I think. After a scrumptious lunch and coffee in the drawing room we went shopping and I ordered a brown tweedy skirt and coat, to wear with sweaters and blouses of which I have a good supply. I really needed something else as my green skirt, my old standby, is pretty shabby and the mauve one is rather light for winter wear. Then I bought an envelope-shaped bag to embroider in tapestry — don't faint! I almost did at the idea!

Wednesday afternoon I went with Henriette and four of the others to the "Salon D'Automne" an exhibition of furniture, jewelry, pottery, sculpture and painting. Almost everything very "Art Moderne." Some of the things were awfully attractive and interesting. They had whole rooms built and furnished and lighted in the modernistic style — bedrooms, dining and sitting rooms and even a gorgeous bathroom in black, silver, gold and pale pink! And I liked a great many of the statues — especially two models for war memorials which were very striking — but the paintings! The less said the better. Room after room of the most awful daubs, terribly out of proportion, hectic colours and weird subjects. They say that the autumn exhibition is always like this and that the more conservative artists exhibit in the spring salon.

Whenever Betty had the chance to study an exhibit of fine art, she was genuinely excited — more so, she noticed, than most of her contemporaries. Betty and Win's grandfather was a well-known Canadian artist named Thomas Mower Martin. His paintings hung throughout their family homes, and, having been exposed to superb art from an early age, Betty now found it both fascinating and comforting.

Their grandfather had been a charter member of the Royal Canadian Academy of Art. He'd painted in both oil and watercolour and managed to support his family of nine children by selling artworks and teaching about art. Some of his works were too enormous to hang in private homes and ended up in museums and art galleries.

During her enchantment with royalty when she was a little girl, Betty had learned that Grandfather had given a painting to Queen Victoria, which still hung in Windsor Castle. She had boasted about it to some of her friends, but nobody seemed that impressed.

Betty's curiosity about art led her to the many art books in the Harbert home library. From them, she had learned how to evaluate an artist's work. She could critique exhibitions with confidence and zeal, having developed "an artistic eye."

"Win, you were so smart to skip the Salon d'Automne," she declared after the trip. "The paintings were simply awful! If Grandfather were here with us, he'd have developed a headache."

"You're so right," Win replied. "I probably would have gotten one too."

(Letter continued)

Now to answer your letter. I heard from Ted this morning — giving his version of the weekend! Amusing to hear of them looking at furniture at this early date. The proper thing to do, of course, is to buy during sales and then the store will keep your purchase until you want it.

Just finished lunch and now I must get to work, and then do an hour's practice as I have my lesson this afternoon. Some of the others are going skating at an indoor rink, and the rest to the Louvre. Poor Cecilia has a two-hour lesson in dress-making every Friday afternoon, which she hates. She is the only one taking it this term and I haven't seen or heard anything about the cooking lessons. The little booklet about this school certainly did give false impressions on actual conditions.

We took some snaps in the garden the other day which are supposed to be done today. If so, I'll stick them in before I post this. About presents, please don't bother about sending us things. I don't intend to send anything, except perhaps hankies or something like that which could go in an envelope.

Best love,

Betty

38 Rue de L'Yvette,
Paris 16e
Nov.9, 1930

Dearest Mother,

This morning we went to the American church to the Armistice Day service. Very nice with lovely music. Yesterday afternoon I went with Henriette and Cecilia to the Museum of the Legion d'Honneur, all sorts of medals and decorations and pictures, clothes, etc. of the famous men and women who had won and worn them. Afterwards we walked part way home along by the Seine — very enjoyable in spite of a fine drizzle. There has been so much rain all over the country that the Seine is very high and muddy. So high in fact that the bigger boats can't pass under the bridges, so traffic is more or less held up.

It has taken me about an hour to write this as there are six of us sitting about one long table ostensibly all writing but someone makes a remark, all work is stopped and we talk for ten minutes — then silence and our pens fly rapidly until the next outburst of conversation. It's rather amusing — Vera writing in Serbian, Cecilia in Swedish, Eldred in French, and the rest of us in English!

XX Tea happened. Then I wrote to Ted and Aunt Mary, then despairing of ever getting anything done downstairs, left the warmth of the fire and the noise and (now in my cozy blue dressing gown) am writing in peace — comparative peace that is! With someone practicing singing in the room next to me, Florence Hackett on the other side attempting Largo on the piano and a gramophone across the hall. A nice quiet Sunday afternoon!

Marjie has been so good in writing weekly letters but her last one was very low. She had seemed so happy with her beloved Pete and really serious about him, but now she says her family have made her break up with him entirely. She seemed to feel awfully badly but to be surprisingly meek, saying she supposed families knew best, could see farther than young people, and so on. Didn't give any reason for her family's attitude but said she would tell me all about it later. Naturally I'm very curious as I thought they liked him, but of course it may all blow over!

Last night I was playing French contract bridge with one of the American girls, Henriette, and Roger De Broin, the son who came home for All Saints' Day. I was mistaken in thinking he was at college and just here for the weekend. It turns out he was working in Brussels but has come back to Paris to stay. He is quite nice and plays awfully good bridge. They play contract with almost the same score as auction 6 for clubs, 7 for diamonds etc. but give a bonus of 50 for every extra trick as we do, and 50 for making your contract as we do in auction when it's doubled! We have learnt all the French names and expressions — a "levé" is a trick, "la manche" is the game and "le mort" is the dummy.

The most amusing of the English girls has a male friend here for a few days who asked her to go out to dinner — they are going tonight accompanied by a chaperon! Also one of the boys at the party invited the other English girl and she is to be chaperoned by Henriette and his sister! So ridiculously old-fashioned. They say that even French girls don't go out without a chaperon, at least not properly brought-up ones.

Tomorrow there is a party going to Montmartre to see the churches, so Win and I hope to go too and spend our time in the fascinating little shop where we got our Christmas cards. The etchings are really awfully good and ridiculously cheap compared to ordinary ones.

Best love,

Betty

On her way to Monday's lunch, Betty checked the mail as usual. Her heart leapt as she came across an envelope addressed in strong, vaguely familiar handwriting. She ripped it open to find a short note from David inviting her out to dinner later in the week. *Yes! A real date*, she thought. He again asked her to respond by telephone, so she called him that evening and they agreed to dine together on Wednesday.

It was unusual to be stepping out with someone who hadn't been properly approved by Mother and Daddy. But she knew that if they were able to meet him, they would be impressed too, and would declare him suitable company for their youngest daughter.

Being a midweek date, she wore a soft red cashmere sweater and a black knee-length skirt rather than a dress. David appeared at Le Gui at seven on the dot, and they headed off arm in arm to the restaurant he'd chosen on Avenue Mozart. As he'd remained physically distant on previous dates, Betty had assumed that he had a sweetheart waiting for him somewhere. *How delicious!* she thought excitedly when he took her arm. She leaned in a little closer, enjoying their physical closeness.

At the restaurant, David removed his raincoat, uncovering a grey-speckled tweed jacket, white shirt, and a green tie with white stripes.

After looking at the extensive menu, Betty said, "I've never been to this place before. What do you recommend?"

"My favourite dish here is coquilles Saint-Jacques," he replied. "Would you like to try it? The scallops melt in your mouth."

"Sounds divine!" Betty said, so David ordered two portions along with green salads and a bottle of sauvignon blanc from Sancerre.

After the wine was poured into chilled stemmed glasses, the two began sharing extensive details about their lives prior to coming to Paris. Betty found David amusing and attentive. He was interested in her Canadian family life, places she'd lived, what her siblings were up to now, and her favorite sports and hobbies.

"I think it's impressive that you know how to play golf!" David exclaimed. "Very few women that I know are willing to chase after a ridiculous little white ball." When she described Aunt Barbie's private golf course in Vermont, he was clearly envious.

"So where did you live as a child?" Betty asked, feeling it was time to learn about his early life.

"I was born in Guildford, Surrey," he replied. "Father commuted daily into London to work in a bank, but my brother and I were lucky enough to stay in the countryside to be educated. We went to Charterhouse School. Perhaps you've heard of it? It was founded over three hundred years ago, amazingly. Mum didn't mind driving us to school most days. That left her free to do plenty of horseback riding and gardening." Betty could easily picture his idyllic, privileged childhood.

Sitting across from each other at a small table made it easy for the couple to hold each other's gaze. A white candle in a pewter holder sat between them, its light adding ambiance to the already romantic setting. The more wine they consumed, the more intimate their friendship became. The first time their knees touched under the table, Betty shifted away, but eventually she felt emboldened enough to just stay put.

Her feelings of romantic attraction to David became so strong that Betty fully expected him to passionately embrace and kiss her on the way back to Le Gui. She sighed expectantly.

It never happened. In fact, after strolling back to Le Gui with only arm-in-arm contact, he merely shook her hand goodnight. "Thanks for coming out with me, Betty. I hope you're willing to do it again," he smiled. He'd thrust a pin into her balloon of excited anticipation.

She frowned slightly and replied coldly, "I had a lovely time, David. Goodnight."

After completing her bedtime rituals, she got into bed feeling both disappointed and puzzled. *How could I have misread him so! Tomorrow I can tell Win what actually happened without having to edit out anything shocking,* she pouted inwardly.

38 Rue de L'Yvette,
Paris 16e
Nov. 13, 1930

Dearest Mother,

We are at last having some perfect autumn weather — today has been gorgeous, cold and bright, giving you such an energetic feeling. And we have accomplished quite a lot in it. To begin with four of us started off right after breakfast and went by taxi to a very grubby and crowded part of the city inhabited mostly by wholesale houses. Here we entered a grimy courtyard, climbed a flight of narrow stairs and found ourselves in the tiny office of a glove merchant, where we proceeded to order numerous pairs of gloves. They were so nice and so reasonable I got several pairs for gifts — guessing at the sizes. I hope they prove correct.

Then, while the others shopped, Win and I had our lesson — only a short one as Mlle. Nizan was playing in a matineé and had to leave early. We hope to see her sometime as she has promised to let us know when she is acting in something amusing that we could understand.

Right after lunch, the same party started out on a shopping expedition and succeeded in getting a very snappy ski outfit for Win (very dark red whipcord) and I ordered breeks which exactly match my leather coat. She also got ski boots, then we went to the same dressmaking establishment where she had her dress made and there I ordered a gorgeous flame-coloured georgette — simply made, fitted waistline, long full skirt and like this at the back [butterfly shape] — two sort of butterfly wings, fastened with a flat buckle — really quite pretty. (There are exactly 13 people talking and a gramophone playing in the room so excuse hectic tone.) Then we had our usual tea — toast and little cakes, came home and I practiced till dinner — which is just over.

Monday afternoon we went to Montmartre again to buy more cards and etchings. Then walked about (in the rain) peering at the old streets and houses. The artistic inhabitants, students, artists, etc. have all moved away so now it is really just a show place for tourists. We were late in getting back, only time to grab some tea and leave for my singing lesson.

Yesterday I stayed home, feeling lazy and the nice hot fire looking more attractive than the prospect of going out to see some historic old house and garden the other side of Paris! The others came back, having walked miles, frozen and starved, to find me toasting myself cozily by the fire!

About the cold — please don't worry. We are always warm enough down here and though our room is like an iceberg we can wear sweaters. My favourite method is to wear my dressing gown upstairs over a sweater and skirt so I'm really quite comfy. Last night Win, Anne and I went with Mlle. St. Opportune to the opera to hear The Master Singers which we enjoyed so much, more than any of the others we've seen so far. It was wonderfully sung and staged. It is an awfully long opera starting at 7:45 p.m. and lasting till nearly midnight — it was after 12:30 a.m. when we got home — such rashness!

Best love,

Betty

> 38 Rue de L'Yvette,
> Paris 16e
> Nov. 16, 1930

Dearest Mother,

Having just finished a rather faulty letter in French to Dick, it is such a relief to write in English. Friday was quite uneventful. I stayed home all afternoon until my lesson, which was quite successful and I was given two new songs — one by Mozart and another a lullaby. I can't remember the composer. Yesterday afternoon we went to a rather interesting museum — the house occupied by Victor Hugo from 1833– 48; furnished as it was then and containing an exhibition of his books and a great many drawings, pen and sketches and water colours done by Victor Hugo as illustrations for his stories.

Then last night a number of us, accompanied by Madame, went to the Marigny Revue — rather a contrast from our Wednesday evening expedition to the opera with such marvellous music and singing! However, it was very colourful and amusing. There were two excellent girl dancers, three men who did wonderful roller skating and a Tiller chorus of 16 girls exactly the same size who danced with such precision and exactness. We were late getting home — well after 12:30 a.m., so this morning Win slept late and didn't go to church. This afternoon is rainy so as usual we are occupying ourselves in various ways — reading, writing, knitting, and doing Swedish crossword puzzles!

Very best love to you all,

Betty

38 Rue de L'Yvette,
Paris 16e
Nov. 19, 1930

Dearest Mother,

We are waiting for our class in verbs to commence so in the meantime I'll start this. This morning is dull and damp after a rainy night and everyone is feeling more or less in tune with the weather — not damp exactly, but slightly grumpy — the grumpiness accentuated by the fact that there was no mail this morning and hasn't been since Sunday. However, there are three more deliveries today to look forward to!

This afternoon a big event is happening. We are going to a lecture on the Theatre — a series of lectures is starting on a variety of subjects to be given by professors, priests, and academicians so we'll probably attend one or two a week. We have a list and can pick out the ones we think would be interesting.

Yesterday we had our weekly lecture on Paris, starting to study Notre Dame cathedral. Our lecturer is really quite interesting — he knows his subject thoroughly and adds numerous little stories and legends. He is also the drawing teacher, so his blackboard sketches to illustrate the lectures are very clear and realistic.

After tea yesterday we went for a fitting of our ski outfits which are going to be very smart. Then to the dressmaker's for the first fitting of my evening dress, of which I am enclosing a sample. Win also ordered a short white evening coat of bunny fur — very pretty and only $52.00. Imagine! Tomorrow is our "congé." We are going in to do some shopping in the morning, then to Madame Ravel's for the afternoon. We are in rather a quandary as when she asked us two weeks ago she didn't mention if she wanted us to lunch again or not. However, Mlle. Jeanne is going to phone and be very tactful. As we don't want to give the impression we are hinting to be asked for a meal!

Things are considerably more cheerful now, as a nice big mail arrived at 11 o'clock! I was so glad to get your long letter which contains so much interesting news. Glad to hear old McGill has snapped out of it at last and actually won a game. Surprised to hear of Queen's beating Varsity. I thought Varsity had their clutches on the championship this year.

About my coming home before the others. I have been thinking about it a lot lately as Aunt Barbie wrote and asked me to let her know definitely what I wanted to do. She plans to leave here about March first, spend a few weeks in the south of France, Holy Week in Seville and then tour around Spain until about June 1st. Then, I imagine, spend three or four weeks in England and get home about the middle of July.

Don't you think it would be alright for me to stay just until they leave Paris, then go to England to see Aunt Mary and then home? Because I really feel I don't want to stay any longer. If you think I really should stay, I will, but after we leave here I don't think Aunt Barbie will need me any longer.

There, thought Betty as she wrote. *I've finally put it in writing.* Ungrateful thoughts of having had enough of this travel arrangement had been running around in her head for days — while she tried to fall asleep, when she first awoke, and when she waited for classes to start.

By boldly stating, "*I don't think Aunt Barbie will need me any longer,*" she'd admitted to Mother and to herself that she was, in fact, a paid companion and not simply the niece of the grand dame Munderloh.

Her heart felt lighter as soon as the words were on paper, but she was also uneasy knowing that there was the possibility of repercussions.

(Letter continued)

She is always so fussy when travelling. She likes to attend to things herself and Miss A more than seconds her in the matter. It is so hard to decide what to do so early, but they are already making their plans with Cooks. Rather unnecessary really as Spain is not so thronged with tourists — at least that early in the season.

XX Thursday night. The end of a very wet but really enjoyable day. This morning we left right after breakfast and went to town — first to Cooks to see if our reservations are all in order for Christmas, then in search of an evening dress for Win. After going miles, to the other side of the Seine and back while employing five taxis, we finally chose a very pretty model for her which she is having made in a red georgette. We came home, changed and went to lunch with Madame Ravel.

During the afternoon we went into town and shopped about looking at all sorts of fascinating things and buying a few Christmas gifts and more wool for Win — beige this time — to wear with her ski outfit. We had tea and took a taxi home about 6:30 p.m. I must stop now and do some work — having a whole composition in "Un souvenir de mon enfance" to write — am very short of ideas — but think perhaps I can imagine enough about the cyclone in Redcliff to fill the necessary three pages.

Best love,

Betty

38 Rue de L'Yvette,
Paris 16e
Nov. 22, 1930

Dearest Mother,

There is a stormy wind blowing tonight, howling in the chimneys in a melancholy fashion, whipping the bare branches of the trees in the garden, banging the shutters, blowing occasional gusts of rain against the windows — altogether behaving like typical November weather. But in contrast to the tempestuous outside, I am very warm and comfy — sitting up in bed wearing my cozy blue dressing gown, with a fire (of tightly rolled pages of the Montreal Star) burning in our little stove and to complete the picture of bliss — a cigarette in my left hand (as I told you before I hardly smoke at all, but now and then I feel like an odd cigarette!)

I wrote on Thursday after our visit to Madame Ravel — she has asked us again for next week. This time there is no question, we know we are asked for lunch. She is really awfully kind to bother with us so often. The Americans are the only ones who have real friends here — they seem to know quite a few and go out every Sunday and often a couple of times during the week.

Oh! We're feeling very gay and giddy having received permission from Aunt Barbie to go out alone in the neighbourhood. It really did seem foolish for me to have a chaperon to go to the hairdressers just around the corner and to have to wait to be called for like an infant. Please don't imagine we'll do anything rash, however. You know we'll always be most circumspect! Not, if I do say it myself, like the Americans — who go out to tea or lunch with friends, then leave them and dash all over the city alone while the De Broins think they are being safely looked after.

This afternoon I went with five of the others to the Petit Palais to see the exhibition of painting, sculpture and tapestries and really enjoyed it. A very good collection of pictures — all by French artists and comparatively modern — in date I mean, not style, about 1850 on. Tonight is the Sergei Rachmaninoff recital. I thought of going but found the tickets are $7.00. As there were only two others going, by the time the price of the chaperone's ticket, the chaperonage, and taxis were totaled it would be at least $10.00. Rather high! Especially as we'll probably have the opportunity to hear him again at home.

XX Sunday after dinner. Today is a pleasant change from our stormy night — clear and still. We went to the British Embassy Church this morning and find that the clergyman we heard before or, at least, couldn't hear, was only supplying and that the permanent rector is back after an absence of four months. He didn't preach a very interesting sermon but at least he has a pleasing voice. There is also a new assistant, quite young and apparently rather "green" — he gave out the wrong psalms, and then as soon as the sermon was finished, hopped up and announced a hymn instead of waiting for the offertory sentence and the anthem!

Now we are in our room. Win is curled up on the bed, chuckling over something in the Literary Digest, which arrived this morning. It is so convenient that all the newspapers and magazines arrive on Sunday which gives us occupation for the afternoon.

We didn't go out at all at night last week, but this week we are going to hear Pablo Casals on Wednesday, and to Madame San-Gene on Thursday. Our first theatre, but as we know the story, we hope we'll be able to understand it. Then on Saturday is the famous dance! About 50 to 60 of the "young French aristocracy." We're not awfully thrilled at the prospect however it may be more interesting than the Hallowe'en affair. My new evening dress arrived last night and is really lovely — very simple and beautifully made.

I'm sending home a parcel of guidebooks which Aunt Barbie suggested mailing to you to save carrying them about. You will probably be interested in the Oberammergau pictures. The large book on Merano has really some lovely illustrations. It was given us by the head porter at our hotel as a souvenir. Also, we are going to try sending our letters via New York. You might let us know if there is any difference in the time it takes for them to reach you. I think it would be quicker when they start going to and from St. John's. It is hard to realize that you have had snow at home and that it is just a month until Christmas. Here, although the trees are almost bare, there are still green shrubs, grass and even chrysanthemums. They say the grass is quite green all winter!

Best love,

Betty

While enjoying a relaxing warm bath, Betty took the opportunity to privately weigh the pros and cons of touring Spain. She realized that she really didn't want to go. She didn't know anyone who had been there, and she'd never heard any stories about the country or gotten tips about any must-see attractions. Before going to Rome, she'd heard about things like the ancient Colosseum and Saint Peter's Basilica, which sounded amazing, but she knew nothing about Madrid or Barcelona.

In her letter about spending Holy Week in Seville, Aunt Barbie had quoted what the Cooks people had told her about what was happening in Spain. Apparently, King Alfonso was desperately clinging to power, while Spanish citizens gathered in huge crowds to protest his rule. Naturally, Cooks said they would be sure to keep the party comfortably safe, but Betty was skeptical. *Obviously, Cooks would say whatever it took to keep Aunt Barbie's business.* Betty preferred to head back to Canada by the summer but decided to keep that to herself for now. *I'm really only asking Mother's opinion to be polite*, she thought. *I want control of my own daily life again. I'm tired of living at Aunt Barbie's beck and call.*

Another factor contributing to her disinterest was unfamiliarity with Spanish culture. Before her voyage that summer, she hadn't really met anyone from Spain, and the few Spaniards on the ship to England looked grumpy and upset most of the time, pointedly keeping to themselves. Plus, she found the concept of being innocent tourists in the middle of noisy demonstrations rather unsettling. *What if we get caught up in some protest?* Betty knew that wherever they went, she'd be looking over her shoulder all the time instead of having fun. She sighed and rinsed off. She decided she'd just bite her tongue for now.

The fact that she was in Europe only because Aunt Barbie paid all her expenses was starting to grate on Betty. She was clearly beholden, with little freedom to choose her own path. Whenever anyone invited her out to dinner or a concert, there was an unspoken expectation that she would check their schedule with her aunt before accepting. After revelling in a date on her own, her mood would darken the minute she got back to Le Gui. She found it took her real effort to be bubbly with Win when she recounted the events of her evening and that the level of detail she shared continued to diminish.

"Yes, I had a nice time, thanks," became her usual abrupt comment.

> 38 Rue de L'Yvette,
> Paris 16e
> Nov. 30, 1930

Dearest Family,

We should be feeling very much like "the morning after the night before" this a.m. as last night was our dance and we didn't get to bed till 2 o'clock! However, it's a gorgeously sunny day (the first time we've seen the sun for a week) and I received five letters so things seem quite bright and cheerful! I was so sorry you didn't get down to the Lake, but perhaps you could manage it again.

By the way, Aunt Barbie sent us the part of your letter to her about us going out alone. Please be sure we'll only go out in daylight and we haven't been to the "bois" yet, but if we do we'll only walk in the open and much-frequented parts. It's just like Mount Royal on Sunday or Saturday afternoon, everyone walking their dogs and babies, really quite respectable. Of course, I can quite understand and we won't do it if it makes you nervous, but really now that we can speak and understand French pretty well it's almost the same as being alone in Montreal!

My last letter was on Tuesday, I think. Yes, I was in bed with a cold until Thursday afternoon. Unfortunately I missed the Pablo Casals cello recital Wednesday night, but went to see Madame San-Gene on

Thursday. It was very well acted and beautifully costumed. Of course, we missed quite a few words but understood pretty well on the whole and quite enough to thoroughly enjoy it. Friday afternoon Win and I went to Avenue Mozart, the shopping street at the end of Rue L'Yvette, where we bought a few Christmas gifts, finding a small stationery store with awfully nice note paper. I also ordered a new black hat to be made for $6.00 at a little millinery.

Yesterday was a big day. No work, as everyone was occupied in preparing for last night. We had breakfast at 9 a.m., after an extra hour's beauty sleep, then in the pouring rain, Win and I and Mlle. St. Opportune went "en ville" for fittings for our ski things at one place, Win's evening coat at another and her evening dress at a third. All very successful. Our ski things are finished and look very smart. When we came home we found all the furniture cleared away, floors waxed, and everything decorated with flowers — pink carnations and ferns and a huge mass of bronzy mums in the hall. In the afternoon we went to the cinema, a French talkie, La lettre by Somerset Maugham, which was played in London by Gerald DuMaurier. Very good but hard to understand as the reproduction was very poor.

The party was in the evening. None of us were very enthusiastic after the Hallowe'en affair, but it really was heaps of fun. They had a pianist and saxophone for music. There were about 50 boys and 15 or 20 girls invited as well as six or eight elderly ladies — chaperons I suppose — very gorgeous and imposing who sat around the edges and gazed benignly on us. Win wore her blue crepe de chine and I my new red one, which is really quite lovely.

At first various people were introduced to us (Many titled ones about. Think of your Betty dancing with Viscounts, etc. Ha! Ha!) but as we couldn't remember their names or they ours after a while they just asked you to dance anyway. Some of them spoke a little English, some none at all, and one man I danced with a couple of times was an Oxford grad — with a beautiful accent! But another awfully nice tall one I danced with several times, couldn't speak a word of English, yet we discussed unemployment and the crash in the stock market quite intelligently. This house is really ideal for a party as all the rooms open into each other, like this floor plan. Afraid I'm not much of an architect.

Poor Win was feeling very scared and shy but she really enjoyed it when she got going and conversed away nobly. She danced with one very shy youth, a military student (there were three here in uniform) and as they were both shy — she made an effort and charmed him, so he asked her to dance again. They had a buffet supper "on tap" all evening — punch, sandwiches, and cakes. It lasted until 1:15 a.m. (it said 9 – 12 on the invitations), then we descended on the remains of the eats in approved fashion, after the guests had gone. There were three girls who stayed all night and Roger came back for the occasion. We didn't go to church this morning several of us sleeping till about 10:30 a.m. I woke at 8 and got up a little before 9 a.m.

Marjie told me all about her break with Pete. It is quite final as they discovered some rash acts on his part! She asked me not to say anything about it, so I'll just tell you that much. Poor darling. I'm so sorry for her. They had been going out so much together that everyone had started asking them to bridge and dinners together, so now it's very awkward to explain things.

About my coming home. I've decided to do so about March, if you won't be too disappointed and think me too foolish? You say my letters have been so cheerful and interesting — I'm awfully glad if they have been. I wanted them to sound happy but must admit I didn't always feel that way — in fact quite the contrary at times. I didn't mean to do or say anything about it, but Aunt Barbie wrote and asked me to let her know what I wanted to do about the spring and advised me to go home if I was homesick. I think Win must have told her I wasn't exactly feeling cheery! I know it's so silly of me but I'm afraid I can't help it. Don't get the impression I'm pining away or anything like that, but I really don't feel like staying that extra three months and though the trip to Spain would be wonderful I think I could get along without it. That's all very involved but I hope you understand what I mean.

Best love,

Betty

In telling Mother about returning home in March, Betty wrote, *"if you won't be too disappointed and think me too foolish."* It had become a chore to continuously be cheerful and engaged. For heaven's sake, many of her Montreal friends were falling in love or getting engaged and here she was being cared for like a baby flower in a greenhouse: fed, watered, kept safe, but not allowed to blossom. Because she was benefitting from Aunt Barbie's generosity, she felt rude and ungrateful when she longed for adult activities, but the gulf between the way she acted and the way she felt was becoming too stark to maintain. It was easier to say that she was homesick and let that be what people believed, but that wasn't exactly it. *I just want my independence back*, she thought. *And I miss my friends!*

Although they were genuinely fond of each other, the two cousins had little in common socially. Not only was Win quiet and withdrawn, she was seven years younger than Betty. Being the only child of a rich, older couple, she had everything material she could possibly want but lacked Betty's charm, easy sense of humour, and lightheartedness.

It helped that Betty had brothers. Ted was five years older than her and Dick was seven years younger, and they both had gently teased her on lots of occasions. Learning to not take herself too seriously had built her self-confidence. She also loved to make her family laugh, and she was able to take that sense of humour with her out into the world. Expert at describing funny vignettes she'd witnessed, her audience often found her stories amusing and her laughter contagious.

But she was less sure of herself at Le Gui. Ever since sailing over here last August, Betty had been constantly aware of the others' opinions of her behaviour. Thoughts crowded her head when she was interacting with people — *Am I being too loud? Did I appear to be criticizing? Am I too concerned with my appearance? Will I be late for dinner? Must I go on yet another sightseeing tour? Can they not see how genuinely bored I am?*

She also felt uncomfortable having to always be on around her aunt and Miss A. She would often catch Aunt Barbie scowling, and she wasn't always sure if she was annoyed at her or at Win. She remembered feeling incredibly worn out some days when they were on their grand tour before landing in Paris. Some days she would make up a headache in order to avoid going along with them to see yet another ruin, church, art gallery, or historical site. She was surprised that her boredom wasn't more evident to them. She tried to hide it most of the time, but some days she just couldn't feign interest any longer. So Betty was pleased that she'd told her mother that she was going to skip the trip to Spain. She'd be able to avoid fake smiling and always having to second-guess her own behaviour.

Since the late-November dance, she'd often thought about a German lad named Wolfgang — she never caught his surname. Wolfgang was tall, blond, and blue-eyed. He spoke excellent English and enjoyed showing it off. Betty often caught herself remembering his perfect waltzing, and she longed to step out with him. She couldn't believe the attention he paid her: They danced together three times and he was deliberately slow letting go of her hand when the music stopped. Betty felt blissful. It was lovely to be touched and valued.

"It was a pleasure to meet you, Miss Harbert," he said as he was about to leave. "I hope we meet again."

She blushed and looked at the floor, murmuring, "So do I."

Over the next week she checked her mailbox for messages more than normal and she daydreamed about the German beauty. *I'd like to call him Wolfie*, she thought whimsically, then she giggled at the idea.

38 Rue de L'Yvette,
Paris 16e
Dec. 5, 1930

Dearest Mother,

When your cable arrived yesterday morning and Madame gave it to me after prayers, I was awfully surprised but, as you can imagine, delighted to get it. I'm pleased to know that you don't disapprove too much of my decision. I was afraid you'd be awfully disappointed and think me foolish, as I suppose I am to give up a wonderful trip, but I feel so much better now I've decided. I have made up my mind to work extra hard and make the most of my time until March. That will be another three months, about the same time as has already elapsed and it already seems years since Aug.27th!

Yesterday morning Win stayed in bed with a cold, so I went in to do some shopping then to lunch with Madame Ravel alone. Today she is up and about again. Though really this place has been more like a hospital than a school the last ten days — I think eight out of 11 of us have had colds. The weather has changed from rain, to very cold and foggy. Say what you like I certainly like our winters better — long and cold though they may be, they are much more agreeable than this penetrating dampness.

To go back to Madame Ravel, I had a very nice lunch with her family, then went with Monsieur to the Rue de Rivoli where we met her niece and did some window shopping. We crossed the river to a fascinating little store where we found all sorts of necklaces and odds and ends. I ordered a very snappy wooden and nickel one to wear with sports things (wooden jewelry is all the rage here to wear with sweaters). This afternoon I made an expedition to Avenue Mozart — my favourite hunting ground!

XX Saturday a.m. Tonight I am going to see some Paris night life, with Vera, Mlle. Jeanne and three boys who were at the party! And tomorrow Win and I are being taken to tea at a friend's — a famous doctor who has been to Canada and dotes on Canadians. We'll have to do our best to make a good impression. I'll write tomorrow and give you details. And thank you again for the cable. I did love getting it!

Best love,

Betty

38 Rue de L'Yvette,
Paris 16e
Dec. 7, 1930

Dearest Mother,

Just finished dinner and I'm now settling down to our usual Sunday afternoon bout of letter writing. So glad to get yours of the 26th this morning and also the Montreal Star, Daily Mail and Good

Housekeeping. I have just glanced them over but will have a good read tonight, I hope. Yesterday afternoon I went into town and succeeded, at last, in getting a new pair of black slippers. It has been awfully difficult as they are all cut so low, however I found some with straps at the sides which hold my ankles pretty well, and of course I won't be walking in them at all. Then in the evening was the big event.

To start at the beginning: Mlle. Jeanne, Vera, and I were called for at about 8:30 by the three "jeunes gens." One shortish, very nice and amusing who spoke English and went by the name of Xavier. The other two were both named Jacques — one tall and nice-looking with a most romantic-looking scar on his cheek, who did not speak any English, and the other, red-haired and a bit older, who seemed to be quite a friend of Jeanne's.

They had two cars so we drove to a tiny theatre in the Montmartre called "Les Deux Ans." A very funny place where we saw a most amusing revue. Not the usual type at all. I mean with no dancing. There was a cast of about 12 or 14 and they put on a series of skits — very clever and original. They introduced all sorts of local characters — political, Coste and Bellonte, etc. and a very clever satire on Briand who is not at all popular. Of course, I know I missed a great deal, both through not understanding and not always recognizing the people mentioned. However, Xavier explained things now and then and I could follow enough to be amused.

Then we went to what is supposed to be the oldest house in Montmartre. We went through a tiny hall to a room — about the size of Aunt Barbie's downstairs bedroom at the Lake. Absolutely blue with smoke, lit only by two dingy lights and crowded with very ordinary looking people (I mean not freaky) sitting on small wooden stools and listening to the music. We were passed small glasses, containing brandied cherries (at least that's what I think they were), which we ate by the stems. There was an elderly man in a sweater who seemed to be the master of ceremonies, though everything was very informal and casual. There was one man at the piano, another who sang and passed drinks in the intervals, and an elderly woman and a younger one with a really lovely voice and a girl who played the harp. We stayed while they sang about eight songs with the crowd joining in whenever they felt like it.

At 2 a.m. we left and drove across the Seine to the other side of the city where we searched for a certain nightclub but couldn't find it so went to one called Coupula — very modernistic in design, with a mirrored ceiling. There were two orchestras — one of Negros and one of Argentines who played most marvelous tangos.

We only indulged in orangeades while the boys had a glass of wine each! It was really heaps of fun and so nice to dance again. The party last week had whetted my appetite. And it was striking 4 a.m. as we entered the door. Nice goings-on for a school — tut! tut! Mlle. Jeanne is really an awfully good sport and quite enjoyed it. This a.m. Win made me stay in bed while she brought me up a huge cup of coffee, a banana and some prunes — which I ate while studying my memory work for our diction lesson at 11. As the family had to go to church, we went in alone — on the Metro, making one change en route and feeling very big and bold and brave. It really is the simplest and easiest thing — as the stations are so plainly marked and there is a list in every Metro so you know exactly where to get off.

Thrilled to finally go out with other young adults, Betty took special care with her hairstyle and makeup, then donned her prettiest black dress, pearls, and new evening slippers. All she knew in advance was that they would have "a taste of Paris night life," which probably meant rather risqué entertainment. *Wouldn't Mother be shocked? Well, she won't be hearing about this!*

No one in the group was romantically involved, so everybody relaxed and mingled without judgment or agenda. The fact that Win wasn't coming along gave her the chance to truly be herself. *Nothing I say or do will be reported back to Aunt Barbie*, she thought, thrilled.

The three men were all great fun and had superb manners, but her favourite was Jacques with the scar on his cheek. It was stimulating to flirt in French with a man unable to speak any English.

She'd described Jacques to Mother as *tall and nice-looking*. His blue eyes sparkled with humour, and he hung on her every word, leaning close when loud background noise interfered with their conversation, which made Betty glad for the disruption.

The sequence of events was electrifying: the revue, the nightclub in Montmartre, the Coupula with two orchestras. Finding the tango an extremely sensual dance, she revelled in dancing with a partner who knew how to properly lead. As Jacques escorted her to their table, she felt drops of perspiration run down the centre of her back.

The three ladies sneaking into the house at 4:00 a.m. was particularly exhilarating as Betty had never been out so late. As she tried to fall asleep, she kept reliving the delicious highlights, so it was likely another hour before she dozed off. Across their room, Win snored lightly.

(Letter continued)

XX Later. Have just had tea, read part of a story and had a long talk. The enclosed piece of material is a sample of my new skirt which you see is nice and warm. I'm getting a new afternoon dress too as I decided I really needed another good one and might as well have it before Christmas. Black crepe de chine trimmed with bright green! I sound as if I'm getting a lot of clothes, but I really would have done so if I'd been home as all my things are leftovers from last spring.

Best love,

Betty

CHAPTER 4

Stemming, Christianas, and So On

It took Betty and Win about fifteen minutes to ride a little train up from Lauterbrunnen to the village of Wengen, which had no automobiles. As soon as they disembarked, they spied the Hotel Regina, where they were going to be staying, situated just a few hundred yards from the station. Betty caught Win's eye, and they both smiled, excited for their ski holiday and amazed by the gorgeous hotel. A porter transported their luggage on a pushcart while the girls walked beside him.

Betty already knew a bit about the hotel from studying the brochure. She had read that it had opened in 1894 and that the hotel's deluxe lounges and bedrooms were deliberately situated to highlight the spectacular views of the mountains of the Jungfrau region and the Lauterbrunnen valley.

Betty and Win stood by the front desk as reception registered all the new arrivals and handed out room keys. Betty looked out over the crescent-shaped lawn facing west. She noticed about fifteen hotel residents relaxing in sturdy wooden chairs as they watched the sun sink behind the opposite mountains. She said to Win, "I can't wait to sit there basking in the sun too! A bit of suntan will do wonders. Let's replace our Parisian pallor with a healthy glow."

"I've always found sunbathing too boring," Win said, "but it may be different in December. And we have an amazing view to study while we sit. Did you bring your dark glasses?"

Regina-Hotel,
Wengen, Switzerland
Dec. 20, 1930

Dearest Mother,

Well, here we are settled in Wengen after our long time of looking forward to it and happily we can say it more than comes up to our expectations. It's so lovely to see the snow and real, warm sunshine after damp, grey Paris.

To begin with Wengen is situated, not in a valley, but on a broadening out at the base of the mountains. We can look down over a thousand feet to the tiny village of Lauterbrunnen and up I don't know how many thousand feet to the various peaks which completely surround us. The highest, of course, is the Jungfrau, but we get quite a different view of it than we did at Interlaken in '27 and of course it is much snowier at this time of year. It is all so different from our summertime impressions but so lovely it is impossible to describe. I do wish you could all be here to enjoy it with us. Being so shut in by mountains we only have sunshine for about five hours from 11 – 4 (that is actually on the village) but it is wonderful watching it come over the tips of the mountains an hour or so earlier and creep gradually down. It is very hot, and during the middle of the day we find one sweater is quite enough for skiing — no hats and just thin gloves. We saw the most beautiful effect yesterday while we were out walking about 5:30 p.m. — the snowy mountain slope with a line of inky black fir trees against a sky which was creamy at the horizon, shading into pinks and then blues.

This hotel, the second largest in the village, has accommodation for about 160. There were only a dozen when we arrived but new people appear every day and they say it will be quite full by Christmas. It is very comfy and very informal, more like a club. Everyone stays in ski clothes all day — just dressing in time for dinner. Everyone seems to be English so far, except one Frenchwoman and her little boy.

We arrived here about 3 on Thursday, spent the afternoon unpacking, then tea, a walk with Win, dinner, and to bed early.

Yesterday a.m. we explored the village which consists of a few houses, one street of stores (sporting goods, candy, cameras, films, etc., two hairdressers, drugstore), a darling English church, two big rinks and about 15 hotels. Then we rented skis and made arrangements for a lesson at 2. We decided it was the best policy to have a few lessons on turns, stops, etc. We had a very nice young guide to teach us — a marvellous skier and a very good instructor. He teaches up on the Jungfrau all summer so is as much at ease skiing as walking.

We had our second lesson at 9 this a.m. and spent the rest of the morning practicing. We have been out all this afternoon too, so enjoyed over four hours of skiing today. We feel we want to be outside all the time to make the most of our precious three weeks of winter.

I haven't told you of our trip from Paris. Wednesday afternoon we went out to tea with the girls, then home in for dinner at 6:30. Mlle. Jeanne escorted us to the station. Luckily we had a very agreeable porter to whom we gave a good big tip and he looked after everything for us. We gave him our passports and key to the trunk so didn't see or hear anything of the customs which we passed about 2 a.m. I think. The train was not very full, so he gave us two lower berths on either side of our little washroom, and we were very comfy. We made our change without difficulty and arrived in Interlaken to find Aunt Barbie and Miss A waiting for us. So nice to see Auntie Barbie again. She looks very well and not any thinner. We had lunch in Interlaken then wandered about a bit coming on up here on the electric cog-wheel train at 1:45.

XX Sunday. The mail arrived when we were at tea yesterday and I was so surprised to hear about Daddy's eye operation, but so glad he did well and hope by now he is quite all right again. The idea of an operation of any kind is always worrying, and as your letter to me in Paris had not arrived this was the first news I'd had — even that there was a possibility of anything! It makes me feel awfully selfish to be enjoying myself in this lovely spot and to know you've been busy and worried. Today was another heavenly day. We were out from 9 a.m. to noon and have just come in from an exploring trip to the valley. Now we are going to have tea and go to church at 5:30 p.m.

Best love,

Betty

Regina-Hotel,
Wengen, Switzerland
Dec. 24, 1930

Dearest Mother,

Two nice letters from you and the cable to answer! The cable arrived at breakfast time yesterday morning and I was so glad to get it and to hear Daddy is better. It's rather hard to realize that news is about two weeks old when it reaches us by letter and a cable is wonderful and seems to bring everything so much nearer. Rather strange the doctor making such a quick decision, but really rather a good idea, I suppose, as it doesn't give one time to think about it beforehand. Your parcels have arrived safely, but we are being very strict with ourselves and have everything put away to open tomorrow. We are planning to go to early service then have breakfast and open presents, to make it as much like a real Christmas as possible. Thank you so much for renewing my Good Housekeeping.

We had rather an interesting time on Monday morning taking the train up two stations (about 2000 ft.) and having a wonderful run down — of course, with numerous spills and hair-raising moments! We were taken up by two Englishmen staying here — both awfully good skiers — but very nice and patient with us showing us quite a lot and not minding our slow progress. We stopped about ¾ of the way down at a tiny chalet and had piping hot chocolate, very welcome as we were an hour late for lunch. This is the fourth foggy day. It started on Sunday when all the valley below us was filled with billows of white fog, though there was bright sunshine here. On Monday it was foggy here but clear on top of the mountain. Yesterday we were out on the hills nearby, but the fog was so dense you could only see clearly for a few feet. It was a most weird effect to see ghostly skiers dashing in and out of sight. Today is much clearer and they prophesy snow tomorrow! Really quite badly needed as the hills are all so packed down and the grass is showing through in exposed places.

This morning we had another lesson, so we are becoming quite proficient in stemming, Christianas, and so on. Hope we'll be able to remember them until next winter and be able to pass on our knowledge to Dick. Have just had lunch and are about to go out again.

Best love,

Betty

Betty was both surprised and encouraged by her progress on the ski slopes. Risking life and limb doing any sport was not exactly her usual style, but so far, she'd had no serious mishaps. Staff at the hotel had carefully fitted her rental boots and skis, and the skiing instructors were patient and gave clear instructions to their pupils. The ski classes were divided according to ability and spoken language, and the maximum class size was only five.

"Isn't it marvellous to be learning to ski on top of the world?" Betty said to Win while they were getting changed for dinner after a full day of skiing. "The Alps make the Laurentians look like baby hills. And taking the train up to the top of the slope is so much more relaxing than hanging on to a rope tow."

"How right you are! It's marvellous," remarked Win. "Why don't you take your bath first?"

Betty peeled off her dark-green breeks and light-grey sweater and hung them up to dry. Their ski wear got rather damp whenever they took a tumble.

Regina-Hotel,
Wengen, Switzerland
Christmas night

Dearest Mother,

Just came up to bed after a very pleasant Christmas day. At least as nice as a hotel one could be! We all went to early church this a.m. — a very nice service, the little church absolutely crowded and strange to say, a large proportion of men and boys arrived on skis from the further hotels. It looked so odd to see a big pile of them outside the door! It was gorgeously clear and frosty after our several misty days. It doesn't get light until about 7:30 a.m. so was quite dusky on the way over and when we came back the sun was just beginning to slant over the mountains.

We had breakfast downstairs, then went up to open our presents. Everyone was so good in remembering us. Thank you and Daddy for the collar and cuff set. They are lovely and I think will fit my new black dress. Auntie Barbie was, as usual, awfully generous, bringing me two lovely slips, a handbag and some beads from Florence and buying me a pair of opera glasses in Interlaken — small gray mother-of-pearl ones with awfully good lenses. Miss A gave me an initialed hankie, in fact I received 14 hankies altogether and many other gifts. I loved Dick's book and think the De Broins would find it interesting. They seem very keen about Canada, especially as one son is out there. I'll buy something with Eleanor's money when I get back to Paris.

XX Friday. Today Miss A wrote the final letter to Cooks about Spain and Aunt Barbie asked me for my final decision which has remained the same. She does not seem to mind my not going at all and thinks it would probably mean my leaving about the first week in March! She said she would take me to England but I said I could leave from Cherbourg so as not to give her extra trouble.

Best love to you all,

Betty

Regina-Hotel,
Wengen, Switzerland
Jan. 2, 1931

Dearest Mother,

Glad to hear of Daddy's satisfactory progress, as far as his eyes and appetite went, but too bad about the rheumatism and hope it was merely temporary. Eleanor's letter was written during Ted's trip to Toronto, giving an account of their visit to Ted's-in-laws to be! So nice that he could use the faithful Hupmobile for dashing about and for his business in London.

Today has been lovely with a heavy snowfall until noon and then bright sun. We had great need of additional snow as with the mild weather and such mobs of people skiing, it had become very thin in spots. Yesterday morning Win went for a walk with Aunt Barbie while I wrote letters and then escorted Miss A who is very ambitious about climbing to see views, but very wobbly and has fallen several times.

In the afternoon Win, an awfully nice Australian girl, and I took the train up one station and had a very nice run down, stopping ¾ of the way home to watch a ski competition being run off. Several wonderful skiers participated including the British woman champion. On New Year's Eve we did have a party after all. Practically every hotel held a Masquerade dance and I was invited to go with two Australian lads (both attending Cambridge) and the same Australian girl, to view the various celebrations.

During one of her skiing lessons, Betty noticed a particularly attractive man in her group of four. After everyone removed their skis to have lunch, he casually strolled over to introduce himself.

"How do you do? My name is Jack Graham. I'm impressed with your stem turns. You've obviously skied before." He smiled, removing his glove to shake her hand.

"Well, yes, I have. Nice to meet you. I'm Betty Harbert from Montreal. I've been lucky enough to ski a few times in the Laurentians," she said.

She noticed he spoke with a slight accent, but she couldn't place it. *That was silly. He's probably never heard of the Laurentians*, she thought, tucking her gloves into a pocket.

Before she knew it, she was sharing a small lunch table with him and devouring steaming bowls of chicken vegetable soup with crusty baguettes. When Win later arrived carrying her tray, Betty shifted over to give her space too.

Jack explained that he was in his final year of law school at the University of Cambridge, England, although he'd grown up in Sydney, Australia. He and his roommate, Klaus, were spending the Christmas holidays at the Hotel Regina, like Betty and Win. But they had no older family members travelling with them the way the girls did. *What I wouldn't give to be that independent!* Betty thought, but she was careful not to indicate her envy because Win was present.

Jack had sandy-blond hair, dancing green eyes, and a hearty laugh. Betty found him deliciously charismatic. *Part of the appeal*, she thought, *is that we can speak English together, just like when I'm with David McKay.* After all those slow, relatively formal conversations in French with boys in Paris, she loved being able to chat away without needing to search for any French vocabulary. *It also makes it easier to flirt*, she realized. They picked up on each other's sense of humour and had a lovely time chatting.

He must be awfully clever and fairly wealthy to be able to travel all those thousands of miles to England to study, Betty thought. *Australia is on the other side of the world!* He was the first citizen of the Southern Hemisphere she'd ever met.

That lunch was the first of several impromptu meetings Betty and Jack enjoyed over the next few days.

It doesn't take psychological training to interpret potential lovers' body language: lots of eye contact, torsos positioned toward each other, frequent brief touches, and laughter over minor things. The air crackled every time they were together, and their mutual attraction was obvious to any onlooker.

On New Year's Eve, Jack and Klaus invited Betty and an Australian girl to go to the Hotel Regina's masquerade dance. They politely included Win, but in her typically shy fashion, she opted to just go upstairs to bed after New Year's Eve dinner. Betty was pleased with the freedom from her cousin that night and didn't even try to persuade her to change her mind.

Betty quickly transformed herself into a gypsy. All it took was a scarf tied tightly over her hair, knotted over one ear; brass curtain rings worn as earrings held in place with loops of string; a blouse tucked into a full skirt; and Aunt Barbie's Spanish shawl draped around her shoulders. And voilà!

The first time Jack took her in his arms to dance, she was overjoyed. He was about eight inches taller than her and a marvellously smooth dancer. *What a delicious treat!*

To prolong the fun after the Hotel Regina party, the foursome toured several other Wengen hotels. Somebody then suggested going luging after the dancing finished. The two girls hurried up to their rooms to change into ski clothes. One could hardly go luging as a gypsy.

After the first run, Betty's fingers and toes were numb, but she ignored the cold. She was glowing with excitement. Pulling the luge behind them, Jack took her hand as they struggled back up the hill for the next run. *Thank goodness Win is safely out of the way,* she smiled to herself.

As the two sat on the luge together with her in front to steer, he wrapped his long legs outside hers. Betty hoped the others were too distracted by all the laughing and sliding to notice this intimate posture. At the bottom of the run, they rolled off into the powder snow. Jack helped Betty up and surreptitiously kissed her cheek. The moon shone brightly on the Alpine snow, and for once, there was no wind.

(Letter continued)

We stayed here until about 11:30 p.m., dancing and participating in the parades of costumes for the choice of the best — most original, etc. Win wouldn't dress and I only decided very late in the day, so improvised a gypsy outfit — very unoriginal but easy. From here we went to the Silberhorn for a few dances, then on to the Palace (the biggest hotel here), for a few more. On the way home we organized a luging party — heaps of fun as it was a gorgeously clear starry night and an almost full moon made it very light. We arrived back about 3:30 a.m. after a very good time. Everyone full of fun.

Many people are starting to leave but there are others arriving and they say the hotel will be quite full until the end of January. All the English schools and colleges have holidays until about the 20th. We are talking of staying a day or so longer. It seems foolish to go back on Wednesday and spend until Monday in a hotel in Paris, but Miss A doesn't want to stay so I don't suppose we will!

She made a point of being cautious when arguing her case for "staying a day or so longer" in Switzerland. She ached to spend more time with Jack and get to know him properly, but she couldn't tell Aunt Barbie and Win that. She hadn't felt such a warm glow in a man's company since her romantic dinner with David McKay, and she was still feeling the sting of that intimacy turning out to be a mirage. She was really hoping that things with Jack would solidify and become something she could hold on to.

(Letter continued)

I'm gradually getting my Christmas letters written, though I still have a great many more to do. It's hard to write here as we are outside all day, then have tea and generally a bath and lie down till dinner. Very lazy I know, but so much fresh air and exercise does make you sleepy. Then in the evening there is music and so much talking going on it's hard to concentrate.

They quite frequently organize some amusement for the evenings as well, such as games, musical chairs, and balloon races. There was to have been an Ice Carnival tonight but it is so mild they have had to postpone it. Tomorrow night there will be a dancing competition. I was tangoing the other night with a German who did it beautifully and I'm more intrigued than ever. I'd love to learn the dance properly. Perhaps I'll have some lessons in Paris, though I don't suppose I'd ever dance the tango at home. I wonder if Dick enjoyed his frat dance. There is a boy staying here who is sitting at the other side of the writing desk at this moment, who reminds me awfully of Dick, though older and of course, not so nice looking. How I wish old Dick were here now — I know he'd enjoy it so.

XX Saturday. Today has been another gorgeous and very energetic day. We went up one station on the 10 o'clock train and skied down, but it was so bad — after rain last night and then frost — that we each rented a luge and went up again on the 12:10 p.m. train — arriving back about 12:50 p.m. After lunch we went up again, farther this time to Wengen Alp, and down just in time to catch the 3:10 p.m. This time we made a record run, coming down in only 14 minutes. Sounds like a lazy day, but really you get so hot climbing in weather like this.

We then had tea and a game of bridge, our first here. We played with a very nice Mrs. Smyth and her son of 17. Now I'm dressed and waiting for the others to come down to dinner. Here they are. Must stop.

Best love,

Betty

Although he was busy dashing about doing winter sports, Jack habitually stopped for lunch at exactly the same time the girls did. On the final day before departure, Betty was delighted when he wandered over to share their table. As she put on her ski jacket again for the afternoon, he blurted out a logical reason for them to meet on their own.

"Betty, you've asked me to tell you the titles of some of my favourite novels. Let's meet in the lounge about six thirty and I'll give you a list of books I think you might enjoy," he said with a twinkle in his eye. It was clear the invitation didn't include her young cousin.

Wearing a simple dark-green dinner dress with no jewellery — *this was not a formal occasion*, she reasoned — the dark-haired beauty descended the wide staircase into the hotel lobby. Christmas decorations were still in place. Betty glanced at the antique luge mounted on the wall near the bar. She held her breath. Jack stood at the bar — in a navy suit, light-blue dress shirt, and navy tie with white polka dots — waiting for her. His hair was still wet from a shower and neatly slicked down.

"Here's the list," he smiled. "May I have the honour of buying you a drink, on our last night in this heavenly spot?"

"That would be lovely, thanks." She tucked the list of books into her purse.

The couple settled onto two tall stools at the bar where she ordered a sherry; he ordered Scotch and water. Their hands and knees touched briefly as they sat there, relaxing into the glow of the alcohol and the joy of being together, finally alone and sitting quietly. She caught the pleasant scent of his subtle aftershave.

"You mentioned that you're coming over to England on your way home to Canada. I have a car in Cambridge and would love to meet up with you in London. Perhaps dinner and the theatre or even more dancing?" His grin matched his smiling eyes.

"That would be simply wonderful, but I'm not exactly sure when I'll be coming to England. I've decided to skip the trip to Spain with the others, so I'll probably be in London sometime in March. Why don't we write to each other so I can tell you when I'll be arriving."

"What's your address in Paris?" Extracting a pen and little notebook from his jacket pocket, he jotted down the address at Le Gui as she recited it. "I will write to you first," Jack said. "In fact, perhaps I'll just arrive at your door one day."

Betty blushed with pleasure and averted her gaze. *I can't wait*, she thought.

An hour later they sneaked several brief kisses in the hallway before parting, hidden from other hotel guests' view by an enormous potted plant. Then she climbed slowly up to join Win in their room, as dinner was at 8:00 p.m.

CHAPTER 5

The Last Lecture at the Sorbonne

38 Rue de L'Yvette,
Paris 16e
Jan. 10, 1931

Dearest Mother,

Well, here we are back in Paris again — all unpacked and so settled down we almost feel as if we'd never been away. No, I should not say that. We did so enjoy Wengen and have such happy memories of what we did and the people we met there. The ones we were most friendly with were some very nice Australians — a father and daughter and two friends and a mother and son and one friend, so we have all sorts of pressing invitations to go and see them, if and when we go to Australia.

We arrived here Wednesday night at 11:30, after rather a long day on the train, which we helped to put in by reading aloud a thrilling mystery book — each one taking turns. We went to the Hotel Majestic, spent the night there and came here Thursday after dinner. We were called for at the hotel at 8:30 a.m. and arrived to find just the four who had spent the holidays here — Anne, Florence, Eldred, and Cecilia and one new English girl. Win and I are in the same room again, but if we stay we are to have another English girl with us later. As we have the chance of moving to a smaller and much warmer room, we think we'll do it.

Yesterday a.m. we unpacked then Win and I went with Henriette to the Sorbonne where we arranged to go for lectures Monday, Tuesday, Thursday, and Friday mornings — so will just have two classes a week here. Win's Italian is to be Wednesday a.m. and my singing Monday and Friday at 5. I am very glad about the lectures as I think they will be much more interesting than the classes here. It is a course in French only for foreigners — 3 lectures a morning starting at 8:30 a.m. (we'll have to leave the house at 7:45 a.m.!) You pay the same price, about $9.00 for one or all — so we will just take the ones we are interested in.

Today we had our classes as usual and this afternoon went to the Rodin museum, which I greatly enjoyed. Aunt Barbie and Miss A are staying at the Majestic Hotel, although Miss A is not very keen about it — she thinks it's too far from the shops and not fashionable enough, which we consider a great joke as she sits in her room most of the time anyway. She is a great trial to poor Aunt Barbie because she's always fussing about something. She is making all the arrangements for Spain so if anything goes wrong, she'll only have herself to blame, which brings me to the subject of the Spanish trip. I'm reconsidering my decision.

After your various letters saying the Spanish tour would be good for me, and that one should not consider one's likes and dislikes and personal feelings too much when something is to your advantage. And as I feel so much better physically and mentally after Wengen, when Aunt Barbie asked me if I wouldn't change my mind and stay, I decided I could stick it out so said I would — providing you don't need me to come home! I mean if Daddy isn't well and I could help, or you'd like me to drive him about or stay with Dick while you take him to the country or anything — please do tell me. Otherwise, I'd be home about the first week in June as Aunt Barbie says I can go home as soon as we get back to London — and she may take a trip around England and Scotland before returning. If you'd rather I came home about March 15, please cable (don't cable otherwise) and please don't feel I'm longing to stay if you want me or that I'm staying against my will. It's so hard to explain my feelings. I know this is very faulty but I hope you understand.

Very best love,

Betty

When writing to her family, Betty did her best to sound conflicted about staying on past March. She would be heartbroken to leave Europe without seeing Jack again but purposely kept mum about her new feelings. He had talked about seeing her in London, and it lifted her spirits to imagine him coming to see her in Paris before then as well. Being a natural optimist, she fully expected to see him within weeks.

She had never felt so wobbly when reliving tender moments with a man. She thought about Jack every time she soaked in a bath of deliciously warm water and every night in bed before falling asleep.

She found his slow Australian drawl relaxing to listen to and pictured him arguing an important criminal case in court. She couldn't help but smile when she thought of him.

38 Rue de L'Yvette,
Paris 16e
Feb. 4, 1931

Dearest Mother,

Just came in from spending an afternoon with Aunt Barbie and Win looking over a most attractive collection of new spring styles, soft frilly printed silks and tailored ensembles. Here are a few hints:

Three-quarter length coats worn with a dress of the same material, wool crepe or some such.

The application of frills — especially to the sleeves, at the wrist or just below the elbow, or at the hips.

The printed things have both large and tiny patterns, not many flowers — mostly abstract designs.

We haven't made any decisions yet as we are going to Miss A's dressmaker tomorrow "to look her over." It really was most amusing. We took Aunt Barbie to Charlotte Appert's where both Win and I had our dresses made — not very expensive but very well done and quite good enough for anyone — least of all Miss A, who doesn't dress so awfully well herself. Aunt Barbie ordered a very pretty plain afternoon dress — black with a tiny blue thread, which was nicely made and suits her wonderfully. But Miss A insisted that she go to her dressmaker Frances who has a very swish place as she did not think ours was fashionable enough. There poor old Aunt Barbie ordered another dress — just about twice as expensive, which turned out the most awful wreck — it makes her look fearfully stout and is having to be made over. So naturally Win and I rather laughed up our sleeves.

Last night was the occasion of the grand dinner party at Madame Ravel's. It really was awfully nice. We arrived at 8 p.m. (I in my black lace and Win in her new red dress.) The other guests consisted of two married couples, of whom one wife spoke very fluent English and both husbands a little — so all went well. We had a most scrumptious dinner lasting from about 8:30 p.m. until after ten — soup, fish, meat, poultry, salad, ice cream, cheese, fruit and coffee and liqueurs served in the drawing room. Oh yes — cocktails first and three kinds of wine during dinner — all of which we did not indulge in, naturally. Madame Ravel is leaving next Monday to visit her mother in the south — taking the little girl to try and get her strong enough for a tonsils and adenoid operation in March. The poor kiddie is very thin and pale and always seems to have a cold.

XX Thursday. Have just come in again from viewing Frances's style show. All sorts of gorgeous things but some very extreme. We took Madame Ravel with us and afterwards to tea on the Champs-Élysées. It is very cold today. Actually a few flakes of snow fell this morning though they melted on touching the ground.

I was so glad to find your two letters waiting when I came in from the Sorbonne at noon and it was most tantalizing to have to sit through lunch with them unopened in my pocket. I had only time to wash my hands before the bell rang. I'm very glad you approve of my decision as I was almost sure you would. We expect to arrive here in Paris May 25th, have a day or two here, if the weather is good; if not, dash right over to London. Going west at that time of year, travel is very light so I would be able to get a berth on very short notice.

Tonight we are going to see "Cyrano de Bergerac" at a small theatre where one does not have to wear evening dress. Lucky as it is bitterly cold and Win's short bunny coat, though so pretty, isn't awfully warm. I find my green one as nice as ever, though the velvet is beginning to show signs of wear — naturally enough after three or four years. But it was so successful perhaps we can make another and transfer the fur? A short black velvet evening coat, without fur, is one of the things I'm ordering for the trip — as it will be warm — or at least we're fervently hoping so!

Went to the Sorbonne this morning but instead of arriving at 9:45 a.m. for our lecture on the History of Ideas we were sadly "en retard" and didn't get there until 10:05 a.m. So instead we went to the Pantheon which is nearby and wandered around until time for the second lecture at 11 a.m.

Best love,

Betty

38 Rue de L'Yvette,
Paris 16e
Feb. 6, 1931

Dearest Mother,

Your letter of Jan. 28th arrived this morning, again at a very tantalizing time just as we were leaving for the Sorbonne, so I stuck it in my bag and read it on the bus. Funny that so many of my letters arrived in a bunch. I think the mails this way seems to be getting better — just eight days for your last to arrive.

I'm writing this at M. Razevet's, while waiting for Diane and Brenda to have their lessons. Poor Diane is so pathetic. She will never have any voice but insists on taking lessons. Brenda, on the other hand, though only 16 has really a lovely voice. She has been having lessons for four years (much to M. Razevet's horror) and means to have her voice tested in a year or two and really study it as a profession. Her voice is surprisingly full and very sweet but rather has that "mouth full of hot potato" sound just now, which she will probably get over. I am singing about an equal quantity of French and English now — going over the things I brought over with me.

Today we were very thrilled on getting up to find the ground and trees covered with snow and a few flakes still falling! Of course, it didn't last and we found the streets in a very wet and slushy condition. This afternoon we went to the lecture "Aux Anales: Education de la jeune fille" or some such title. Very uninteresting. At least the man who gave it had one of those sleepy voices, very difficult to listen to and I must admit after the first few minutes I didn't try very hard and almost slept the rest of the hour. I was rather tired having had a latish night last night. We enjoyed Cyrano very much.

Tomorrow night is Le Jongleur de Notre Dame. Was so glad you enjoyed Il Trovatore. Who sang it? The American Opera Company I suppose! Very many thanks for the birthday wishes. I will get myself a new bag I think, from you — as I want a black one very badly.

Betty strolled down Avenue Mozart to take a look at the shops. How delightful she found it to go out to the shops alone! She could browse for hours, and nobody stated an opinion on whether or not something would be a good purchase. Being totally independent gave her pure pleasure. She had already visited two separate shops before finding the perfect evening bag.

She spotted "the one" through a shop window. It was a black satin evening bag with a simple silver-toned clasp. *It's so very modern looking*, she thought. Betty had noticed the most elegant women at the opera with similar bags. It was called a clutch. *I suppose because you have to clutch it*, Betty mused — as there was no handle, you had to tuck it under your arm when going out for the evening.

Betty bought the extravagant item as her parents' present to her for her twenty-fifth birthday. It was only big enough for her new opera glasses, a comb, lipstick, and a hanky, but it would go beautifully with all her evening clothes. It felt a little odd to be buying their gift herself, but she did love the chance to choose something she truly wanted. So often she received gifts that she would never have chosen herself, but thankfully, she had long ago mastered the art of hiding disappointment after unwrapping something she had absolutely no interest in. She wouldn't lie and say, "Oh! It's lovely. Just what I've always wanted." Instead, she was purposely vague — "What an unusual colour!" worked well. Ted and Dick especially struggled with selecting items she found tasteful, but she was always touched when they tried to get her something to bring her joy, even if they ultimately missed the mark.

(Letter continued)

XX Sunday night. It was time for my lesson then, so I had to stop and have not had any time since. To continue the subject of birthday gifts, Aunt Barbie gave me a very pretty brilliant clip — to be worn on a hat or dress, and Win gave me some of my favourite Evening in Paris perfume.

We spent a very pleasant day today. Church at 11, then walked over to the hotel. After a delicious lunch we taxied down to the Louvre and spent almost two hours — mostly among the Dutch and Flemish painting — one room of French — Gros, Dela Croix, Ingres and a few Spanish in the long Gallery between. It was a very good day as the sun was actually shining making the light very good. Then we walked along through the Tuileries Garden to the Place de la Concorde and up the Rue Royale to the Place de la Madeleine for tea.

As they walked through the Tuileries Garden, a little girl of about four ran by Betty, followed closely by a slightly older boy. They appeared to be playing tag. The girl was sucking on a lollipop while they played. Seeing kids running with sticks always reminded Betty of the tragic event that had befallen her sister Mary.

Betty said to Win, "Oh dear! I want to tell that little girl how dangerous it is to do that."

"Well then, go ahead and speak to her," replied Win. "It can't do any harm."

By this time, the kids had stopped running and were settling on a park bench with a grown-up, so Betty decided not to approach them, but seeing the little girl had left her feeling troubled.

Before Dick was born, Betty's only younger sibling was Mary — three years her junior. The girls shared a bedroom and were inseparable. Betty's active imagination sparked the most wonderful games and plays, which the sisters would perform for the family.

Tragedy struck when they all briefly lived in Redcliff, Alberta. One autumn afternoon, the two girls were playing in a stable. Betty didn't notice that Mary was absentmindedly chewing on a wooden stick she'd found. *If only I'd paid closer attention, I could have stopped her*, thought Betty whenever she recollected the event.

When Mary lost her balance and tumbled off a bale of hay, the bacteria-laden stick pierced the inside of her cheek. The wound became infected, and five-year-old Mary died weeks later.

Betty felt the loss particularly deeply, having been her little sister's constant playmate. For months, she could only fall asleep lying in the upstairs hallway, listening to her parents' voices below, and not tucked up into her bed.

Whenever she spied any little "kiddies" nearby in a park or restaurant, Betty felt a pull in their direction. Anything remotely dangerous in a child's mouth made her want to tell the caregiver to take it away.

(Letter continued)

This evening we are quite comfy with a nice warm fire. We are all gathered at our usual Sunday night pursuits: one game of bridge, three writing, and the rest reading. The gramophone is playing of course, but we are having the treat of some lovely music — records belonging to the Belgian girl.

I am enclosing a copy of the Itinerary for Spain — of course subject to change and I'll send you a list of hotels as soon as possible.

Yesterday afternoon I went in with Henriette, Eldred and the new English girl (who, by the way is awfully nice — a big improvement on the others) to see Notre Dame and a tiny church nearby, St. Julien des Pauvres — one of the oldest in Paris and very quaint. In the evening we went to the Opéra-Comique to see the "Le Jongleur de Notre Dame" — very well sung, but so short! Only from 8 to 10 p.m.!! So they gave a second short opera "La Vie Brive" — an awfully colorful Spanish thing — fairly modern. The girl who sang the heroine was very Spanish-looking and sang beautifully.

When we arrived home a little after midnight, we met Mlle. Jeanne just coming in who announced that the little nephew had arrived about 9 p.m. weighing 7 lbs. "Mother and child doing well!" I think I told you that the other married daughter, had arrived about three weeks ago in anticipation of the event. Of course, everyone is very thrilled and we are to see the baby tomorrow.

Best love,

Betty

Betty received a second letter from Jack. As soon as she read his name on the envelope's return address, she slipped off to a corner of the drawing room to rip open the envelope. This exciting moment required privacy.

My dear Betty, he wrote, *I can't seem to concentrate on the paper I need to write this evening. It's about wills and trusts, and I have a pile of books and papers I need to research but I prefer to write to you instead.*

Just holding notepaper he had used made him feel nearby. *What strong, decisive handwriting*, Betty thought. *Messy and urgent — like he wrote it in a passion.*

He asked her to mail him a photograph of herself — *a close-up, if possible*. She told Win about their new friendship because talking about him somehow brought him closer. She got a thrill whenever she mentioned his name. Betty decided, *I'll just leave out the romantic feelings that we're developing. Just pretend we're good, platonic friends who like to ski, dance, laugh — oh gosh, I'm probably being so obvious.*

Once she was back in their bedroom, she hid the envelope in her underwear drawer, along with the short note — *How are you doing? May I please write to you?* — that she'd received the week before.

À la Sorbonne
Le 12 fev., 1931

Dearest Mother,

This was supposed to be a model letter to make up for the untidiness and meandering of the last one, but I'm afraid this won't be much better as I seem to have been so busy and I am writing this between lectures.

Yesterday was quite a busy day. Because of the christening of the new baby, Bertrand de Verdun, we were all given a holiday in the morning after our 9:30 a.m. lecture on History, and the house was tidied up and decorated for the reception. The ceremony was at 3 o'clock at a small church near by — very short and simple attended just by family and most of the girls. Then from 4 to 6 p.m. all kinds of friends and relations came, saw the baby who "received" in the arms of the nurse, and congratulated the proud papa, then feasted on cakes, tea, chocolate or champagne! Catholic babies are supposed to be baptized "toute de suite" — at least before they are five days old, but it seems rather a shame to do it before the mother is able to be present.

Win and I could not go to the church because she had a dentist's appointment to treat a very bad tooth. At 4:30 p.m. we left for our second-to-last dancing lesson. You should see us tango now! Pretty hot!! In the evening I was very noble — mended stockings, washed gloves, tidied my drawers and cupboards. Monday — nothing special except a trip to the hairdresser's for a shampoo, friction with l'eau de cologne and Marcel wave all for the sum of $1.16! I'm really getting very spoilt having my hair washed all the time, but it's really impossible to do it myself without running water and no means of drying it.

We have just had a lecture on "L'histoire des idées," not very interesting and so abstract and theoretical that it was very hard to take notes. There is really a most astonishing range in age, nationality and appearance among the people who attend these lectures. They are only open to foreigners — about a third at least are Americans, the usual college age and type, and also half a dozen old-maid schoolteachers from small American towns — obviously so thrilled to be living in Paris and being as French and "Latin Quartier" as possible. There are about 4 or 5 middle-aged men, one old English couple (very drab and shabby), one nun, one dear old man with snow-white hair who always wears a large red plaid muffler — I don't know if he's Scottish or not. The rest are made up of English, German, and a few Scandinavians, I think. And one Japanese girl!

This afternoon we are taking the Hacketts to the movies, to hear Laurence Tibbet in "The Rogue Song" and, of course, out to tea afterwards. We are so lucky having Aunt Barbie to go out with, so try to take some of the others out occasionally.

This last has been written during the taking of notes on history. Our old professor being in fine fettle this a.m. — full of anecdotes and stories. But it is nearly time to go, so I'll stop and post this on the way home as there is a boat going tomorrow.

Best love,

Betty

Just before dinner time, Mireille, one of the house's maids, knocked on their bedroom door announcing in French, "Mademoiselle Harbert, there is a telephone call for you."

Betty hurried down the stairs to the residents' phone stationed prominently in the front hall. As soon as she heard Jack's deep voice say, "Hello, Betty," she felt her tummy drop to her knees. *It sounds as though he's next door! Is he really here in Paris?*

Recovering her usual poise, she said, "Why, hello, Jack. What a lovely surprise to hear from you!"

"It's wonderful to hear your sweet voice too. Mother arrived from Sydney last week and she wants to see Paris too. We are here for three or four days," he said. "Could you have dinner with me — just me — tomorrow evening? I'm rather keen to see you again. Sorry about the very short notice!"

"That would be absolutely marvellous! Win and I have invited some friends out to the movies and tea tomorrow afternoon, but I should be available at seven, if that works for you," she answered.

They agreed they'd meet at seven, then Betty described the route Jack would need to take to Le Gui from the metro station.

Throughout Thursday's tea party, Betty surreptitiously glanced at her watch to see if it was yet time to leave so she could get changed for her date. She didn't want to reveal how excited she was to the others. If they knew she had a romantic attachment to Jack, they'd be not only envious but possibly slightly shocked as well. And she wanted to keep Jack a secret for the time being, even though she was bursting with anticipation.

She pretended to listen to all their gossip as innumerable cups of tea were consumed, along with too many little iced cakes. Betty's stomach was tied in nervous knots and she only took a few small bites of one of the cakes.

The tea party finally ended and she headed back to the house to freshen up her rouge and lipstick, then she slipped on her black cocktail dress with the long sleeves. The simple art deco silver brooch pinned at the centre of the V-neckline was the finishing touch. Tucking her new satin evening bag under her arm, she appraised the outfit in the full-length mirror and thought with a little giggle, *Wow! Who is that sophisticate?*

Mireille knocked on the bedroom door at 7:09 p.m. and announced there was a gentleman waiting in the front hall. Betty grabbed her cloche hat and warmest coat and floated down the stairs, being sure to not trip in her dressy black patent shoes. *Thank goodness we're not in Montreal. I would never get away with wearing these shoes there*, she thought. *Any outing in February would require clunky snow boots instead.*

When she reached the bottom of the stairs, she saw him: her darling Jack, standing in the entranceway, holding his fedora in his hand, with a huge grin on his handsome face. His black overcoat was slung over his arm, and he wore grey flannels, a navy-blue blazer, a white shirt, and a Cambridge tie. Following the French custom, he tenderly kissed Betty on both cheeks. She blushed with joy, happy that she'd applied a little Evening in Paris perfume behind each ear. *I hope I didn't overdo the scent.*

"I've made a reservation on Avenue Mozart so we can easily walk there," Jack said.

"Perfect," she replied as he helped her on with her coat. *Here I am, twenty-five years old and experienced at dating men by myself back home*, she thought. *So why do I feel as though I'm only fifteen and nervously going out on the first date I've ever had?*

For the last six months, she had existed under the watchful eye of Aunt Barbie, Win, Miss A, or the de Broins during evening outings — often feeling like a bird in a gilded cage. Everyone around Betty was convinced that Paris was full of unsavoury types keen to take advantage of young innocent girls, and Aunt Barbie had assured her sister that Betty would be properly shielded from unpleasantness.

Betty slipped her hand into the crook of Jack's left elbow as they left the house.

Jack was twenty-seven and he was well-educated, charming, and from an upper-class Australian family. During one of their lunches in Wengen, he'd explained that his mother was born in Germany and he figured he inherited his skiing ability from her.

The young couple had waited weeks to be alone like this, and as they strolled to the restaurant, conversation was light and effortless. They shared stories about their doings since being together, how much they missed Wengen, how their respective studies were going.

Betty was pleased that Jack had chosen a different bistro from the place David had taken her. When they arrived, the maître d' showed them to a table nestled in a bay window and took their coats. After they each studied the menu, Jack offered, "Would you like me to order for both of us?"

"That would be excellent, thanks." *That way*, she thought, *I don't need to worry about choosing something too expensive.*

They dined on consommé, green salad, and sole almondine. They shared a bottle of French Chablis and, of course, a fresh baguette with unsalted butter accompanied the meal.

Throughout their date, Betty felt like Jack's good character and trustworthiness shone through. *Of course*, she thought, *this is just a dinner date. There are no dilemmas or tests of character really going on.* Nevertheless, Jack acted unfailingly polite but far from stodgy. *His sense of humour would appeal to the whole family*, she thought, and she could even picture Dick taking him out for a sail.

After dinner, the couple wandered over to a bar with live music where Jack ordered a whiskey, Betty a demitasse coffee. Betty felt comfortable on the tiny highly polished dance floor with Jack because they were familiar with each other's moves. It was blissful. As they strolled home, she felt deliriously happy to be with him, yet sad that they had to soon part.

They paused several times on the way back to Le Gui, ducking into shadowy places along the sidewalk. His kisses felt passionate, urgent. She sank into his final embrace around the corner from Le Gui's front door — just in case anyone was peering out looking for her.

As they parted, they made a plan to spend most of the next day together.

"I'll telephone at nine to discuss the schedule," Jack promised. "Mother will join us for luncheon, but we should have a chance to be alone for much of the day."

"I can't wait," Betty said as she headed inside.

She rushed upstairs, feeling light as air, and found Win already in bed asleep. Betty couldn't stop smiling as she undressed. She climbed into bed, but she lay awake for hours, reliving every magical detail, too stimulated to sleep.

38 Rue de L'Yvette,
Paris 16e
Feb. 15, 1931

Dearest Mother,

We are down at the hotel, have just finished dinner and now are cozily settled in the little sitting room — Aunt Barbie and Win knitting, Miss A reading The Times and of course, we're all talking.

When we got home on Thursday, I found that Jack Graham (the Australian I told you about) had telephoned having arrived here on

Wednesday night. We went to the movies with the Hacketts, as arranged — and in the evening I went out with Jack, getting home at 12:20. Such a good girl! He had meant to stay 3 or 4 days but his mother, who was with him, was not well so he went back to England on Friday morning. It was really such fun to step out again!

Friday was quite uneventful and yesterday too. Last night Aunt Barbie went to the Russian opera and heard Feodor Chaliapin. She said it was wonderfully staged, acted and sung with all sorts of gorgeous costumes. We are going to hear Lohengrin tonight and I hope to hear Carmen next week. Win has seen it twice, so she is not going. Tuesday, being Mardi Gras, we are having a holiday and are all invited to spend the day at the home of Madame's brother — the Count de Freligoude, who has a gorgeous old chateau about 50 miles from Paris. It is the occasion of a family gathering and a picnic — weather permitting — so should be lots of fun.

I suppose you are following the news of the threatening revolution in Spain. Poor Miss A is so hot and bothered about it and will be so disappointed if we can't go. Aunt Barbie intends going to Cooks in London and if they advise not going perhaps make arrangements for about six weeks trip in Italy. Then to England for May!! Which sounds very nice to me.

Aunt Barbie is all packed up, or at least all her arrangements made, for her little trip to England and now is anxiously watching the weather as to prospects for the crossings.

Best love,

Betty

38 Rue de L'Yvette,
Paris 16e
Feb. 17, 1931

Dearest Mother,

I've just got into bed after a most satisfactory and enjoyable day and now, being warm and cozy with a hot water bottle and wearing my pink knitted jacket, I must tell you all about it. We got up at 6 a.m. and dressed in all sorts of winter woolies — I wore my brown dress, green sweater, scarf, fawn beret, heavy stockings and brogues — and at 6:45 we embarked in a large omnibus hired for the day and set out on our excursion to Chautemerle. There were 18 of us — 11 girls, Mlle. Jeanne, Henriette, an aunt and uncle and two cousins of 16 and 11 and the cutest boy cousin, about 13. Our destination — the home of an uncle, M. de Freligoude, was 140 km. away and our route lay through Versailles and Chartres.

The country is very flat with small villages, farms and groups of scraggy woods — in fact it reminded us a great deal of the country around Montreal. There was a heavy rain last night and great pools of water lying in the fields. It must be awfully damp all the time as most of the trees were absolutely green with moss — very lovely to see, but not very healthy. We experienced every variety of weather during the day — showers, heavy rain, four heavy snow flurries and occasional gleams of sunshine. The coloring was really lovely in spots — the wet trees a blue-y black, all sorts of low browns and reds and the grass surprisingly green.

We arrived at 10:15 a.m. I was not particularly stricken with the chateau which has been in the family since 1760, or some such date. It was most oddly laid out like this [sketch of floor plan] only one room deep and with six huge French windows in the drawing room — making it awfully cold. They are having a lot of redecorating, plumbing and central heating done so things were rather in a mess. The downstairs, of course, was all in order and contained some beautiful old furniture.

We walked for about an hour and a half, then back to a picnic lunch — most of which we had taken with us — soup, cold meats, peas, rolls, cakes, tangerines, and very bitter wine — the two liquids being supplied by the hosts. We had lunch in one room with Henriette, the cousins, and the daughter of the house and the rest of the grown-ups dined elsewhere. Then to the drawing room for coffee and cigarettes.

At two o'clock we left, going on a few miles to see the ruins of another chateau, then on to Chartres to see the Cathedral. Very beautiful architecturally and with such marvelous windows — sad to say the sun was not shining, but we hope to go again with Aunt Barbie before we leave. We will try to pick a bright day. Then, very cold and wet, we all gathered in a small tearoom and left half an hour later, much warmed and refreshed by hot chocolate and pastries! It got dark almost as soon as we started again and we did not get in till about 8:20 p.m. The last couple of hours the driving conditions were very bad, a sleety snow which froze on the windshield, so the poor chauffeur had to open it — then quite a heavy mist. Luckily, he was a very careful driver.

Now dinner is just over and we're all pleasantly tired and will be ready to sleep early. It is funny to think of Aunt Barbie over in London tonight. I do hope they had a good crossing and am sure they will enjoy the change.

Great rejoicing yesterday when our hopes were realized and we all got mail from Canada. I received four letters and a most mysterious Valentine from Toronto!

Thank you for the "kindly thoughts" on my birthday. I have bought a very snappy black evening bag which I consider my present from you all and like very much.

I must stop. I'm really almost asleep. Win has finished her note to her mother and is ready to put the light out.

Best love,

Betty

The valentine that arrived from Montreal was signed *Guess who?* Betty was pretty sure it was from Ralph Spencer. She recognized the precise, pinched handwriting. She sighed. *Ralph is a nice enough man, but he's deadly dull.*

Thankfully, Betty thought, *I have a much more exciting prospect.* She smiled as she looked at Jack's valentine, which was gorgeous — a drawing of a large red heart with lace trim, roses, and a sentimental printed message. He'd written, *Where have you been all my life? Be my Valentine!* and signed it, *Your loving Jack.*

Chez M. Razavet
Feb. 20, 1931

Dearest Mother,

Such richness, five letters again today! From Aunt Barbie and Eleanor, by the morning mail and three from you which were brought in just before we left so I read them en route in the taxi. It is a full half hour's trip but too bumpy to make a habit of reading as we do in the buses and Metro. I reckoned up the other day that I spend over three hours every Friday dashing about the city — 1 ½ hrs. to and from the Sorbonne, about 40 minutes for the lecture, and 1 hr. to come here and return!

The "Anales" was very interesting this afternoon and rather different. It consisted of a sort of debate between an architect and a professor of art — the subject being modernistic houses and their furnishing. The architect is a very noted one - the designer of several ultramodern buildings — one of them a huge apartment house near us.

You say you get so tired of thinking of things to eat! I don't see how you've stood it all these years. I know how I feel after only a month of it. I'm picking up some ideas over here, however, especially for lunch or supper dishes, and perhaps I'll collect more in Spain. How do you think the men would appreciate French and Spanish cooking?

Today was the last lecture at the Sorbonne. I may have told you we are not starting again, as you have to pay for the whole month and we would only have a short two weeks. The exams take place between the two terms so the next one does not start for about 10 days. I did not go this morning being tired, so I stayed in bed until noon.

Yesterday to another, smaller dressmaker's shop with Eldred to help her choose her dress for confirmation and I ordered a small black velvet evening coat — a short three-quarter and without fur — for Spain. Wednesday afternoon I went with Win to the dentist and then to have a fitting of my dark red georgette dress. It is made with long sleeves for dressy afternoon or informal evening wear. I also chose the material and design for a spring coat and suit of brown. I have samples at the house which I'll enclose in my next letter. Wednesday night Win and I went with Mlle. Jeanne to the Opéra-Comique and saw "The Tales of Hoffman." Of course, quite a change from Wagner, but we did enjoy it — lovely music and beautifully sung and acted.

At the performance of *The Tales of Hoffmann*, two German-speaking couples sat right in front of the three young women. Everybody waited for the performance to begin, perusing their programs in the usual fashion. Betty had remembered to bring her opera glasses, so she scanned the audience to pass the time. She didn't recognize a soul, which wasn't all that surprising.

Suddenly, the two men in front of them began talking loudly. It must have been about something they'd read because one kept stabbing his program with his index finger. Betty heard "die Dame," which she knew meant *lady*. *Do they mean the soprano singing the lead role?* she wondered. Then she heard "Jüdin," which meant *Jew*, and it looked to her like the couples were arguing about whether to stay or go. The two men soon overruled their wives and the four stood up to leave with much commotion and putting on of coats. *What was that all about?* Betty wondered. *Better that they not stay if they're going to be loud and rude. And now I won't have to look over anyone's heads to see the performers!*

(Letter continued)

The trouble with so many of the things we've seen at the opera, though wonderfully sung, is that they are very mediocre with regard to acting. So often the parts of the young beautiful heroine and stalwart hero are taken by fat, chesty old people, not at all convincing to watch. Parsifal, for instance, was supposed to be a young and innocent youth, so pure and good he became a knight and priest of the Holy Grail, but the part was sung by a frightfully pudgy man who, in trying to appear innocent, looked feeble-minded and laughable.

The story of "Les Contes d'Hoffman" is done in a prologue. Hoffman, a young poet, enters a tavern, meets his friends and stays to drink and sing. He is very sad and when asked why he says he will tell them of his sad love affairs. Then follow three acts of his three loves. Act I: A doll who has to be wound up all the time by a delightfully funny footman — but the doll breaks so he loses her. Act II: A beautiful Venetian lady. The scene was on a balcony overlooking the canals and the music of the Barcarolle ran all through the act. The beautiful lady spurns Hoffman and elopes with another. Act III: A beautiful girl (really lovely with a gorgeous voice) who is ill and dies. The curtain goes up once more to show the scene in the tavern with Hoffman just finishing his story — and starting to drown his sorrows in drink.

The second singing lesson is just about done, I must stop and take mine.

Very best love,

Betty

Following Jack's visit to Paris, Betty and Jack wrote to each other as frequently as they could manage. Because Cambridge and Paris are relatively close geographically, with excellent postal service (each correspondent received two deliveries a day), the sweethearts waited to receive a letter before writing again. This avoided the frustration of unanswered questions or crossed letters.

Correspondence was gradually getting longer and more intimate as they explored each other's origins, past relationships, hobbies, social opinions, and value systems. Betty moved the treasured stack of letters from her underwear drawer to her empty suitcase to ensure privacy. *I doubt Win would snoop*, she thought, *but why tempt her?*

Betty was pleased to be getting to know Jack better. She learned that, although his Christian name was John, he preferred to be called Jack. His older brother, Hans, would soon graduate in engineering from Ludwig Maximilian University of Munich. As children, their mother spoke to them only in German, so they were completely fluent. Their Scottish-born dad owned an enormous lucrative sheep farm in New South Wales with thousands of sheep, so it was no financial hardship to send both sons to university overseas. Hans, aged thirty, was just as good a skier as Jack and headed to the Alps whenever he could. Betty knew that Hans was fascinated by politics. On New Year's Day, he and his girlfriend were thrilled to attend the opening of the new Nazi Party Munich headquarters. Why they were so excited by that, Betty had no idea.

She shared similar facts about herself: Her full name was Elisabeth with an s, but she preferred to be called Betty. Born in Toronto, Ontario, she spent several childhood years in Alberta and moved to Montreal, Quebec, to complete high school. She enthusiastically recounted stories from her glorious summers spent by a lake in Vermont at a cottage built by Aunt Barbie — or at least by Aunt Barbie's money — for the Harberts. She told Jack that, after living in Europe for months, she genuinely missed her close-knit family, and she complained about how tiresome the role of paid companion had become, with its expectation of unwavering acquiescence to every plan.

As she wrote about her troubles with her role, Betty considered that her current existence had one major advantage: Without Aunt Barbie, she would never have met Jack. Thanks to her, they were confidants and possibly becoming lovers.

As with other men she'd dated seriously, trying to find out about his previous romantic attachments was like pulling teeth. *There must have been plenty of girlfriends in his past*, she thought. *He's too attractive and charming for there not to have been!* Betty knew that McGill had plenty of female students, but Jack said all Cambridge students were men. *Even so*, Betty thought, *local girls probably mingle at events like rowing competitions and cricket matches.* She knew Jack had plenty of opportunities to meet and charm women.

Jack had explained that all students wore black academic gowns to class. *Every Cambridge man must own a dinner jacket*, Betty considered, *and wouldn't Jack look dashing in his?*

It was pure joy to write to a man she was fond of. It offered a sharp contrast to the tedious descriptions of all the travel and

Parisian doings she was obligated to post to Montreal. Even though it was more exciting to write to her new beau, she forced herself to write to "Dearest Mother" first. *It's rather like getting my compulsory homework done before picking up an absorbing novel,* she thought.

Jack's letters made Betty's heart sing. The handwriting was always dishevelled because time was short. Earning a law degree entailed masses of writing, which took precedence, so he allowed himself only a few minutes at the end of the day to scribble to Betty.

Betty's family did not drink wine, beer, or spirits, so she was rather curious about the amount of drinking Jack seemed to do with his friends — *not dismayed,* she told herself, *just curious.* He frequently recounted stories of pub crawls during which he imbibed too much beer and whiskey, and he told her of the ensuing massive hangovers. *Why drink so much if it makes you feel awful the next day?* Betty wondered. Then she answered herself: *It's the pressure of his final-year law studies. Alcohol helps him relax. If I were there, I could entice him to take long walks and go to movies to unwind instead. He wouldn't need his alcohol.* Then Betty's mind started to wander to another peaceful activity she enjoyed. *There's nothing as tranquil as a paddle in a canoe. Of course,* she thought with a smile, *in Cambridge, it would be a spin in a punt.*

One evening Jack placed a long-distance telephone call to Betty, but it took several tries for them to connect. It was marvellous to hear his voice again, but she felt almost tongue-tied. The house telephone for residents was in the front hall, so she knew that anybody in the vicinity could eavesdrop. Betty knew she sounded formal, distant, and boring on the phone. She updated Jack on her classes, the weather, and everyone's health.

"Never mind what's happening there, I just need to hear your voice, sweetheart," he said. "I'll call you again in exactly a week." Betty looked forward to hearing from him, but the second call never happened, and although she was slightly disappointed, she never mentioned it to him.

38 Rue de L'Yvette,
Paris 16e
Feb. 22, 1931

Dearest Mother,

I am not at all in a letter-writing mood today, but as usual have a long list that must be written so will start in. It feels rather odd to be spending a Sunday afternoon here. The first since our return from Wengen. Four of the others have gone to the movies and the rest of us are at our customary tasks, knitting, reading, and writing. It is gorgeously sunny day and we have just come in from a half hour stroll in the garden — quite warm enough, in the sun, with only light coats, minus hats and gloves. And yet I suppose the mountain is crowded with skiers and the slide in operation. How I'd love to be going up with Dick!! We met one of the American girls at church this morning, who said Violet is in Switzerland now and having a marvelous time. Being from the southern states, she has hardly ever seen the snow and, of course, knows nothing of skiing or skating.

Yesterday I was not out at all except for a few minutes in the afternoon when I went to Avenue Mozart to buy some fruit and have a breath of fresh air. The others went out in two parties — one lot to a museum which I was not keen on seeing and the other shopping. Eldred and one of the English girls returned each with a canary in a little wooden cage. They bought them on the street for 25 and 60 francs! The 25 f one is very young and does not sing yet, but Eldred pipes away at it at a great rate. It is rather a nice idea to have a pet, but also rather an encumbrance for travelling.

It's almost impossible to believe there are only three weeks to go before we leave and start our trip. When I started marking off the days on the calendar, there seemed so many I thought they'd never pass.

Did I tell you there is to be another dance the night before we leave? The occasion is mid-Lent when it is quite "the thing" to have a party. We quite look forward to it now after the good time we had at the other one.

Aunt Barbie suggested that we might go down to the hotel a day or so before we leave, but we have decided not to, as it would be rather difficult getting down to the hotel so late after the party. Tomorrow night we are going to the Russian Opera — Chaliapin in "Boris Godouna" — supposed to be his best. The tickets are very expensive and we were not going, but Aunt Barbie saw it and said was really a shame not to go. So, we talked it up and enthused four others to come too.

XX Tuesday. I managed to get up enough energy to write five letters on Sunday and now have my list down to respectable proportions. We heard from Aunt Barbie again saying they were enjoying London but also containing some awfully sad news about poor Miss A. It seems that she has had a pain in her arm and chest for nearly two years which could not be accounted for. When she went to the eye specialist in London, she said something about the pain and he advised her to go to a doctor who says it is cancer. Isn't that terrible? And coming on top of her other trouble.

She has decided to go home, sailing on the S.S. Olympic from Cherbourg on March 4th, as they say she should have an operation at once. Of course, Aunt Barbie feels terrible, as we all do, and we are giving up the Spanish trip and going to Italy instead. Miss A was the moving spirit with regard to Spain and, with the rumours of trouble there, I think Aunt Barbie is just as glad not to go. I feel awfully wicked, as I did not want to (as you know) and hoped we would change our plans. Though, of course, I didn't wish for anything to happen like this. And I'm so sorry for thinking how cross and peculiar Miss A was — no wonder, with this hanging over her. Miss A has cabled her family but did not want anyone told until her own letters arrived, so please don't say anything about it or our change in plans until you hear from Aunt Barbie.

Now I'm writing on the bus en route to the Louvre, as I want to post this. This a.m. another gorgeously sunny day. Thank Dick for his letter, I'll write soon.

They are coming back from London tomorrow and Miss A will have a week to get her dresses finished. It seems so sad. All the lovely clothes she picked out with such care and such high hopes for Spain! And she has been talking, thinking, and dreaming Spain — reading up all sorts of books on the subject for months. And now the disappointment of not going and the lonely trip home. Aunt Barbie offered to go with her, but of course she wouldn't hear of it.

Best love,

Betty

Even though Jack neglected to call Betty in "exactly a week," his correspondence did not slow down. In his letters, Jack frequently asked Betty about life in Montreal. She started to wonder if he wanted to live there one day because he would enquire about things like law firms, types of law practised, winter and summer sports, and types of accommodation (apartments, duplexes, houses, summer cottages). McGill was the only Canadian university he was familiar with, so he asked her all about it too: location, campus layout, architecture, faculties, student population. She found it exhilarating to know more about these topics than a well-educated — slightly older — man, so she took pleasure in filling in details for him.

As a member of the Cambridge University Air Squadron, he had his pilot's licence. He asked about Montreal's airport and the types of planes flown out of it. She was at a loss on that topic but described yacht clubs on the island of Montreal and ski clubs in the Laurentians. Having never flown, she was petrified at the idea of going up in a plane. *I'll keep my feet on solid ground, thank you.*

Whenever she asked him about Australia, Jack's answers were short and factual. He seemed completely smitten with life in Europe and with English cultural events, like theatre in the West End and Wimbledon. Now it seemed he wanted to explore North American ways.

As her affection for Jack grew, she decided to start studying German properly. His Germanic heritage was clearly important to him, and she wanted to better understand it. On the Sorbonne lecture notice board, she found an introductory German course and signed up as a guest, even though she'd missed the early lectures.

Perhaps Win will want to come too, she thought on the way home. *We leave Paris in just a few weeks, but at least I'll have a chance to practise speaking in a safe classroom setting.* She considered what she already knew about the language: *I think German nouns are capitalized. I noticed this on our travels through Germany before we arrived in Paris. So that's a start!*

Hotel Majestic,
Paris
March 8, 1931

Dearest Mother,

I feel very well up on home news, having received your two wonderful letters yesterday and having read your lengthy epistle to Aunt B today. This has been such a nice Sunday — to begin with we rejoiced to have brilliant sunshine after several dull rainy days. We came down here to the hotel before church, but Aunt Barbie was not ready and Win has a sneezy cold, so I went over alone — to a very nice service. They have just had a new organ installed. It cost I don't know how many thousands of dollars and is supposed to be one of the best in Europe, but I don't care for the organist. He plays in a very flashy and blare-y manner.

We had a guest to lunch, Isabel Rowat. She is awfully sweet with pretty red hair, graduated from McGill last year and is now living with a French family, going to the Sorbonne, and writing a thesis for her M.A. We talked until 3:30 p.m. Then we walked out to the Trocadero, down under the Eiffel tower, as far as the Ecole Militaire — beautifully sunny but a cold wind. Then we taxied to a place on Le Champs Elysées for tea. And now we are sitting in Aunt Barbie's room very cozily.

Yesterday afternoon I went with Aunt Barbie to the Louvre, wandered among the statuary and had another look at the Venus — who I still think is too fat. Then along the Long Gallery and through the small Dutch pictures. We went to tea at Smith's — over the bookshop on Rue de Rivoli — so English — scrummy hot buttered tea cakes and such a nice home-y atmosphere.

At 5 p.m. we had our last lecture from our old absent-minded professor of art. There will not be one next week on account of the dance. It seems almost impossible to realize we will be leaving in just a week.

Au Gui once more, have had dinner, and now are gathered around the foyer discussing the approaching dance. It will really be quite fun, I think. We are going to have some of the girls down to dinner at the hotel before — aren't we stylish having a dinner party? — even without any males! On Wednesday night we are going out to see some more night life — Mlle. Jeanne, Win, Eldred, Roger, and three other "jeunes gens." I'm so glad Win is coming this time as I'm sure she will enjoy it.

On Friday night we went to the Comédie-Française and saw a play called "La Belle Adventure" — well done and so amusing. The story of a girl who, all dressed in her wedding dress, is just about to leave for the church when a former suitor, from whom she had been separated by her cruel family, appears on the scene and they elope — all sorts of amusing situations follow.

This morning I had a permanent wave — leaving here at 8:30 a.m. to go miles to a little place where all the De Broins go — ridiculously cheap but my hair was very carefully done. I was there until 1 o'clock and arrived home just as they'd finished dinner. However, Jean, the very good-natured man, got me something and I gobbled it in time for the lecture at 1:40 p.m.

Yesterday we went to town with Aunt Barbie in the morning and at last succeeded in getting some shoes. Both Win and I wanted walking shoes and had hunted high and low. It is most disappointing. They have such attractive-looking shoes and so cheap, but Win could not get any narrow enough and I could not get them with good support for my ankles.

In the afternoon we went into a lecture at the Louvre. It was supposed to be on the Barbizon School and was advertised to be given in a certain collection which has been closed ever since we have been here. But, much to our sorrow, we found the collection still closed and the lecture on Millet alone, by a very blah American woman, who kept talking about "We Americans" and used a whole lot of words like "symbolism," "synthetic realism" — which sounded very high hat and intellectual but didn't really convey a thing. It's so wonderful to think that this time next week we'll be down in the sunny south and how we're hoping it will be warm!

Best love,

Betty

Betty returned from her blah Saturday afternoon lecture to a letter from the charming David McKay. He invited Betty for another evening out on the following Monday. She was curious to see how he would treat her this time. She telephoned immediately to accept the invitation and decide on a time to meet.

When Monday came around, he was as warm and chatty as usual, but any romantic intentions were completely absent. *Either he's engaged to a phantom lady back in England or he prefers the company of men*, she decided. *Fine with me. In fact, I'm relieved that our friendship is platonic. It means I'm not torn between two men. Although … would that be so terrible?* She smiled wickedly at the thought.

The platonic atmosphere in David's company eliminated any feeling of being unfaithful to Jack. While the new sweethearts were far from a committed relationship, in her heart they were becoming an item. It wasn't beyond the realm of possibility that Betty and Jack would marry someday, given their ages and obvious compatibility.

She still enjoyed spending time with David, who was incredibly smart as well as kind. He was so well informed about world events that he could make a country's complex tensions or leadership issues remarkably easy for Betty to understand. It was no secret that she never got around to reading newspapers, so she loved it when he would bring her up to speed. He never pontificated or talked down to her.

Tonight, his topic was German politics. He had just finished reading volume one of Adolf Hitler's book *Mein Kampf*, which he explained translates to "my struggle." Although the book had been published about five years earlier, Hitler's rise to power was more recent, and David wanted to learn what kind of philosophies Hitler was espousing. In it, David explained, Hitler outlined anti-Semitism and anti-Communism as the heart of his political philosophy and made clear his disdain for representative democracy.

"So that means Hitler wants to be in charge of everything — like a king?" Betty asked.

David said, "Hitler sees Germans as the Aryan master race, so he wants to deny citizenship to Jews. He wants them to just disappear."

"That's ridiculous," Betty said. "I have several Jewish friends in Montreal. They are such warm, engaging people. How appalling for Jews to be discriminated against like that!"

"Hitler believes Germany should expand its territory by invading other countries," David continued. "Have you heard of the National Socialist Party? They're also called Nazis."

Betty tried to recall, *Where have I heard that term recently?* "Yes, I think I have heard of Nazis before," she told David. Then it came to her, *Oh, right — Jack's brother was going to a Nazi meeting in Munich. Does that mean that Jack's brother is a Nazi?*

As he continued to talk about all these alarming policies, David raised his voice, and his cheeks turned pink with emotion. Betty could see that he was worried about Hitler's power and the danger the Nazis posed. Betty was silent and kept listening. A knot of dismay began to form in her stomach.

Hotel Majestic,
Paris
Sat. Mar. 21, 1931

Dearest Mother,

Such richness — three letters from you this week! So nice to hear so often of all your various doings which seem as many and varied as usual. I'm afraid my letters have not been as interesting or lengthy of late, but soon as we get started on our trip I will have more news.

It was awfully nice of Miss A to phone you. By now you will have heard that it was not cancer after all. Such a blessing and comfort. Her sister cabled Aunt Barbie who of course was much relieved to hear the news.

Well, here we are still Paris-bound, but am glad to report my patient is very much better and we'll probably leave Monday night. We have not decided if we will go directly to Rome or cut our time there in half and spend five or six days in the south of France. Aunt Barbie has not really been awfully sick (luckily) — just suffering a very bad throat and a temp ranging from 99 – 100.2. We had a very nice doctor who rather took the worst view of things and said we could not leave for days. But the temp has been practically normal all today and we're hoping it will continue the same tomorrow.

I have been staying down here at the hotel since Sunday night — just going out once or twice a day for walks, so have not much to relate. The weather has been simply gorgeous — really warm. I've been out several times in my new suit and have been quite comfy.

Oh, yes — one event of the week was the occasion of a French play given by the girls on Thursday night. Roger picked us up and took us to Le Gui to watch the play. It was really very well done — two acts lasting about an hour. Eldred played the hero and Vera, the Serbian girl, played his wife. Eldred really acted awfully well. She had a very long part and was on the stage all the time. About halfway through the second act, catastrophe occurred. Her sideburns unstuck and fell off — first one and then the other — however she carried it off very well and just ignored the fact.

By this time, Betty knew that her outgoing nature and sense of humour were enjoyed by the girls living at Le Gui. She took along her opera glasses to watch the plays and made a point of ostentatiously using them to peer at the performers from time to time. The size of the theatre didn't warrant the glasses, of course, and she was seated in the first row! She enjoyed hearing the audience laugh at her silliness.

Eldred's ability to act in French well enough to be understood combined with Betty's ability to follow the plot made their post-performance hug sincere. "Eldred, you were absolutely wonderful!" Betty exclaimed. "I understood everything. And the way you carried on valiantly when your sideburns hit the floor was both professional and hilarious. I commend you, skilled thespian!"

"Thanks, Betty," said Eldred. "It would have been fun if you'd been in it with me. Next time." They both knew there would never be a next time. The residents of Le Gui were about to disperse across the globe and would likely never be in the same room again.

(Letter continued)

Of course, Win and I had not expected to be here, so we were not in it. After it was over we indulged in orangeade and cakes, then played musical chairs and other childish games — assisted by Roger, Francois and Jacques (two of the boys who were with us the other night) and the four other girls who had worn men's pants and stayed on in costume — looking so quaint in old-fashioned clothes — with wigs and whiskers. Then Roger took me out to dinner and brought me home at 12 o'clock!

Anne and Florence Hackett left for Montreux and Italy this a.m., the Belgian girl goes home tomorrow and the holidays start officially on Wednesday. There will be six of us still "au Gui." Win, Diane, the other English girl, and I are the only ones not going back, but there are to be another Swede and a Dutch girl instead — quite a mixture of nationalities. It was so funny at the dance. The opening remark of each new partner was "What country do you come from?" and such funny ideas some of them have on our dear Canada. Of course, to a great many it seems to just be part of America! However, we did our best to enlighten their ignorance.

Two weeks from tomorrow is Easter Day. This will probably arrive after you have returned from Toronto and probably dear Eleanor will be home.

It's only ten o'clock but I seem to have become so sleepy — having had fairly disturbed nights all week, I suppose. I have slept on a sort of chaise lounge at the far end of this huge room. The beds are so close together in a sort of alcove and I was not at all anxious to catch Aunt Barbie's germ.

Best love,

Betty

CHAPTER 6

This Quaint, Old-World Place

On board the "Rome Express" 11 a.m. just past Genova
March 26, 1931

Dearest Mother,

Here we are actually on our way. We left Paris at 5:30 yesterday afternoon and half an hour ago had our first view of the Mediterranean! It is all so thrilling and lovely. My letters from now on will probably be rather incoherent. It's really hopeless to try to describe such beauty and I do so wish you were all here to enjoy it too. The sea is not the famous blue one always sees in pictures. I suppose because it is so sunny and the sky full of misty clouds. Even less than 24 hours from Paris the character of the country is quite changed. It became almost tropical, at least to our northern eyes — magnolias, palms, lovely rugged pines silhouetted against the sea.

To go back to Paris, Aunt Barbie was feeling so much better on Tuesday that we decided definitely to leave the following night. I went out to the house Tuesday to finish up my packing. I spent the early part of the evening having a last game of contract bridge with Eldred, Vera and Roger. Then a long gossip with Mlle. Jeanne and a new Dutch girl who had just arrived. Then we started to go to bed but took a long while doing so — stopping for chats with numerous visitors and ending up by eating some wonderful Christmas cake.

Betty recognized that, when women gossip with each other, they are sharing opinions, feelings, intimacies, dreams, and disappointments.

She'd become close with the girls at Le Gui and the de Broins and was sorry to have to say goodbye. *How terribly I will miss Jeanne!* she thought. *In spite of her inability to speak English, we have really become close friends and confidantes. I guess that means I must have developed a strong French vocabulary,* she considered. *Talking about personal emotions in a second language takes both talent and patience — not exactly my strong suits. Good for me,* she smiled. *I've stopped worrying if my tenses and gender are correct. Who cares! Jeanne smiles and nods regardless.*

(Letter continued)

On Wednesday a.m. we shut up our trunks which we are leaving at the house. Then I walked in the garden for about an hour — a gorgeously sunny day — the leaves and early flowers looking so springy. After lunch we took numerous snaps, then bid fond farewells and left about 3 — going to the hotel to meet Aunt Barbie and Mr. Addison (Addie). I really was a bit sorry to leave Paris and very sorry to leave Le Gui. The De Broins have all been so nice and we've become very fond of them all.

We left from the Gare de Lyon. The Rome Express is a "train deluxe" and we are really very comfy. We each have a small sort of one berth compartment with doors between — very nicely decorated and complete with all the latest devices — reading lights, fans, special lever for opening and shutting the windows, etc. I slept very well, though it feels odd at first to be lying across the train — instead of lengthwise. I woke up about 2 a.m. Such a lovely night — the stars seemed so bright and close. We passed the frontier about 4 but, having given our passports to the porter, were not wakened until 7:30 when I heard a loud banging at my door and I opened it to find the porter, a customs official, and blackshirt soldier peering in at me. They asked if I had any cigarettes and being assured on that point, departed at once. Then I opened my blind and found we were passing some lovely snowy mountains — I suppose the Alps.

When I re-awoke about 9, I found a complete change — very flat, rows of pollarded trees, villages of white stucco, red roofed houses. Now it is quite rugged and hilly with long tunnels every four or five minutes. There are said to be 108 tunnels between Genova and Pisa. The country seems fairly dry, but so carefully cultivated — every inch of land is used. Even quite high up the mountains you see terraces of vines or fruit trees. The ground is covered with wildflowers in places and ever so many peach and plum trees in full bloom.

We are running along very close to the shore now. The sea is so sparkly and dotted with numerous small sailboats — fishing boats, I suppose. We've just passed a group of bare-legged men pulling in their nets and spreading them to dry on the sands. A little while ago we saw women washing clothes in the water of a small lagoon. How can they get them clean in cold, saltwater? And standing in the water in their poor bare feet! Very picturesque but not very practical or comfortable.

I suppose it was no wonder the poets loved Italy so and found such inspiration here. I feel quite in the mood for Browning and wish I had a copy of him with me! Just passed a tree laden with ripe oranges.

XX 2:30 p.m. Just came through Pisa but sadly could not see the famous tower. The country has quite changed again since lunch time when we passed some good-sized snow-capped mountains. Now it is flat, green fertile fields and many trees. All the farmers seem hard at work — ploughing with teams of creamy white oxen — picturesque but not very speedy.

We had a very nice lunch — hors d'oeuvres, scrambled eggs, veal, potatoes, artichokes, dessert and cheese, fruit figs and raisins — all so nicely cooked and served — not thrown at you as they usually do here. They waited until everyone had arrived and rushed the courses quite speedily. We are due to arrive in Rome at 7:45 and we are pretty well on time, I think. I hope you can read this epistle. I know it's rather wobbly, although I've tried to write during stops.

Hotel Quirnal,
Rome
March 28, 1931

Dearest Mother,

The end of our second day in Rome and what a busy and interesting time it has been! We arrived at 8 o'clock Thursday night and with our nine pieces of luggage (3 of them Addie's) were driven the three or four blocks from the station in a large and luxurious hotel bus. This hotel, a medium-sized and quite comfy one, is on one of the main streets of Rome. Just a block away is a huge square or "circus" with a fountain in the centre. They say Rome is called the city of fountains, which seems very appropriate as I'm sure we've already seen a dozen. They also say there is a church, a wine shop and a fountain in every street so all their needs are supplied.

When we reached here on Thursday, we were all frightfully grubby and rather tired — so had dinner sent up to our room. Then we relaxed in long, hot baths and "so to bed" where I, at least, slept soundly until 9:30 the next morning. After a leisurely breakfast, served by a very polite and cheery Italian, speaking awfully good English, Win and I went out for a short walk — to see what we could see.

While out on their short walk, the girls made a point of carefully peering down each block from the intersection before committing to walk down a narrow street. This method made sure they avoided beggars and any of the threatening types who saw tourists as prey. Having sellers aggressively pitch things at them — like cheap souvenirs, postcards, and beads — when they didn't have Addie's protection was most distressing.

Before she'd left Paris, David filled her in on some of Italy's history. He'd explained that the country had emerged from the Great War in a poor and weakened condition and suffered inflation, massive debts, and an extended depression. By 1920, the economy was in terrible shape, with mass unemployment, food shortages, and strikes. Since the beginning of the Great Depression in 1929, economic activity had slowed even more drastically. Betty noticed the poverty around her, but mostly wanted to avoid anything unpleasant. Betty, Win, and Aunt Barbie relied on Addie to provide educational excursions, stunning views, and protection from the poor. They all thought he did an excellent job.

(Letter continued)

The first thing, of course, upon which to comment is the weather — such a blue sky and really hot sun. We walked for about half an hour, then seeing some large and imposing ruins and a sign became curious and entered what we found to be the ruins of Diocletian's Baths. After lunch Aunt Barbie went to lie down and we went for another walk — about two hours — this time with Addie who pointed out all the sights. The Marcus Aurelius Column, Victor Emmanuel Monument, a huge affair of white marble and gold — commemorating the union of Italy. We were shown exteriors of several churches — also the house where Keats lived and died. We also saw the main business and shopping district.

It's very odd, but Rome does not impress me as being a large city, although it has nearly one million inhabitants. Of course, there are no skyscrapers, very few motors, though the few there are make a terrific din — blowing their horns continuously, and the streets seem very bare and quiet. Perhaps it's the sharp contrast of coming directly from Paris, where traffic is certainly lively!

After we reached the hotel, we had a call from the Hackett girls who came down via Montreux. They are staying here alone during Holy Week, and are being picked up and taken back by another party about the 9th. They are very devout and strict Catholics, but it does seem odd for their family to arrange to leave two girls of 16 and 17 alone here for two weeks — even for religious reasons, especially they are such unsophisticated young innocents.

When checking into the Hotel Quirnal, the concierge presented Betty with an envelope with Jack's return address. She ripped it open the minute she got upstairs.

My dearest Betty, he wrote, *I can't stand being so far away from you. Paris was bad enough, but now we are separated by about 1,200 miles.* He shared his angst about all the papers he had to complete before Easter and told her the dates of his upcoming exams.

Now that you are safely settled in Rome, I am going to telephone you. I simply must hear your voice again. So be sure to regularly check for messages at reception and eventually I'll be successful!

Won't that be a thrill, Betty thought. *Now Win will definitely pick up on our feelings for each other. That is, if she hasn't already!*

(Letter continued)

Today has really been quite hectic — sightseeing, accompanied by Addie and a local guide, an Australian named McGee from 9:30 — 12:30 and from 2:30 to 5! The idea being to dash about and see all the principal things early, then go back again to any we like.

First, we visited the Pantheon — a huge circular place — built 27 A.D. and intended as a temple of worship for 12 gods. It is a marvelous construction, its only light and ventilation being from a window about 30 feet across in the very centre of the dome. Of course, it is open and when it rains, the rain runs off the floor which is raised slightly in the centre.

Then we drove up, through the edge of a lovely park, to an observation point to take a view of the city — picking out the seven hills, St Peter's and the Vatican. After this we drove out to the Vatican — an immense pile of buildings supposed to contain over 1000 rooms. We walked through a great many — seeing all sorts of interesting things — Roman remains, manuscripts, sculpture — and various gifts to the Popes from all over the world: alabaster vases, inlaid boxes, tapestries, brocades, mosaic-topped tables. Of course, we did not see everything and will go back again.

Then to the Sistine Chapel — with its wonderful ceiling and wall by Michelangelo. It was the last time it would be open to the public until after Easter and was consequently swarming with people — tourists,

Italians, two girls' schools, and a great many theological students. One sees them everywhere. There are all sorts of colleges here — German, Spanish, Scottish, and each college wears a different uniform — long cassock and broad-brimmed hats of black piped with red, or purple. The Germans wear plain scarlet ones — very picturesque and striking. We did not go into St. Peter's but came home for a much-needed lunch.

After which we visited the Coliseum — needless to describe it — except that it quite came up to my expectations as to size. Then to a wonderful old church, St Paul's Outside the Walls — a great bare place, very long with forty pillars on each side and life-sized medallions of all the 260 popes with their names and dates.

In one of the smaller side chapels we saw a baby being baptized. They put salt in their mouths — signifying wisdom and oil on their backs — and, if a baby girl — on their ears. This one was being conducted in a quiet, orderly fashion by two priests — with several friends and relatives, but later in the day at the Baptistery we saw another. A faded old priest, in very crumpled vestments who was baptizing a baby girl — assisted by a moth-eaten grubby old verger. There were two poor-looking women and a little girl. I've never seen anything done so speedily in all my days. The priest mumbled so fast I'm sure no one could understand him — while the old verger muttered the responses and an occasional loud Amen!

After St. Paul's we visited St. Peter ad vincula and St. John's - called the Mother Church of all the Catholics — a terribly ornate and ugly affair — converted from part of the Palace of Constantine on his conversion to Christianity. After we had seen the Scala Sacra or sacred steps — supposed to be the steps up which Pilate led Christ to show Him to the multitude — and which people mount on their knees, we drove around the town a bit, arriving home about 5:30. We had tea then I went to the hotel hairdresser to have a shampoo — the first since my permanent — and I'm glad to say it seems very successful.

XX Sunday night. Another interesting day though not quite as energetic as yesterday. We woke fairly late, had breakfast, then Win and I went to church — to an American Episcopal church about a block from the Hotel. A very nice ordinary service with a boys' choir of such cute looking little lads. Unfortunately, the clergyman was a ranting American which rather spoiled things. He was most dramatic — putting sobs into his voice, thundering forth, then dropping down to a whisper. Most aggravating. There is a British Embassy church here too, quite a distance away, but we are going to hunt it up.

This afternoon we were taken by McGee, as a very special treat, to see the state apartments at the Royal Palace. He knew someone from whom he could get a ticket. Of course, it was very interesting — just a succession of gorgeously furnished rooms, and some lovely old tapestries. After that we hailed an open two-seated cab and drove for about an hour through a lovely park full of people enjoying the sun.

Rome is full of soldiers. You see them all over the place in such gorgeous uniforms. A great many varieties wear long, full capes — most romantic and picturesque — and they are covered with gold braid and buttons. The black-shirts are most intriguing and Addie says they are the paramilitary wing of Mussolini's Italian National Fascist Party.

Tomorrow we are driving to Tivoli in the Sabine Hills and the next day more dashing about with Mr. McGee. He is most amusing — a not very well educated Australian, about 38 — who did some sort of interpreting during the war and so, speaking several languages, drifted into a job with Cooks after the war. He is very good-natured and willing to do his best, but his facts are not always strictly authentic, as Win discovered on reading up the guidebook after our return. However, he reels off his dates and data in a glib manner — quite good enough for the usual tourist, I suppose.

Best love,

Betty

At one point during the Rome sightseeing, Betty and Win found themselves with about forty minutes to stroll without accompaniment, which was a rare treat. As they climbed up the Spanish Steps to enjoy the view from the top, brilliant sunshine deliciously warmed their backs. Italians and a few tourists relaxed on both sides of the famous steps — just people-watching. The girls' descent was especially slow because there was no handrail to help with balance. Halfway down, an Italian man in his twenties walked over to speak to them, smiling broadly.

"Excuse me, *signorine*," he said. "I was asleep over there" — he pointed to his friend sitting on a step, leaning against the side wall. "My friend woke me up after you went by earlier and said we simply must meet those two beautiful ladies."

Purposely not smiling in response, Betty said, "That's interesting. Goodbye," and she kept moving toward the fountain at the bottom. Having already experienced aggressive attention from young Italian men, she knew how to firmly dismiss them.

As soon as they were out of earshot of their admirer, they giggled at his unique pickup line.

Hotel Quirnal,
Rome
March 31, 1931

Dearest Mother,

We have just come in from a damp but interesting morning seeing Rome. We woke to find it pouring rain and though it started before seven, it did not act according to rule and "clear before eleven." Aunt Barbie's throat is still bothering her a bit so she decided not to go out in the wet. Win and I left in state at 10, guided by nice Mr. McGee, chaperoned by dour old Addie, and driven in a big, shiny Fiat by a very good-looking, cheery Italian chauffeur.

We went first to St. Peter's — so huge and impressive as regards size, but really very disappointing otherwise. The decoration is very heavy and ornate — all sorts of marbles, bronze, and gilt. We went down into a dear little low-ceilinged chapel — part of the church used by the early Christians 1st — 4th centuries. We finished the morning by visiting a museum in the palace of Pope Paul IV. It contains some lovely mosaics found at Tivoli, some Titians, some Raphaels, and one drawing by Leonardo da Vinci.

Yesterday we had our all-day trip — leaving here by car at 9:30 and driving about 25 miles to the ruins of Hadrian's Villa. Such huge piles of stone and brick and really in a marvelous state of preservation — at least in parts. There were ruins of the baths, council halls, temples to various gods and goddesses, courtyards, living quarters, the soldiers' barracks and even the hospital. We saw some lovely mosaic floors. Of course, they found all sorts of busts and statues, gold and bronze ornaments which have been used in decorating the churches or placed in museums. It was really a perfect morning — not too sunny but quite warm.

We wandered about for about 2 hours, then, warned by the pangs of hunger we proceeded to Tivoli — a quaint old town perched in the Sabine Hills and supposed to be even older than Rome, whose date of founding is given as 783 B.C. We went to a very picturesque hotel built on the edge of a deep ravine into which a huge waterfall tumbles, with such a roar and clouds of spray. Our table was at the edge of the balcony so we ate a very greasy Italian meal while feasting our eyes on a wonderful view of the falls, with the valley and the gray-green hills in the distance.

About 2 o'clock we drove through the town to the Villa d'Este, a wonderful garden built on the side of the hills by Cardinal d'Este, the son of Lucrezia Borgia. It is beautifully laid out and contains all sorts of ferns and rock plants, wonderful old cypress trees — supposed to be the oldest in this district — great, gray, gnarled old fellows — and about 1000 fountains. All kinds and sizes all fed by the natural waterpower. There is one long walk said to be lined by 200 jets of water. Of course, they looked lovely in the sun and made such a musical tinkle falling and splashing on the stones. The water flows into three square pools at the bottom of the garden, where they keep a few ducks and geese, but unfortunately no swans. Mr. McGee brought some crusts from the hotel for us to feed them. It really was a fascinating place and we hated to leave it — which we did about 5 p.m. — picking up Addie who had spent the afternoon with friends and coming back to Rome.

Last night we walked up to see the Hacketts who are at a hotel fairly nearby. They seem to be enjoying everything immensely.

Yesterday afternoon we continued our sightseeing with Mr. McGee. Aunt Barbie staying in again on account of the dampness and Addie dashing off to the Cooks travel agency office. He spends so much time there for no apparent reason that Win and I have decided he must go to play poker with his old cronies!

First, we went to the Capitiline Museum where they have all sorts of statues found in various excavations. We saw the huge, beautifully carved sarcophagus in which they found the famous Portland Vase — which you probably saw in London. Also, the "Dying Gladiator," the Little Boy taking a thorn from his foot, and a perfectly lovely Venus — in perfect condition and, to my mind, much more wonderful than the Venus de Milo. We walked to the town hall and from its balcony got a lovely view of the Forum — so much bigger than I imagined. It was still drizzling so we did not go down. It really was a good idea to have a view of the whole, and we will probably go there on Friday, as of course all the museums will be closed.

We drove out the Apian Way to the church of St. Sebastian built over the home of St. Peter and the commencement of the catacombs. Win and I were given candles and taken down by a dear little old monk. The passages are very narrow — on each side openings in the rock where the Early Christians were buried. Here and there you saw skulls and bones — very spooky. Our guide spoke English of sorts — very sing-songy and hard to follow. The catacombs extend for miles and there are thousands of graves still closed. It does seem rather a shame to disturb their bones after all these centuries. On the way back we stopped at a tiny, bare little church built on the spot where Peter is said to have had the Vision of Christ — where he said Domine Quo Vadis.

It was still rainy this a.m. though it cleared about noon. We took a taxi up to the Vatican to see the Picture Gallery. Then Addie took us to see a dear little church — Santa Maria in Consedine — very early Romanesque. After lunch we went out on our own — first to the Capitiline Museum and took another look at the Forum — flooded with sunlight and full of people dashing about with Kodaks! Of course, Rome is the mecca for all Catholics, regardless of nationality, and so is always full of strangers at all times of the year. And you are continually hearing different languages: French, German, even Chinese.

Betty enjoyed eavesdropping on French-speaking tourists and was pleased to find she understood about eighty percent of what they were saying. Because the Italian and French languages are both direct descendants of Latin, Betty managed to get the gist of many Italian words without too much effort. And she loved the way Italians used extravagant hand gestures for emphasis. It turned out that the stereotypes were true in that regard.

Having had only a very few German lessons, she understood little of German, but every so often something would click and she'd feel encouraged. Observing physical interactions — like having a meal or making a purchase — while hearing the language helped her understand the context of the conversation, and from there she was able to pick out some of the vocabulary she'd learned already. Most German tourists she observed seemed to have plenty of money to throw around, so Italian restaurateurs and shop owners did their best to accommodate their needs.

If Jack and I ever manage to get together, he can help me learn German. It's easiest to pick up a new language with a personal coach, and he'd be sure to make it fun, she thought. *He makes everything fun.*

(Letter continued)

We peeped into another church, which Aunt Barbie remembered visiting with Uncle Henry the last time she was here. It contains a figure of the infant Christ, said to be carved from olive wood from the Garden of Gethsemane — which is absolutely covered with jewels — chains, rings, bracelets — given as thank offerings from people whose children have been cured of illnesses.

We walked part way home — past Trajans Forum — and a great lot of ruins which they are just excavating. As we stood there looking at the remains of the civilization of 2000 years ago, a flight of planes — 18 great silvery things — went by. I wonder if the old Romans ever imagined a time when men could fly!

We had rather an amusing time on the way back. Aunt Barbie was tired so we decided to take a cab. We approached one standing in the square, prodded the sleeping driver and got in. What a ride! Win said the old lad must have been dreaming he was Ben Hur, he whipped up his steed and we came home at a terrific rate — dashing from side to side, bumping into the curb, being narrowly missed and thoroughly cussed by taxi drivers and even reprimanded by a policeman. We finally arrived but have decided to stick to taxis after this!

Best love,

Betty

Rome
Friday, April 3, 1931

Dearest Mother,

I've just come up to bed leaving Aunt Barbie and Win chatting to Addie downstairs. He really is a funny mixture — awfully down on a lot of innocent things and people, very fond of bullfights and children, very skeptical and sarcastic, and an ardent Catholic. Of course, he is really very clever, well-educated and well-read and we have some very keen arguments and discussions. He knows Greek and Latin and of course, everything about the Catholic faith — the rites and symbols, legends of the saints, so he is really an ideal guide for Rome.

This afternoon we spent about an hour at a museum nearby, then he took us to a church where we heard them singing mass — a lovely choir of men's and boys' voices singing without accompaniment. It was a huge bare church and the service was being held in a side chapel. We went in for a few minutes, then wandered about — the singing sounded so beautiful echoing and ringing through the vast spaces.

We stayed in this morning as it was dull and rainy — but we went to the Three Hour Good Friday service at the American Episcopal church nearby.

Betty found three hours a very long time to sit still being pious. *Why are all these Bible readings about the crucifixion so long?* she wondered. *And why can't we hear a different version? I've heard the same words so many times!*

Just as her mind began to wander, she found herself looking at the back of a young man's head, admiring his hairstyle and thinking it was rather like Clark Gable's. This American fellow — *he had to be American with that haircut*, she reasoned — must have popped into the pew directly in front of her while she'd had her eyes closed in prayer. He wore a smart grey suit and seemed to be about her age. She found the last two hours of the service not only bearable, but in fact, slightly intriguing.

I wonder if I'm about to meet an American version of David McKay. She felt almost giddy at the thought. Betty thought he looked like an expatriate resident of Rome. *He seems very familiar with these surroundings*, she noticed.

Betty was dismayed when the man picked up his hat and hurried away at the start of the final hymn, leaving without even glancing in her direction and dashing the hopes she'd built up over the last two hours.

(Letter continued)

Let me see what we did yesterday. Seeing and doing so much one is apt to get rather confused. Aunt Barbie has become an indefatigable sightseer — dashes about with a guidebook at a great rate. She is certainly much better and stronger and can keep it up almost longer than Win and me.

Yesterday morning we saw two churches. First St. Clement's, a perfectly fascinating place. You enter a fair-sized church built 1180 and nothing out of the ordinary, except for some lovely old frescoes and beautiful mosaics. Then, guided by an Irish Dominican monk speaking with the most musical brogue, we went down to a second church underneath. This one dating from the 4th century. Then we went lower still to a tiny chapel and part of a house — the home of St. Clement and visited by Peter and Paul. The Chapel is built on the site of a temple to the god Mithra and below that again are massive stone constructions — dating back to Republican Rome about 4 centuries B.C. Really rather wonderful, isn't it? But you do wonder how each building could get so covered with earth and debris that they could build over it. The under structures were discovered only about 1860 by an Irish monk, so now the church belongs to them.

In the afternoon we went to a museum built inside the ruins of the Baths of Diocletian. The building was part of a monastery designed by Michelangelo. A cypress tree he planted is still growing in the garden. Now they have all sorts of odds and ends there — scraps of mosaics, wall frescos, statues, as well as a few lovely pieces. It closed at 4 p.m. so we went into the church where we heard the singing. Then taxied up to the Hacketts' hotel and went out to tea together.

Very best love to you all,

Betty

Rome
April 6, 1931
Easter Sunday

Dearest Mother,

We are sitting in the train having arrived 35 minutes ahead (as usual) so I'll write this and post it before we leave. I'm afraid we'll all be grey with the excitement of travelling. It really is terrible. Addie is so fussy and tells us to be ready hours ahead of time, then Aunt Barbie goes him one better and gets us up practically at dawn. It's all very hectic and nerve-wracking.

We were so thrilled to have your cable and Ted's which arrived as we were having breakfast. It was odd to think that you were all slumbering while we had already been out to church. We went to the American church at 8 and to All Saints at 11, the latter is one of two English churches in Rome, a very nice Gothic building. A bishop preached and the service was very nice though the music was very slow and mournful — not at all like Easter music.

Win and I are thrilled. A large and very smart Italian soldier with a flowing blue cape has just reserved a place in our compartment, leaving a large and shiny sword to keep his seat.

Yesterday afternoon we tried to go to the Forum — our intention being to wander about and explore in the nice warm sun. But we found it closed so went up to a park, quite high above the city where we drove for a while, then dismissed our taxi and walked. Such crowds of people and soldiers listening to the music of a large band. We walked down to a very cozy little English tearoom where we indulged in a large tea.

XX Naples, Monday night. Our train left then so this did not get posted. It is very odd. They give absolutely no warning before they start — no bell or whistle — no "all a-b-o-a-r-d!" You have to keep a very keen eye on the train if you get out at stops and be ready to make a flying leap. The trains seem much more comfy and cleaner than I remember them and if you travel first class you generally have lots of room. It was very crowded this a.m. perhaps on account of the holiday. Besides our snappy officer, we had such a nice looking, spick and span Italian businessman sitting with us.

We arrived about 2 p.m. and it's lovely to be here. Our rooms are at the front of the hotel, only separated from the sea by a wide road. The view from our windows is gorgeous and very familiar from pictures — the wide curve of the shore dotted with gaily-colored houses. Vesuvius on our left was covered with clouds when we first arrived. They soon cleared and we could see the thin spiral of white smoke curling up into the blue, blue sky! The sea is a gorgeous color with the island of Capri right opposite. We are hoping to go out to it, if we can get a smooth day, but they say it's been very rough lately.

After lunch we walked along the waterfront stopping to watch some very tanned, barelegged men setting their nets. Then we took a taxi and drove about the town a bit, going up to quite a height to see some lovely views. We find the taxi drivers are so obliging and take such trouble to point to all the things and places of interest and look so pleased when you admire them.

This evening we sat for a while after dinner listening to a very good trio. Then we asked Addie to take us out for a little walk. No moon tonight and only a few misty stars but lovely just the same and the air so soft and balmy.

It will be lovely for you to get down to the Lake Memphremagog so early this year. I find myself thinking very longingly of the Lake sometimes. However, it's less than three months now and the time will probably pass fairly quickly when we are on the go so much.

Best love,

Betty

After mailing her letter, Betty wondered about her frank description of the nerve-wracking dynamics between Addie and Aunt Barbie. *On one hand, I've been brought up to never criticize family members in writing, but Mother knows how nervous her sister is. It will give her a good laugh!*

Whenever she wrote to Dick, she pictured gossiping with him on the front steps of Marlowe Avenue, the way they sometimes did on warm evenings. Preparing to describe the highlights of Capri, Naples, and Pompeii reminded her how incredibly privileged she was to even be in Italy. *Just stop complaining and concentrate on the positive!* In only a few months, she and Dick would be together at Lake Memphremagog with only mundane activities like golf or swimming to pass the time.

The Grand Hotel,
Naples
April 9, 1931

Dear Dick,

This letter has a three — no, a four-fold purpose. Firstly, to say "Many Happy Returns" of your birthday and congratulations on attaining the noble age of 18; secondly, to thank you for your very welcome letter; thirdly, to wish you the very best of luck for your exams and fourthly, to relate our many and varied doings since we arrived in Naples. Ahem! What do you think of my new style? Nice and flowery. The result of composing a letter in French to Madame, when long and complicated sentences are quite "comme il faut."

I'd better start with Tuesday. We were very anxious to go to Capri but were afraid to make any definite arrangements on account of the very unstable weather. At 8:10 that morning Addie appeared to say the guide was here and said it looked like a good day and that the boat left at 9 o'clock. We jumped into some clothes, grabbed some breakfast, and left here just after 8:30. We arrived at the dock to find the boat absolutely jammed — mostly with fat, fair German tourists outfitted with cameras, field glasses and being very obstreperous and noisy.

There is a very great reduction on the railways — over 50% and good for 25 days — consequently all Italy is swarming with tourists. The trip took about 2 ½ hours — going straight across the bay to a place called Sorrento, then to the island of Capri. It was really a heavenly day — the sea quite smooth and blue. We saw ever so many sailing vessels — tiny fishing boats with just one or two men, and several good-sized ones. A huge black and silver sea plane flew past us, quite close and low over the water.

The boat stopped about 10 minutes at Capri landing, then went on a little further and anchored near the Blue Grotto. We got into a small skiff, rowed by a husky Italian, and were taken into the grotto. The opening is only about three ft. high so you all lie on the floor of the boat and the man pulls it in by means of an iron chain. Inside the grotto is quite large and the water the most marvelous blue imaginable. After this we transferred to a slightly larger boat — room for eight or ten people and rowed by three boys — and went back to the landing.

Here we took a funicular railway up for about 20 minutes and arrived in Capri proper where we had lunch and wandered about the quaint old town. In the afternoon we drove by motor bus higher still to a second little town called Anacapri — where Emperor Tiberius is said to have had a villa perched on the highest spot 1000 ft. above the sea and from where he is said to have tossed his enemies and prisoners onto the rocks below. We reached home about 7 p.m. having to stand all the way because it was so crowded.

Yesterday was equally enjoyable. Leaving here at 9 a.m. we took what they call the Amalfi drive past the base of Vesuvius and Pompei, climbed over 4000 ft. through a pass and down to the sea again at Amalfi. The road then follows the shore — winding and climbing terrifically to Sorrento and finally home.

We had lunch at Amalfi at a hotel which was formerly a Capucian monastery. It is perched on the side of the cliff with a gorgeous view over the sea. There are about 200 steps to climb, but there are men to carry you in chairs so we persuaded Aunt Barbie to use one.

Aunt Barbie was a rather rotund lady, whom Betty had never seen deny herself a rich dessert. Barbie did her best to minimize her girth by wearing expensive clothes. Betty would never tease or criticize her benefactor, so persuading her to be carried to the former monastery took considerable tact.

"Aunt Barbie, it's the hottest part of the day and you really shouldn't exert yourself climbing all those two hundred steps. Think how nice it will be to arrive feeling calm and cool — so please let the strong men carry you," Betty said. "Maybe you'll like the transport service so much you'll want to be carried down too!"

"Probably a wise idea, but I forbid you to take any snaps!" Aunt Barbie replied with a bit of a scowl. She climbed into the chair mounted on two long poles, and two muscular men picked up their passenger as they grasped handles at each end. Her feet were about three feet off the ground as they walked slowly up to the hotel.

Aunt Barbie decided to be carried down after lunch and declared, "It would be most inconvenient to twist my ankle."

(Letter continued)

The hotel is quite interesting. The dining room was the old refectory — long and narrow with white-washed walls and a vaulted ceiling. The bedrooms are very small and square as they were formerly the monks' cells. The little church connected to the hotel is still used and there is a lovely cloistered garden. Rather a quaint place to stay, though the long climb every time you wanted to go out would be a bother. All day long the scenery was beautiful, very rough and rocky with all the villages built on the sides of the hills. The small stucco houses are sometimes perched at very precarious angles and always with a garden, some vines, and a few orange, lemon, and olive trees straggling up the cliff beside them. Of course, most of the gardens are on man-made ground — a wall of stones built, then filled in with earth — such a tremendous amount of work. It must be lovely to have your own oranges grow by your back door.

This morning we "did" Naples. There is really not awfully much to see — just the Cathedral and National Museum. Rather a relief after the umpteen and one churches we saw in Rome! The museum is really most interesting, containing most of the things found at Pompei and Herculaneum. All sorts of statues and busts, both bronze and stone, but I loved seeing all sorts of household furniture and utensils. Pots, pans, cups, spoons, lamps, tables, an iron bed, stoves, glass vases, and bottles of all sizes and shapes which must have been in the drug store. They even have remains of food, grains, raisins, fruit, eggs (2000 years old!!), loaves of bread, and one small cake with a hole in the middle — proof they even had doughnuts. This afternoon we drove out to see the ruins which already cover a large piece of ground and they are still excavating. There were supposed to have been 20,000 inhabitants at the time of the disaster, of whom 2000 were killed. They have found about 20 skeletons lying in various attitudes — the bones completely covered with ashes which have hardened and become like stone. They have the skeleton of a dog with the collar still around his neck. Rather pathetic!

Some of the houses are in wonderful condition. They have restored one sufficiently to give a very good idea of its appearance. We wandered up and down the narrow streets paved with huge blocks of stone, with deep grooves made by chariot wheels. We saw the forum consisting of a huge amphitheatre, two smaller theatres for comedies and tragedies, a wine shop containing huge casks, bottles and wine measures, the bakery with the mill for the flour and a big oven. Really most fascinating! We bought a copy of "The Last Days of Pompei" and are all agog to read it now.

Our guide has been a nice old Swiss who has lived in Italy for 35 years. He speaks French, Italian, Spanish, German, Arabic, and English of sorts. And our car is another Fiat, a huge thing — wonderfully comfy — which spins along at 90 km. an hour. At least whenever the road is good enough. Our driver is very dark, with a big grin and sparkling white teeth, and goes by the lovely name of Angelo! Luckily he is a careful driver which is very necessary with such narrow winding roads — simply swarming with kiddies, hens, goats, and donkey carts. They are all most casual wandering about the roads quite heedless of traffic. All the people live on the streets: do their washing, mind their babies, comb their hair, eat and sleep at the front door on the sidewalk. I wonder what they do when it rains. I know it seldom rains but it must happen sometime.

Isn't it wonderful to think you have only about a month more at college? Then I suppose you will all be off to the Lake. Win and I are feeling very energetic just now and are planning to play lots of golf and tennis and go swimming. I hope our enthusiasm lasts. And I so wish we had a sailboat. There are so many here and they look so graceful dashing along in the breeze.

Best love from your loving sister

Betty

The Munderloh compound that straddled the Quebec–Vermont border consisted of nearly one thousand acres of prime coastline, forest, and pastureland. Betty's family adored the cottage Barbie had built for them in 1922 on the northernmost tip of the Vermont portion. The Harberts regularly played golf on the private nine-hole golf course and tennis in the court next to Barbie's imposing home.

But there were strings attached.

Barbie was incredibly nervous about water sports of all types, especially sailing. When Nell said to her sister, "We're thinking of buying a sailboat for Dick and Betty to fool around in," Barbie's response was a swift and final, "Absolutely not! Lake Memphremagog is known for its sudden storms and gusts of wind, and they would drown in an instant."

So they all stuck to swimming at their family beach or canoeing up north to Canada — in the opposite direction from Barbie's viewpoint. But even so, the Harberts knew that the advantages of being beholden to Barbie outweighed the disadvantages.

Grand Hotel,
Naples
April 11, 1931

Dearest Mother,

All packed up and ready for our next move! Leaving here at midnight and due to arrive in Messina about noon tomorrow. I believe they put the train, or a portion of it, on the boat for the crossing. Rather nice to avoid the two transfers of baggage, etc.

Today has been gorgeous — the warmest day yet. We spent most of the morning at the Aquarium, then sat in the sun in the garden of the hotel. This afternoon we packed, read, wrote letters, then I slept while Aunt Barbie and Win were out for a short walk. The things at the Aquarium were most interesting — all varieties of fish, crabs, lobsters, three horrible squirmy octopus — or I suppose the plural is octopi! Not very large but simply foul-looking things. Then there were cases of star fish, sea anemones, jelly fish, etc. One kind, coloured pale mauve and purple, looked exactly like shaggy chrysanthemums. Another case was filled with corals — white, pink and different shades of orange.

Yesterday afternoon we took a drive — first calling on Florence and Anne who came on from Rome on Thursday night. We then drove to the crater of a small volcano which erupted about the 15th century, I think. There is evidently volcanic activity going on below even now as the ground is quite warm with lots of sulphurous gas escaping here and there — one great open hole about 25 feet across full of boiling black mud. It is the most gruesome thing to watch it bubbling away, making a loud gurgling sound and sending up great belches of smoke. Talk about Inferno — it gives you a pretty good idea of it. At another place there is a hollow filled with boiling ashes. That is, they jump up and down as if there were a fire beneath and are much too hot to touch.

From there we drove to Lake Avernus which Vergil wrote about and Dante visited. Then we saw the ruins of a temple which has sunk 16 feet due to volcanic disturbances and is still sinking at the rate of 1" a year. It is now filled with water and, being surrounded by houses, is used by all the kiddies of the neighbourhood as a pond.

Best love,

Betty

Grand Hotel & Des Palmes,
Palermo, Sicily
April 13, 1931

Dearest Mother,

We arrived here just at 6 tonight, came right upstairs for tea, then unpacked and took a much-needed bath before dinner, so have not seen anything of the city. Palermo is quite a good-sized place — over 300,000 inhabitants and the capital of Sicily, so will probably have a full day tomorrow "doing the town."

Aunt Barbie wrote you last night so probably told you of our trip over and our stay in Messina — such an unfinished-looking place, rather reminiscent of a small Western Canada city. Of course, the earthquake happened about 20 years ago, and practically everything was destroyed and 80,000 killed out of a population of 100,000, so they have not had much time to rebuild.

We left there at 9 a.m. in a huge Isotta Fraschini limousine, with nine bags piled on top. The road followed the coast almost all day, very winding and hilly and bumpy in spots. They are working to improve it — great gangs of dark-skinned men and boys and carts drawn by small grey and brown donkeys. The carts are most amusing, painted all over the sides with brightly-coloured figures. The horses are very gay too, with bells and bows, almost all with a big charm on their collar to keep off the "evil eye." The island people are said to be awfully superstitious and great believers in charms and portents.

We had lunch at a terrible little hotel — said to be the only place possible. We alighted at the door, being met by a greasy-looking young man badly in need of a shave, who welcomed us in and showed us up to the "washroom"!! Then he proceeded to set the table and wait on us. Apparently, he was the whole show — except for an enormous old woman we glimpsed in the kitchen. Addie and the chauffeur sat at the same table with us, and after surreptitiously rubbing off our glasses and "silver" we set to — and really it wasn't such a bad meal after all.

We started with large soup plates of the ever-present spaghetti. We ate about an eighth of it, but you should have seen the chauffeur gobble all of his! The next items were fish, then meat and green peas, but we did not fancy them and ordered omelets — which, much to our surprise, turned out to be really delicious. Then fruit and coffee and we continued on our drive feeling much refreshed. Incidentally, the whole cost, including the chauffeur's meal, the coffee and mineral water, was 53 lira or about $3.10!!

The natural colours here are delightful with the sea continually changing — blue, green and mauve at the horizon. The land is brown rock, with grey green olives, brilliant green cultivated fields, yellow of broom, and every so often, the most beautiful golden sand beaches. There are quantities of very prickly prickly-pear cactus and long spiky aloes, and quantities of cypress trees. I do love them, such tall, graceful things — I do wish they grew at home.

This hotel is very modern and up-to-date, and said to have a lovely garden. We must discover it tomorrow, though we will have very little time to sit there, I'm afraid.

That afternoon, Betty decided to take a stroll by herself, with no destination in mind. All this sightseeing was getting tiresome, and she craved a chance to wander and let her mind go blank for a change. *Win is resting*, she thought, *so now's my chance.*

Betty changed into walking shoes and plopped a wide-brimmed straw hat on her head. She headed to the hotel lobby, where she ran into Addie. He was nervous at the idea of her going out unaccompanied and insisted that he join her. The two had never chatted one on one before, and she wondered how it would go. She longed for companionable silence, but that wasn't Addie's strong suit. The quiet lasted less than a minute.

"Well, Miss Betty," he began, "how are you enjoying the trip so far? Am I organizing too many outings?"

"You certainly squeeze a lot into every day," she answered.

They passed a sidewalk café with red-checked tablecloths and red umbrellas tilted to protect patrons from the setting sun. Six rowdy Blackshirts occupied a table at the café. They argued with each other and carried on loudly, much to the noticeable dismay of other patrons. Addie took Betty's arm and carefully guided her across the street to avoid the café.

"Sometimes I worry about you and Miss Winifred," Addie continued. "You are both such innocent young Canadian ladies and there are hostile forces at work in Europe that are currently boiling up. It's my job to keep you safe, you know."

"Like what kind of forces?" she asked.

"Like those Blackshirt soldiers we just passed. My colleagues at Cooks say they are stirring up trouble all over Italy. They began as a bunch of disgruntled former soldiers, and then the fascist leader Mussolini organized them into a formal group about ten years ago. We're being advised to avoid Blackshirts as much as possible, and Cooks guides working in Germany have been warned to watch for Brownshirts as well, I understand," Addie told her. "We want to make sure clients like you never feel threatened, so we always watch for signs of protest or demonstrations."

"I've never heard of Brownshirts. Who are they?"

"You've heard of the Nazi Party in Germany, yes? Well, the paramilitary wing of the Nazi Party is called *Sturmabteilung* — or SA for short — which means *storm detachment* in English. These soldiers wear brown shirts, and their job is to provide security protection at Nazi rallies and meetings."

"Why does there need to be security at a meeting?" Betty asked. The only type of meeting she had attended was at the church or the orphanage. She'd never witnessed any physical discord or danger in either of those places.

"As Hitler and his Nazis gain power, people opposing him try to disrupt his speeches. And they're quickly hustled out of the meeting by Brownshirts. Cooks keeps me aware of anything nasty, and the Rome office brought me up to date when we were there. We all need to pay attention, Miss Betty."

Somehow having Addie confide in her like this made Betty feel more grown-up. And it gave her new perspective on their tour guide. *How interesting! Our usually bland, fussy, highly religious Addie pays attention to political undercurrents. He's been great at keeping us oblivious to anything sinister,* she realized. *I can't wait to tell Win. Now that she's eighteen, she needs to pay attention too.*

(Letter continued)

XX Tuesday. Just settling down after dinner to a busy evening of writing. I've been rather lazy lately and am behind. This morning we were very sad to find it pouring rain and although the actual rain stopped about 2 p.m., it remained cloudy all afternoon.

This morning we went to Monreale, just outside the city. It is too lovely even to attempt to describe, but I am enclosing two cards. Then we went to San Giovanni, a very characteristic Norman building constructed in 1132. It is quite small and bare surrounded by a charming little garden. The architecture here is a very odd combination of styles and periods. Sicily was colonized by the Greeks in the first place, who were followed by the Romans, Vandals, Byzantines, Saracens, Normans, then a variety of Angevin, Spanish, and Bourbon rulers until Garibaldi in 1860! Naturally they have all left their traces on the country, though those of the Saracens and Normans are most pronounced. It seems very odd to think of Normans here at just about the same time as their invasion of England (1070) and remaining for 200 years.

This afternoon we just peeped into the museum to see the state apartments of the Royal Palace, very much like other state rooms we've seen — lots of gilt furniture and red silk damask hangings. But the chapel is lovely. It is Norman/Saracenic combination with marvelous mosaics — even finer that those of Monreale, if that is possible. It was built in 1132, by the same Roger II — who seems to have been a mighty busy old lad, judging from the number of places he built.

The Cathedral has a lovely exterior, though rather ruined by a hideous dome added about 1800 by some misguided architect. The inside I thought pretty awful too, with a cold grey effect. It's most amusing. Addie is such a strict Catholic that he thinks any church is wonderful. I mean, he enthuses over most awful baroque affairs which we can't stand. We discovered the other day that he was born in Ireland, though educated at Westminster, which accounts for him being so "agin the government" and down on the English.

Our guide was too funny — a most tough-looking "Dago" aged about 40, short, stout, and dressed in a very crinkled suit of a startling brownish-purple, a brown fedora, and shiny yellow shoes! He told us Boston was his hometown. He was a graduate of Boston Tech and a second "Lootenant" in the American army. He came here 11 years ago, married and settled down, but we could not decide if he was a native of these parts or the son of an Italian emigrant. He had his facts down very pat, but his accent was excruciating.

Best love,

Betty

> Grand Hotel des Temples,
> Agrigento, Sicily
> Le 17 avril, 1931

Dearest Eleanor,

One should really write a wonderful letter with such gorgeous paper to inspire one, but it's all so lovely mere words of mine are hopelessly inadequate. [a drawing of the hotel printed in colour takes up a third of the page]

I was very glad to receive your letter written March 29th, just before your holidays. I have not written you for some time as I knew you would be home and would see the family's letters. Of course, by now you will be back at work, having had a lovely two weeks, I'm sure, with our dear family in "dear old Montreal."

I'm beginning to feel awfully keen to get home. We should be sailing in just two months more — June 19th, I think, is the happy date. I know being on the move time passes awfully quickly and two months does not sound much when you think of the eight that have passed.

So, the old Hupp's being re-painted! Why the same colour? I'm sure you will have a lot of pleasure with the car this spring. Your plans for weekends sound very enjoyable. I wonder who will drive to Montreal with you in June. Perhaps Dick could go up to Toronto and accompany you. It's lovely to think of the family getting down to the Lake so early, but Dick may find it rather quiet with no one to tease or play tennis with.

We are so enjoying Sicily. We go on from here tomorrow on quite a long run to Syracuse where we stay for two nights. Then to Taormina, which they say in the guidebook, is so lovely anyone who goes there is never the same again, so I may arrive home a reformed character.

There are surprisingly few Americans over this year. In fact, very few people of any kind seem to be travelling except Germans. They are everywhere because of an excursion fare — a 50% reduction on railways, good for a month or six weeks. We meet them everywhere, armed with cameras, field glasses, and guidebooks "doing Italy" in a most thorough and efficient manner.

I like the Italians awfully well. They all seem so cheery and good-natured.

Best love,

Betty

Recalling a delicate black-beaded necklace she'd spied in a little shop earlier that day, Betty headed out by herself between tea and dinner to buy it. The shop was only two blocks from the hotel, so she didn't bother getting Win to join her.

Carefully crossing at an intersection, she watched both ways for donkey carts to avoid being run over. Then she heard a dreadful commotion about two hundred feet away. Two men were having a knock-down fistfight! A crowd had gathered to watch, and three Blackshirts approached to break it up. One fighter had a bloody nose, the other a major cut above his eye, and they were swinging wildly at each other. It took at least three minutes, which felt more like twenty to Betty, for the Blackshirts to pull them apart.

What a dreadful thing to witness on a solitary shopping trip. Having only ever seen staged fights in movies, watching genuine fisticuffs made Betty nauseous. Abandoning her mission, she turned around and scurried back to the safety of the hotel.

Betty trembled as she told Win what she'd seen, and she made her cousin promise to keep the experience from Aunt Barbie. "She's nervous enough as it is," Betty pleaded, "and doesn't need to hear about actual violence nearby. She enjoys expecting disaster, so let's not give her the satisfaction of sometimes being right!"

Grand Hotel des Temples,
Agrigento, Sicily
Le 17 avril, 1931

Dearest Mother,

Seven a.m.! Such a gorgeous morning and having been wakened by a small grey donkey braying mournfully outside my window, I decided to sit out on our balcony (the one you see at the right of the hotel drawing) and write. But finding it still rather chilly, I have retreated to bed again. This hotel is situated outside the town, beautifully peaceful and quiet — a marked contrast to our abode Wednesday night.

Castelvetrano was the name of the town, a small but unusually clean and tidy one. Our hotel, also small but spic and span, was on a side street but so noisy. We went to bed at 11 p.m., after a game of bridge, and were entertained until midnight by music coming from a dance or concert hall nearby. About 2:30 a.m. we were wakened by a terrific din — six men on their way home from a big evening all feeling very happy. They took about 20 minutes to pass. Then the roosters started crowing and kept it up for a long while. Finally, "came the dawn" accompanied by church bells, birds, dogs, and children, so we gave up trying to sleep and lay there conversing. However, I later fell sound asleep and was dreaming I was at the Mount Royal Hotel with Ted and Eleanor, when a dark-eyed little maid arrived with hot water and breakfast.

Isn't this gorgeous paper — showing a bit of the really lovely garden? We arrived here yesterday in time for tea on the terrace, then a walk in the garden. Such a profusion of flowers — all the familiar kinds: geraniums, big clusters of marguerites, roses, calla lilies, and of course, tropical varieties like cacti, aloes, palms, etc. I intended to write last night, but we met one of the Americans who was at the Villa in Florence, so talked to her all evening. She seemed very nice, rather attractive with red hair. She has lived over here in Europe for seven years — apparently with heaps of money and no home ties. She is leaving this a.m. but we will meet again in Taormina, and probably in Florence and Paris.

I have had breakfast and dressed and am now on the balcony. Agrigento, like most of the towns here, is built on the top of a hill with the streets straggling up and down in a most haphazard manner. We are a little lower down, and beyond us is a great rolling plain stretching down to the sea. It contains three of the famous Grecian temples — two in ruins, but one almost perfect. There are said to be better examples of temples here than in Greece.

We saw some ruins yesterday — such a mass of stones and rocks, parts of fluted pillars, and capitals. They are all that's left of a group of seven temples built around 600 B.C. and destroyed by earthquake in 400 A.D. One had been partially reconstructed from the original stone which gives an idea of what it must have been like.

Wednesday's drive from Castelvetrano was lovely. We left the sea about an hour out of Palermo and drove through some beautiful country — very rough and rugged, without much growing but olives, oranges, and wildflowers (a small yellowish plant much like a dandelion, and another the colour of Indian Paintbrush, but with 5 petals). There were whole fields of these two with occasional patches of purple vetch. We stopped to see the Temple of Selinus, a huge Doric construction situated on top of a hill, with a glorious vista below stretching down to the blue Bay of Castellammare. We took lunch with us from the hotel and got coffee from a small chalet there.

Yesterday the country was more rolling and fertile with great fields of wheat and beautiful dark red flowers — a kind of alfalfa which is grown for feed. We drove for miles between fields of this, the edges of the road a riot of yellow, white and purple. The colour here simply takes your breath away. It is so vivid! I do wish we could use colour-cameras to properly convey the impression.

Have just come in from a visit to the town with its narrow, hilly streets and yellow sandstone houses. We visited the Cathedral and a small museum containing chiefly items discovered in the various temples. We had such a dear old man show us about. So enthusiastic about everything, talking with great speed and many gestures. It really is wonderful how much Italian one can understand by knowing French and remembering some high school Latin. Mr. Addison is most useful because he knows Latin, Greek and Arabic and is able to read inscriptions.

We leave here tomorrow morning to go on to Syracuse — quite a long run I believe. We have a very good chauffeur called Dominic. It's nearly a month since we left Paris, so there are only two more months to go. Of course, time passes much more quickly when we are on the move. But this lovely summery feeling makes me think so much of Vermont.

Best love,

Betty

Excelsior Hotel,
Taormina, Sicily
April 22, 1931

Dearest Mother,

We are spending a delightfully lazy and enjoyable morning sitting in the warm sun, surrounded by birds and flowers with such a lovely view of the sea below and Mount Etna across the valley. It is really wonderful to sit still and just gaze at the beauty about us after such arduous sight-seeing! At each place we are provided with a guide whose duty it is to show us everything, and as Addie always has a couple of extra churches up his sleeve — which must be seen — we have a busy time.

We arrived here on Monday afternoon and feel as if we could settle down happily for a month. Taormina is beautifully situated on the side of the hills running up from the sea. Our hotel has an especially good position with a wonderful view of Etna. It is still covered with snow, generally wreathed in clouds, and with a tiny spiral of smoke — so white and brilliant against the blue sky. It does not look very high (it is about 10,700 ft.) owing to its being so huge with very gradual slopes.

Yesterday morning we drove to the ruins of a Greek theatre considerably higher up, so we had a view in all directions. We took some pictures and then just sat and absorbed sunshine for about an hour. In the afternoon we drove down to the shore, where we sat on the beach for a long while watching some hardy people swim. It looked lovely — great big waves rolling in and breaking on the beach with a crash and a smother of white foam, but I imagine the water is still quite cold and the air chilly out of the sun.

The people there seemed to be mostly Germans. In fact, they are practically the only nationality we see. Some of them are so objectionable — big stogy, fat men with their heads shaved. Horrible!

This morning we walked through the town down its one narrow street lined with shops. They do the loveliest embroidery here. Pottery and majolica ware are two of their other specialties. This garden where we are sitting was once private property but was given to the town as a park. There are quantities of flowers: a huge bed of tulips, another of pansies.

As well as receiving letters from you and Molly, I heard from Jack Graham — he's the Australian I met in Switzerland. He is writing his last Cambridge exams the end of May and will be in London until the end of June, so said he hoped we could "go places and see things together" which will be rather fun.

Feeling it wise to tell her parents about her friendship with Jack, Betty made a point of dropping his name every so often into her correspondence — carefully reminding them how they'd met. She intentionally avoided any inkling of romance, but it wasn't beyond the realm of possibility that they would get really serious and marry. Of course, this highly conservative young lady wouldn't dream of getting engaged before Mother and Daddy formally gave their blessing to the match. Eleanor hadn't married yet, so the family had no precedent for the marrying process. Appropriate length of engagement and size and locale of wedding were all unknown.

Jack Graham and Betty Harbert were both subjects of the British Empire (as stated in their passports), born and raised in two colonies thousands of miles apart. Betty considered that it might be because Australia and Canada were both part of the New World that their cultures felt similar. She'd noticed that they pronounced some words quite differently, but that neither of them used the precise, clipped diction of the King's English. Each homeland's history was centuries shorter than Britain's. They shared King George V as monarch, yet both had been educated with the forward-thinking optimism common to younger civilizations.

During her time in England three years earlier and then last fall, Betty had noticed wide variation in ways of speaking. British people from different social backgrounds and classes used distinctive pronunciation. It reminded her of George Bernard Shaw's play *Pygmalion*, which she'd been lucky to see years before in Montreal.

Australia and Canada had class systems too, but Betty thought they were more subtle than those in England. Canada became a confederation in 1867, and Australia became independent in 1901 — *only thirty years ago!* Betty considered — so both societies were relatively young. Betty thought, *Career and social opportunities are surely not as restrictive as they are in set-in-its-ways Europe.*

While Betty was not particularly curious about Canadian politics, she remembered the fuss that was made in 1917 when women finally achieved the right to vote. Australian women had been granted it even earlier, in 1902. She was well aware of Australia's climate being much more temperate than what she had grown up with in eastern Canada.

Jack had never been to Canada; she had never been to Australia. Betty loved imagining different options and scenarios for their relationship as she fell asleep each night, but she tended to doze off too quickly to reach any reasonable conclusions.

(Letter continued)

We are leaving here tonight by train, having changed our plans a little. The original idea was to drive to Messina this afternoon, have dinner there and leave at 11 o'clock. But Addie suggested this as there is a train leaving here at 9.24 p.m. which would connect very nicely and save putting in the evening at the most unattractive hotel. It's very odd, but he really is terrified of Messina on account of the earthquake which happened 20 years ago. Yet he is a terribly devout Catholic (is forever going to Mass) and one might think he would have a little more faith. He isn't keen on being in Sicily at all and I know he will be only too glad to leave.

This afternoon we are going to drive out to see the most recent lava flow which is about two years old. We passed one place the other day where the lava had come to within about 25 ft. of the road. It is very dark grayish brown and stretches down into the valleys like great arms. It is astonishing to see how high the houses and villages are built on the sides of the mountain and how they are being rebuilt after being destroyed. I suppose the people living here never think of the possibility of destruction!

Very best love to you all,

Betty

Brufani & Palace Hotels,
Perugia
April 26, 1931

Dearest Mother,

I don't know if Aunt Barbie has told you that we are undecided between the S.S. Duchess of Bedford from Liverpool on the 19th or the S.S. Duchess of York from Southampton on the 22nd. Win is rather keen to see the Liverpool Cathedral, but on the other hand it would be very simple to go from Southampton. Just four weeks from today we'll probably be arriving in London, so you had better think of sending out letters to the Bank there soon after you get this.

We did enjoy our 24 hours in Assisi. It is such a quaint old town — full of atmosphere and of course, very dear to Catholics due to its associations. The Basilica is lovely containing some wonderful frescoes by Giotto and Cimabue, though unfortunately some are very nearly obliterated by time and moisture.

This morning we visited the Cathedral, the Church of St. Clare and the convent where St. Clare (the sister of St. Francis) founded the order of nuns called the Poor Clares. It's rather fun walking about a small town on a bright Sunday morning as the streets are crowded with young and old men gathered in groups. I suppose they are discussing crops, the weather and politics in the usual way of men the world over.

After lunch we took another peep at the Basilica and left at 3:30 p.m. to drive over here to Perugia — only a distance of ten miles. This hotel is perched up very high with the town sprawled out below. Directly in front are two big playing fields full of men and boys playing football. We had a very nice dinner, read awhile downstairs, and now are all busy writing. This hotel is fuller than any we have stayed in yet, and odd to say, not with Germans. There are some very nice-looking English and a few French.

XX Monday. All packed up and ready to leave for Siena which is only three hours away. There we will actually sleep three nights in the same beds! We spent a very interesting morning being shown the town by an excellent guide — an Italian, speaking almost perfect English — so cultured and well-educated. We saw two churches, the Cathedral, the town hall, and chapel of the Bankers' Guild — beautifully decorated with frescoes. In the town hall, a huge old 13th century building, there is a very good collection of work by Italian artists.

It has just started to rain so we will have a wet drive. However, we should not grumble as we have had very little bad weather. The hour of departure is here, so I must stop.

Best love,

Betty

Ever since her chat with Addie in Palermo about Brownshirts, Betty had been searching for an English newspaper. Both David and Addie had made it sound as though the Nazi Party was gaining considerable influence in Germany. She stopped at newsagents to browse whenever she had the chance. She wanted to find out more detail and was thrilled to discover a pile of *The Times* in a corner of the library at their Perugia hotel.

The issues were weeks old, of course, but she managed to locate an article about Brownshirts. She read about the Nazis combining terror tactics with conventional campaigning. Apparently, Hitler was criss-crossing the nation by air to give speeches, and SA troops paraded in the streets, beat up opponents, and broke up their meetings.

Once they returned to their room, Betty told Win what she'd been reading about. She added, "I need to convince Addie to take another private walk with me. What is Hitler hoping to do in Germany? None of this sounds very reassuring, especially how violent the Brownshirts are with anyone who opposes Hitler and the Nazi Party."

Win nodded in agreement, saying, "Betty, I'd like to come along when you talk to Addie. May I please?"

"By all means," Betty said.

Siena,
April 29th

Dearest Mother,

I was very surprised and pained today on looking in the back of my purse to find an unposted letter, but as it wasn't stamped, I decided to be Scotch — and open it up and add this note.

It will be really brief as it is 10:15 p.m. and I must do some packing and be ready for a 9:30 a.m. start tomorrow. These have been two very enjoyable days. Yesterday we did our duty nobly and "sight-saw" under the guidance of a very nice girl, reputed to be the best guide in the city. In the morning we saw the Cathedral, the Baptistery and a small museum. In the afternoon, we visited the town hall and a monastery just outside the city with some Della Robbias. I'm afraid some of my letters are awfully guide book-y, but it's really hard to be anything else. It's hopeless to try and give an adequate description of everything.

This Palazzo Ravizza is a charming place to stay. It is really a pensione or private hotel, with room for about 30 people. Just now it's about ¾ full. It must have once been a lovely home, with a big garden at the back. It belongs to an Italian family who lost their money and were very low, when an American woman appeared with enough capital to get started. Now they run it together and a very good combination they seem to make.

The lounge downstairs is most attractively furnished — exactly like a private home. We have two rooms with beamed ceilings, creamy walls, dark furniture and woodwork, and a leaded glass window opening over the lovely garden. As usual it is on a slope, so below the garden are two gorgeous en-tous-cas courts where we can see people playing tennis all day. Below them is a drill ground where the poor new recruits march, play games, and practice saluting from 6 a.m. on. This is the time of year when new recruits are taken on to begin their year's military service. Pretty raw and rough material some of them look, having been brought in from farms and small villages. The poor lads — some of them seem so hot and bewildered, though I suppose they will soon get used to it.

Today we just "lazed": breakfast in bed, up and out for a walk at 11. And this afternoon, reading, writing and another stroll. Aunt Barbie does get tired but is so keen and does not want to take time to rest. Then she is always so nervous and worried over things that "might" happen but never do. I think she takes a lot out of herself that way.

Best love,

Betty

Grand Hotel,
Florence
Monday, May 4th

Dearest Mother,

I intended writing the day after our arrival here, but somehow felt very lazy and not at all in a letter-writing frame of mind, consequently haven't written a line except the start of a note to Eleanor and the cards I sent with Aunt Barb's letter. She probably told you of our trip from Siena on Thursday but since then, as usual, our days have been pretty full.

Your little note from the Station was here when we arrived and your letter from the lake came Saturday a.m. So glad you and Daddy were able to go down, and I can imagine how you must have worked in your beloved garden. I was so sorry to hear about poor darling Binkie. Of course, I knew there was a possibility of renewed growths, but I hated to even think about it. Am so glad you sent him to Dr. Symes. He always seemed so gentle and nice. I know you must all miss Binkie so much and hate to think of coming home not be met by the little black pup. I wonder if it's really wise to have a dog. You get to love them so and they have to go so soon.

Learning news of Binkie's death felt like a punch in Betty's stomach. The Scottish terrier was the first dog her family had ever owned. He had joined the household on Betty's thirteenth birthday, so his sudden demise devastated her. The sturdy little black dog had been part of virtually every milestone during her teenage years and appeared in countless photos. As she hunted through her wallet for the photo of Binkie with Dick at the lake, she felt tears starting to stream down her cheeks. Betty was angry that she was so far away when her Binkie died. She didn't get the chance to say goodbye and have one last cuddle.

I don't even remember giving him a proper goodbye when I was leaving Marlowe Avenue to board the ship! Betty thought. *Perhaps he was sleeping in the sunny back garden on his favourite warm patch of concrete as I got into Aunt Barbie's Stutz.*

The grief that had overwhelmed her when her little sister, Mary, died came rushing back, accompanied by floods of tears. *It's ghastly to get over the death of a pet you love, so why set yourself up for pain? No more dogs for me*, she firmly decided. *I'll stick to loving people.*

(Letter continued)

I suppose Dick is in the midst of exams at McGill. I'm sure he'll do well and keep up his old Lower Canada College record.

Just two weeks from tomorrow we will be in Paris. Then we can really start to count the days until we sail! We won't make definite arrangements until London, of course, but can get the C.P.R. sailing list and pretty well make up our minds. Aunt Barbie says we can go June 19th, if that would get me home in time for Pittsie's wedding, but even that might be too late, and anyway, I mightn't be invited!

Today has been lovely. We left at 8:30 a.m., accompanied by our faithful Addie, and a guide who turned out to know very little and prove almost useless, and drove to Pisa. The road follows along the valley of the Arno most of the way, running through fertile fields and the usual grubby, though picturesque villages. It was a gloriously sunny day with blue sky and big billowy white clouds— much appreciated after a day and a half of rain. It was interesting to see people making hats as we passed through several villages. They are supplied with straw which they weave and braid into shapes, and then turn them into the factories. All the females seem to work, from quite little girls to old grandmothers — and they do it continually — while out walking, minding the baby, etc. Another industry is making the straw covers for wine bottles. We saw the girls leaving the central depot with little wagons full of bottles and straw and others arriving with their carts full of neatly covered bottles. It certainly seems a good system to have the work done in their homes in the country, instead of herding workers into a city factory.

Pisa was lovely — the beautiful Cathedral, the baptistery and of course, the famous tower. Win, Addie and I climbed up to the top. Such a queer feeling walking up as the slant is quite noticeable. We had lunch there, then came home through Lucca and Pratto, with an old hospital with wonderful frieze by Giovanni Della Robbia. There are five panels showing various charitable deeds, like nursing the sick, and such lovely blues, yellows and greens on a white ground. We didn't get in until after 6, quite a long day. Now we have had dinner and I'm writing this in bed — hence the scrawl.

Now to go back to Friday in Florence. We started off at 9:30 a.m. and went to the Uffizi Gallery and stayed until just time for a short wander through town and back to lunch. The stores are fascinating — pottery, leather goods, linen, and marvelous jewellery. After lunch we explored a bit more, spending quite a long while at an old church with some lovely cloisters and a rose garden. Then we repaired to a tearoom called "The Tabby Cat" kept by an American. We emerged, much refreshed by tea and a huge piece of gingerbread, hailed a taxi and drove up to an old church called San Miniato.

Betty was surprised to find out how useful her opera glasses could be beyond theatres and opera houses. She now made it a habit to carry them in her purse all the time. The views of Florence's cathedral and bell tower from San Miniato were spectacular when seen through her little device — not highly magnified, of course, but pleasingly focused.

Win turned to Betty as they wandered the grounds of the San Miniato basilica. "May I borrow your glasses, please?" she asked. "It's divine the way the setting sun reflects off all the buildings. The combination of red-tiled roofs and light-brown structures is just too much."

(Letter continued)

It's situated quite a distance above the city. The sun was just setting, shedding a lovely golden glow over the city, the river, and the hills beyond. On Saturday we prevailed upon Aunt Barbie to stay in and rest. Win and I "did" the Cathedral — a great bare, dark place — the baptistery, a small museum containing the two groups of singing angels by Della Robbia. Then, joined by Addie we walked past Danté's house to another small church, San Michele. After lunch it started to pour, so we taxied to the Pitti Palace and spent the afternoon looking at the pictures, furniture, and jewels there.

As the visit to the Pitti Palace was ending, Betty spied her chance to have further conversation with Addie about German politics. Aunt Barbie was safely out of the way, resting at the hotel, and Win had asked to be included in their serious conversation. The threesome headed across the street for refreshments.

After ordering tea in a little café, Betty said, "Addie, when we were in Perugia, I found a couple of articles about Hitler in an old newspaper and passed on information to Win. I read that he is flying around Germany giving speeches, while Brownshirts parade in the streets and beat up his opponents. We're both quite concerned. What is he wanting to make happen? Would you mind filling us in?"

"Happy to oblige, Miss Betty," said Addie as he stirred sugar into his tea. "The people at Cooks do a good job of keeping we guides informed. What I've heard is that Hitler's campaign appearances are carefully staged events. Hitler and his entourage always keep the audiences waiting, deliberately letting the tension increase. Finally, Brownshirts carrying golden banners enter, marching in a procession to military music. Then Hitler appears and the crowds shout 'Heil!'" Betty and Win looked confused. Addie clarified, "That means *hail.*"

Betty asked, "What happens next?"

"Next, Hitler begins his speech in low, hesitating tones," Addie continued, "then gradually raises the pitch. His voice explodes in a climax. He skillfully plays on the emotions of the audience as he brings the level of excitement higher and higher, and the crowd ends up adoring him as though he is a religious leader."

Win looked puzzled and asked, "That doesn't make a lot of sense. Religious leaders have a promising message, with God behind them. What does Hitler have that gets everyone so ecstatic?"

"That's just it. He promises an end to these hard times. In his policies, he offers something to everyone: work to the unemployed; an end of class distinctions to young students; and restoration of German glory. He promises order amid chaos. He says he will make Germany strong again; end payment of war reparations to the Allies; tear up the Treaty of Versailles; keep down Marxism; and deal harshly with the Jews."

At the end of this dissertation, Win and Betty sat wide-eyed and stunned. They didn't know how to react to all this unsettling information, so they just thanked Addie for his time and paid the bill.

After they left the café, the girls walked quietly together back to their hotel, and Addie strolled in the opposite direction.

(Letter continued)

Yesterday morning church at 11 a.m. at St. Mark's English church quite nearby. Aunt Barbie had heard it inclined on the high-Anglican side, but when we arrived we found it was Anglo-Catholic and full of candles and incense. Not that it hurt us, but it seemed so different, not as comfortable and satisfying as our own familiar service. It drizzled on and off all morning and poured most of the afternoon, so we couldn't go to the parade and 16th century football game. Rather disappointing as it would have been most interesting and amusing. Perhaps we could have picked up a few pointers to hand on to the McGill team!

The rain seems to have been pretty general and the river is tremendously high and muddy. There is a dam built across it directly in front of the hotel. The water tumbling down makes such a roar — really very soothing and conducive to sleep. I'm about ¾ asleep now as you may have guessed, so I must stop.

Best love,

Betty

Le grand hotel,
Venise
May 7

Dearest Mother,

Well, we've had our first ride in a gondola — or I should say "rides" as we came here from the station in one. Then, after unpacking and settling a bit, we went out again and chartered one for an hour, going slowly up the Grand Canal and ending up for tea on the square before St. Mark's. It really is fascinating but is the sort of place where good weather and sunshine are essential to one's enjoyment. We are hoping for the best, though they say it has rained here a lot lately.

I have not much more to relate about Florence since my letter Monday night as I stayed in all day Tuesday and Wednesday morning. It rained on and off both days and as I was feeling chilly and rather under the weather, I decided to be wise and take a rest. On Wednesday after lunch I sallied forth with Winnie to shop. Such wonderful stores! We wandered along looking into windows and making quite a few small purchases — chiefly pottery and leather things. We went into nine stores and actually bought some little thing in each — much to Addie's amazement when we told him. He apparently has had a great deal of experience with people who go shopping all day without buying anything.

Betty had actually first met Mr. Addison three years earlier when he'd been their guide during her first trip to Europe. In many ways, he felt like a trustworthy old friend. She wondered about what he did when he wasn't on duty.

"Win, do you think he has a wife and kids? What does he enjoy doing beyond hanging out with his cronies? I guess it would be rude to ask."

"When we told him we'd bought something in all nine stores we went into, I think he was absolutely thrilled," said Win. "It was rather touching to see how much he cared about our happiness. Maybe taking care of his clients, and going to church a lot, fills his life."

They sat on their beds to open their treasures. Among other things, Win had bought a small red leather handbag with a matching change purse and keyholder; Betty was pleased with two brown chicken-shaped pottery egg cups she'd bought for Eleanor and the black leather gloves she'd picked up for her father.

"I do hope they're large enough," she said. "I asked the shopkeeper to try them on because his hands are a similar size to Daddy's, and they fit well, so I think they'll be okay."

(Letter continued)

We left Florence at 8:15 a.m., had lunch en route, and arrived here at 2 p.m. This hotel is a rambling old place, full of little passages and steps up and down. It is quite large, having been converted from three old palaces on the Grand Canal. Our rooms are in the left-hand building and to reach them we go over the narrow canal across a little covered bridge. Aunt Barbie has a good-sized room, then the bathroom, and down two steps to our room. The bathroom is most amusing, with very old-fashioned fittings. They seem to have bought up a bargain lot of taps. In the basin one says "Kalt" (cold in German) and the other "Fredda" (cold in Italian), but on trying them we discovered the Kalt was really warm! The hotel seems to be fairly well filled — more Americans and English than there were in Florence. Old Addie is very thrilled because an old Englishman friend of his lives here all the time, so they are hobnobbing together.

Win was just saying tonight how nice it will be to see someone we know again. You know how reserved Aunt Barbie is and we haven't spoken to a soul other than taxi drivers, guides and hotel people since we left Paris! Oh yes, we spoke to Anne, Florence, and Margot Watts, one of the American girls whom we saw for about two minutes in Amalfi. We found a C.P.R. folder here tonight and have been looking up sailings. Still hovering between the 19th and the 23rd, but I think (and hope) it will be the former.

Did I tell you I heard from Jack Graham? He finishes his exams the end of May but is not going home until June so we will see him in London.

We were sorry not to find any letters here, but of course we shouldn't grumble as everyone is so good about writing and there may be a mail in tomorrow.

I am so sleepy I must stop and go up to bed. We were up at 6:30 a.m. though we were all packed except for pajamas and toothbrushes, had coffee and rolls brought to our room as usual, and our train did not leave until 8:15 a.m.! Really, I have never seen such a helpless sort of man as Addie. The idea of his piloting people about is so funny. He is so fussy and worried and needs someone to look after him! I'll write again soon with real "impressions of Venice."

Best love,

Betty

Thrills and more thrills! Betty was counting the days until she saw Jack in London but did her best to sound nonchalant about him with others. *With every letter he writes to me,* she thought, *the space he occupies in my heart grows.*

> Le grand hotel,
> Venise
> May 9

Dearest Mother,

Have just come to bed after twenty minutes of hanging out of the window watching the lights on the water and the shadowy shapes of the gondolas gliding up and down. It is a lovely starlit night and seems a crime to be meekly going to bed at 10:30! I do wish good old Dick was here to escort us about. It's such a bother being a girl on occasions like these. Of course, Aunt Barbie doesn't like going out and it's not much fun with Addie.

The unique city with watery canals instead of paved streets exuded romance. With a sigh, Betty observed the gondolas gliding silently along the canals, waves slapping gently against the wharfs, young couples sitting in gondolas with their arms touching, and relaxed patrons sipping wine at bistro tables beside the water. Betty wished Jack were there too. She knew that in a few weeks, they'd see each other in London, but thought, *Wouldn't we have a romantic time together here in Venice?* Knowing he'd never been to Venice, Betty did her best to describe its glorious atmosphere in the next letter she wrote to Jack.

> (Letter continued)

I was so glad to have your two letters of the 23rd and the 26th, which came in a nice big bunch yesterday. Too bad your lovely warm spell had broken, though it did sound too good to be true for April. So glad you and Daddy enjoyed your time at the lake. I suppose by now, or rather when this arrives, you will be there again. I'll send it to Montreal however, in case anything keeps you there, and if not, of course it will be sent on.

Now that the time to sail is drawing so close I am getting so impatient to get home. We've practically decided on the 19th, though Aunt Barbie seems rather worried about business affairs, having read tonight that the C.P.R. only paid half its dividend and she now talks of going even earlier than that. If we do go the 19th, we should arrive the 27th, so you might want to kill two birds with one stone. Meet us and attend Pittsie's wedding on the same trip.

This morning we woke to rain, as we did yesterday, though both days it cleared about 11 and we had sun and clouds the rest of the day. I always pictured Venice with sunshine and blue sky and water, so I am rather disappointed to find it far less vivid than my imagination painted it. However, we still have another day and a half, so I may change my opinion! After breakfast we wandered up to the Square of St. Mark's — a huge place lined with arcades and under them the most fascinating stores selling leather, beads, glass, and lace chiefly. Of course, they are all very "touristy" but really have some lovely things among piles of junk and are all surprisingly reasonable.

St. Mark's you know from pictures. It is rather ginger-bready but somehow it all fits into the setting beautifully. The interior is very much like a mosque with numerous domes, lined with gorgeous mosaics. Very dark, with lights suspended on chains here and there. We "did" it yesterday, but just went in again for a moment to see a special statue of the Virgin which is only on display on Saturdays. Talk about "idol-worship." The R.C. religion seems to come very close to it, with all the reverence for images and relics. Of course, Addie was very thrilled and insisted on Aunt Barbie going to see the Treasury, but Win and I came out and bought some corn to feed the pigeons. Then we strolled slowly back to the hotel, window-shopping all the way. It's fun feeding the pigeons. Simply hundreds of them are so tame they fly onto your head or shoulders and eat out of your hand. It's sweet to see the kiddies feeding them. We saw an adorable little two-year-old surrounded by birds and having his picture taken by a fond papa.

This afternoon we went to the Art Gallery: most paintings by Titian, Paul Veronese, Tintoretto, and Bellini. Good, I know, but I don't care for their style of painting — too fussy and flowing, though the portraits are wonderful. Then we took a gondola for an hour, ending up at the Square for tea. It is the thing to do. There must be over 3000 chairs set up on the pavement around the edges, belonging to different cafés or restaurants. Almost each one with a five or six-piece orchestra, each of course, playing different things. It's all right if you are near the centre of your particular café, but if you are near the edge, as we were today, you hear a delightful(?) combination of the two selections. The well-known place to go is called "Florians," established in 1720 and patronized by all sorts of famous people. We went there the first afternoon and again today, but after giving our order we were so sorry to see how few people were at the next place, equally nice, but lacking the name and reputation. Of course, people who don't know the difference naturally just follow the crowd. We are going to the next-door place tomorrow to try and give them some patronage — perhaps draw some customers with our charming? and distinguished? appearances!

In spite of the rain and cloud cover, Betty was absolutely enthralled with the unique beauty of Venice. She felt as though she were walking around on a stage or movie set much of the time. The absence of paved streets and motor cars meant that enjoying the water views and people-watching were the main attractions. The lack of motor traffic added a serenity she'd never felt in any other city. There were no honking horns.

Betty wore her floral yellow-and-white day dress with her white sweater to keep off the chill. She found riding in a gondola entirely mesmerizing. All gondoliers wore close-fitting, collarless knitted shirts with either red and white or blue and white wide horizontal stripes. They wore wide-brimmed straw hats, and some also had neckerchiefs in solid colours.

"Isn't it amazing the way the gondolier can move this huge weight with only a single — albeit enormous — paddle?" she whispered to Win during their ride. "He actually makes it look easy."

"I'm sure there's plenty of training required before they're allowed to take out passengers," Win replied. "Venice is such a popular tourist destination that a mishap causing a foreigner to get hurt or, God forbid, drown, would be a disaster!"

Whenever the gondola headed down a narrower side canal, Betty studied the non-touristy residential neighbourhoods. Tantalizing secondary canals were only wide enough to permit two small boats to safely pass each other. Sweet little stone footbridges, spaced about fifty yards apart, curved across the water to serve pedestrians. Occupants of small boats had to stay seated to avoid banging their heads as they passed underneath.

She noticed pedestrians laden with bags of fruit, vegetables, and crusty loaves she presumed were bought at markets just out of sight. *How I long to get out and walk around among ordinary Venetians!*

Their gondola glided past lovely wrought-iron gates protecting tiny gardens. Betty was enchanted by the greenery tucked inside. Ivy and vines spilled over old stone walls, softening their angular surfaces.

"Wouldn't Eleanor love to peer into these gardens?" she said to Win.

"Yes, your sister is such a keen gardener," Win commented. "I'll try to take a photo of one for her."

(Letter continued)

Yesterday we went out at 9:30 a.m. guided by a large, fat Italian, who told us he was a retired opera singer. We saw St. Mark's, then the Doges Palace next door — a wonderful building. We saw the room where the prisoners were tried by the dread Council of Ten. We then crossed the Bridge of Sighs and saw some of the prisons — not very terrible looking, though of course not very pleasant. In the afternoon we took a gondola again, with the guide, and saw two churches and ended up by visiting a place where they make glass, china, and beads, and saw them blowing glass.

Riding in a gondola is a most intriguing, and very comfy, though not awfully speedy, way of getting about. It is wonderful to see how well the men, and even quite small boys, can handle them. They are quite large as a rule, painted black with brass or nickel trim. There are neither horses nor motors in the city, so you can imagine the job it is to transport everything — supplies of all kinds, building materials, food, etc. — by boat. Of course, they are using quite a few power boats now. There is a regular service up and down the Grand Canal, of fair-sized steam launches, with regular stops, just like streetcars. The post is delivered by motor launch; the hospital has several, painted white with a red cross to use as ambulances; the police do their rounds two by two in a gondola; but the military officials have very snappy power boats. Wealthy people have motorboats with uniformed drivers instead of cars — mighty nice-looking some of them are too. Mostly the cabin kind, and not very speedy, I imagine. I have only seen one outboard. Rather a good thing as they would be too noisy for this quaint, old-world place, but I know what fun Dick would have dashing up and down the canals with his faithful Elto.

Tomorrow we are going to church in the morning, then after lunch, for a couple of hours trip by launch to the Lido and some of the other islands. We pack tomorrow night and leave about 11 on Monday.

I did not expect to finish this tonight but seem to have wandered on tremendously. Must stop and go to sleep.

Best love,

Betty

Hotel Pricipe & Savoia,
Milano
May 11th

Dearest Mother,

Well, here we are at the next stage of our journey, having left Venice at noon and arrived here rather dusty and tired at 4:45 p.m. We are just across the square from the station, so walked across accompanied by two porters laden with our bags, went up to our rooms for a wash and powder of our noses, then came outside to the garden for a refreshing cup of tea. We were sorry to not find any mail, but as we were relaxing we saw the postman arrive. We waited hopefully and pretty soon one of the bellhops came out with your letter of the 30th, and the letter containing the Junior League News Sheet. Thanks so much for sending it.

XX We had dinner, then sat in the lounge for a while listening to a good, but rather too loud and energetic, orchestra and are now all in bed. Win is fiendishly playing "Idiot's Delight" beside me. This is rather a nice hotel, though fairly noisy as it is in the centre of the city. It is supposed to be the best one here. It has quite a nice little space in front, surrounded by a high hedge, which shuts out the station and cars, and just across the road is a lovely park with beautifully smooth green lawns and lovely trees. The country we came through today is very flat — being the Lombardy plain which spreads out below the Alps. How good it is to see flat green fields and ordinary trees, much like Ontario or Quebec, as much as we enjoyed the cypresses and exotic Southern plants. Only another sign, I suppose, that we are all ready to go home. We came away with such a good impression of Venice, having had a lovely day yesterday.

XX Wednesday night: We put our lights out then and since I seem to have been so busy, I haven't finished this up.

Yesterday morning we started out at 10:15 a.m. having, with many arguments, prevailed upon Aunt Barbie to stay in bed an extra half hour, and made a bee line for the Art Gallery — a medium-sized one, containing chiefly Italian paintings. Afterwards we took a wander into the Cathedral — so cool and dark after the hot streets. Much as I have enjoyed seeing all the various types of churches (Roman, Byzantine, etc. in the South) there is something about real Gothic which certainly appeals to me. The Cathedral here is very large, beautifully proportioned, with two rows of pillars on either side. The roof is made of stone with such delicately carved tracery. There is a lift which we took to the roof of the nave, then Win and Addie climbed up the tower while I waited with Aunt Barbie. We had a very good view of the city and it was interesting to see the carving and statues of the Cathedral so close.

In the afternoon, Addie had planned to take us to two churches, but what do you think we did instead? We went to a tennis tournament to see the great Henri Cochet play! (He's ranked No.1 in the world.) It was really a very enjoyable afternoon. We taxied out to the Milan Tennis Club, a beautiful place with about 10 en-tout-cas courts and a snappy-looking club house. There we paid the large sum of 15 lira ($0.75) and saw first a game between an American girl and an Italian (the American won), then Cochet and quite a young Italian who was beaten 6-2, 6-4, 6-2, and finally a Frenchman and another Italian.

The occasion seems to be some sort of International Competition and a great many of the players are staying here. The great Cochet is actually in the room next to us! He certainly is a marvel — medium height, dark and slim, graceful, and his playing seems so effortless. At the end of the game he looked as cool and unruffled as at the start, while the poor Italian lad was crimson and so hot. He seemed very nice, quite young but a good player and a good loser.

The idea of running into Henri Cochet in the hallway outside their adjoining rooms enticed Betty. She said to Win, "Do you think it would be too obvious if I sat cross-legged in front of his door with a magazine, hoping he'll trip over me? Either coming or going. I won't care."

"Ha!" answered Win. "I read in the program that he won Wimbledon twice, in 1927 and 1929, and that he's married. So you're too late, dear cousin!"

(Letter continued)

Last night we were very rash. At 9:30 p.m. Addie, Aunt Barbie and I sallied forth to the Galleria, a cross-shaped arcade lined with stores and cafés. There we sat listening to the music and consuming ices until after eleven. Aren't we getting devilish?

This morning we got back on the job: "did" our two churches and a private house and painting collection. We walked home through a park and seeing part of the zoo. After lunch we went back to the same park, saw the animals, then sat on a bench and watched the adorable children and their nurses, a great many of whom seem to be from the provinces and still wear their attractive native costumes. It was just 4 o'clock and most of the kiddies were having their afternoon snack of biscuits and milk which their nurses produced from Thermos bottles.

These two days have been really hot. This evening we were quite comfy sitting outside without coats. We are hoping it stays warm while we are at the lakes. We leave here at 9 a.m. tomorrow. Como is just an hour's run, so we will stop to see the town and arrive at Menaggio in time for lunch. The man brought the car around this afternoon. It looks very big and comfy — a Fiat limousine. Eleven o'clock so I must stop. It will be just 5 p.m. at home, so I suppose Dick has finished his last exam and will be all set to make "Big Whoopee" tonight. Great to hear he is an authorized driver now. Just a month to wait and you'll have the good old Hupp on the job again. I do hope your Finnish maid turns out to be satisfactory. As you say, it would be nice to have someone who really could cook and could undertake more of the other work when necessary.

Best love,

Betty

Hotel Splendide
Lugano (Suisse)
Friday, May 15th

Dearest Mother,

Here we are back in Switzerland again, though sad to say, only for one night. We left Menaggio after lunch and took just about two hours to drive over, a beautiful drive as the road follows Lake Como almost halfway, then a short run across and up beside Lake Lugano. We crossed the frontier at a place called Chiussa — a very ordinary little town with a large and formidable-looking iron fence in the middle of the main street.

The Italians are fussier about letting you out of their country than the Swiss are in admitting you! We all had to get out of the car and go into the Italian customs and have our passports stamped. The Swiss merely looked at Addie's and the chauffeur's passports and admitted us "on our looks." Which, by the way, are getting decidedly dark these days. We are all getting gorgeous tans — especially Win.

We arrived at Menaggio about noon yesterday. It is quite a short distance from Milan, but we stopped for about an hour at Como to take a look at the Cathedral and the town and to let Addie go to mass. Menaggio is a beautiful place. Our hotel was right by the lake, with a gorgeous view of the snowy mountains on the other side. We were really lazy there — sat in the garden all afternoon doing tapestry, reading, and watching boats come and go. This morning, after breakfast outside, we repeated the process and took a short walk in the village.

We have only just arrived here so cannot say much about Lugano yet. The lake is fair-sized, long and narrow, with thickly wooded green sides, coming down quite sharply into the water. Lugano seems to be a mass of white hotels, with a road and promenade between them and the lake. We have two very comfy rooms, each with its own little balcony. As they face East, the balconies will be very pleasant for breakfast tomorrow. It seems such a shame to stay such a short while in each of these lovely places, but of course, it is better than not being here at all, and we don't want to stay away from home any longer.

We have definitely decided to go to The Park Lane Hotel, Piccadilly, where Aunt Barb and Miss A stayed. It is on Piccadilly opposite the Green Park, so fairly near the Stafford and the district that is familiar to us.

Now that their London hotel had been booked, Betty began to daydream about the fun she'd have in her favourite European capital. Jack had told her in a letter that he and his roommate Klaus quite often drove the sixty-five miles into London for a change of scene and break from the pressures of law school, and that he'd gotten to know the city fairly well. *How lucky Jack is to have his own sports car to zip around in*, she thought when hearing about these little getaways. Jack told her that whenever they went to London, they stayed with Klaus's brother, Johannes, who was training to be an accountant. Like Jack's family, Klaus and Johannes's family was German Australian.

Germany was now the "in" place for British aristocrats to send their daughters to finishing schools. Betty thought she wouldn't mind being sent to Germany for school and spending time with the men there. Most of the young German men Betty had met — unlike the older German tourists — were attractive, talented, and polite. She was slightly envious of the young British women who would no doubt end up with some of these charming men as their husbands.

(Letter continued)

XX Saturday: Sitting on top of the world. In other words, on top of a mountain 3000-odd feet high, with Lake Lugano and two other small lakes spread out below us and surrounded by a circle of snow-capped mountains. It is a gorgeous blue and white morning. We feel so lazy sitting here in the sun. This is a very get-at-able place, just 20 minutes ride in a very steady funicular railway, and a few minutes climb afterwards, brought us to this lovely spot. Last night between tea and dinner we took a walk through the town, with the usual stores full of carved ivory, embroidery, and photographs. Lugano is beautifully neat and clean. Even the streetcars are typically Swiss-looking—rather small and quiet and painted a shiny baby-blue and white.

XX Stressa. Sunday, 7:30 a.m. Inspiration failed me then, so now I'm sitting looking across a beautifully misty lake, listening to the numerous church bells, which sound lovely when muffled a bit by distance and water. I'm waiting for the others to wake up and have breakfast.

I'm afraid I'm getting very spoiled about having coffee every morning about ten minutes after I wake! As soon as we are all awake, we ring for breakfast. Then by the time we've had baths, done our hair, etc., it arrives so we eat in our dressing gowns and finish dressing afterwards.

It took us just three hours to drive over yesterday afternoon, coming around the top of the lake, through Locarno and back into Italy just a few miles later. Lake Lugano seems to be quite a bit higher than this one and separated from it by some small mountains. We climbed steadily for the first few miles, then came such a long way down a winding road into a broad valley, crossing the river which flows into Lake Maggiore.

It is rather too civilized here. The hotel is quite large, with almost everyone dressing for dinner in black tie. In front there is a lovely green lawn — very gay with flowers, striped canvas chairs and big sun umbrellas. Then there is a white iron fence, the road, a gravel walk, more grass with a row of palm trees, and the lake. We have certainly been most fortunate with regard to weather these last few days. It sprinkled a bit last night when we were out for some air before coming up to bed, and this morning it is rather undecided-looking — clouds, with quite light patches here and there.

Last night we actually had Addie playing bridge. He said he had only played twice, though he used to play a great deal of whist and was keen to learn. He seemed to have only a foggy notion of what to do, however we did most of the bidding and he got along quite well. Some days he really seems quite human and I like him, but again, he gets what I might call "an Irish fit" very much "agin the government" and makes all sorts of ridiculous statements.

By the way, when we were in Lugano we were playing ping-pong at the hotel, Win and I thought it would be an awfully good idea to get a set for the country. It would be great for playing on rainy days. I wonder if Dick would like to see about it, either in Newport, or from Sears Roebuck. I don't think a set would be very expensive (four bats, the net, and a couple of balls). Then between Dad, Dick and Edwards, a board might be made the correct size and marked, to be laid on the dining room table for playing. If Dick doesn't want to bother, leave it until we get home. It really is quite good fun and gives you a certain amount of exercise.

This hotel, though so modern and up to date, has the most amusing and antiquated collection of books in the library. We looked through them yesterday, discovering a large copy of "Good Works for 1873" and decided the most readable book was "Wild Wales" by Borrow.

Sad to say it has decided to rain — not very energetically — just a half-hearted sort of drizzle, which keeps people hoping it will clear. We were supposed to go out by launch to visit the three Borromean Islands but will probably wait until tomorrow.

I am down in the writing room now, surrounded by people "writing home." There are two Englishwomen at the desk next to mine. One has just said to the other, "If you do, Edith, I'll write to George and Mary." They are members of a large party, two big bus loads who arrived last night, and seem to be thoroughly enjoying and making the most of their "trip abroad."

My next letter will be from Paris. It is nice to think of seeing everyone again, and of course every day past is one day nearer home!

Very best love to you all,

Betty

After mentioning her return to Paris in her letter, Betty thought about David McKay. *I do so hope we'll see each other.* David's friendship had so brightened her life over the winter that she looked forward to having a meal with him again. Betty had written his telephone number in her address book and planned to give him a call as soon as she arrived at Hotel Majestic.

CHAPTER 7

Bags Closed and Locked and Only Our Hats to Put On

Hotel Majestic
Avenue Kléber
Place de l'Etoile, Paris
May 21st

Dearest Mother,

I'm sitting down in the lounge surrounded by a babble of conversation in French, English, and American, so this may be a more-or-less wandering epistle. It's really rather nice to be back here again, and of course, all seems very familiar in spite of the fact that the trees are all in full leaf — so fresh and green and they were just budding when we left in March.

The trip up from Stressa was uneventful, after leaving there in the pouring rain at 6:40 p.m. Monday night. We were not sorry to leave as we had two solid days of rain. The only time we left the hotel during the whole time was to go to church at 11 a.m. Sunday. Such a dear little stucco building and nice service though very poorly attended. It was, in fact, the last day of services as the clergyman announced they were forced to close due to lack of support. Of course, there is no resident congregation, and with so few English and American travelling these days they are naturally affected.

This hotel is really full, strange to say — the first full hotel we've encountered. There are quite a few Americans here, and two lots of Indians; a man and his wife who sat next to us at dinner tonight speaking perfect English, and another couple with two sons. One of the women is really beautiful and they dress wonderfully. All European clothes, except for a heavily embroidered scarf over their heads.

We had a busy day Tuesday, starting out soon after breakfast for the Bank, and to choose a hat for Aunt Barbie, a dress for Win, then to the Bank again for letters. In the afternoon, more shopping, and to the hairdresser's. Yesterday we continued our shopping in the morning, then the others stayed in while I went out to see Madame Ravel, then to Le Gui.

I only found Monsieur at home. Mlle. Jeanne, Henriette, and all the girls were away on a five-day motor trip to visit the chateaux de la Loire and Madame was out. The girls will be back Friday night and we are going out to tea on Saturday, so we will see them all. I conversed with Monsieur for a while, then got a taxi and came back with our two trunks and Win's valise which we had stored in the trunk room.

The garden looked lovely. Such a change from all the bare, black branches we saw all winter. There are several horse-chestnut trees, one of them full of lovely pink blossoms. Everyone had told us how lovely Paris is in May, but we seem to be rather unlucky and have had three dull, cold days. We are planning to go to the Exhibition Coloniale tomorrow, so are hoping for some sunshine.

Today we had Madame Ravel to lunch. After she left, I went out to a modiste that she told me about and ordered a new hat. I only took one with me on the trip and having worn it every day for two months, in rain, dust and sun, it is naturally pretty nearly done for.

XX Friday: We have had a most gorgeous time today, going by Metro to the Exhibition at 11 a.m. and returning rather tired at 6 p.m. The weather was ideal, not too warm, sunny, with an intensely blue sky — a perfect background for the buildings and exhibits. It is a huge affair, spread over acres of the Bois de Vincennes, and contains far too much to hope to see in one day.

It is divided into four general sections; administrative offices (housed in the most gorgeous modernistic buildings), French colonies (Maroc, Tunisie, Martinique, Indo Chine, etc.), foreign countries (Belgium,

U.S.A., Holland, Portugal, Denmark), and amusements (all the usual things concentrated on two islands in the lake in the centre). Oh, I forgot the zoo — small but so well-arranged. All the animals, including the lions, are right in the open, on raised places. Their houses are made of artificial, though very natural-looking, rock. They are separated from the public only by deep ditches with straight sides, wide enough to prevent jumping across. There were three sad looking giraffes, five elephants, and dozens of monkeys climbing up and down a big rocky arrangement like the one in the London Zoo.

Each of the colonies has a building with the exports of each displayed inside. There are several native villages with people living there and carrying on their usual trades of weaving, pottery, etc. It must be rather hard on them to be transplanted to a strange land and be expected to "act naturally" under the gaze of so many curious eyes. They seem to feel the cold greatly, and their picturesque-ness was sometimes marred by rather incongruous additions of knitted caps and sweaters.

We had lunch at an African restaurant, served by black waiters, but we did not indulge in African eats! Then we had tea in a sunny spot beside the lake. The grounds were very well laid out and most attractively lighted with ultra-modern lights. They say it is well worth going out at night to see the illuminations and fireworks, but of course we won't be able to go.

A month from tonight we should be midway across the ocean! Thrills and heart throb!

Best love,

Betty

Thrills and heart throb, indeed. Finally, being less than four hundred miles away from Jack in Cambridge, Betty was beside herself with anticipation. They had kept up their written correspondence with snowballing devotion. Occasionally when missing him, she imagined the trials that loving couples must have endured during the war. Not only were the soldier and sweetheart miles apart, the real possibility of his being wounded or killed in battle must have been excruciating.

Upon opening every envelope addressed to her, a soldier's beloved might have been thinking, "Is this the final letter I'll receive from him?" The only struggle her dear Jack was facing was his final exams. He gave the impression of being incredibly smart, so he'd no doubt breeze through with flying colours. This was his final year studying law; after his studies, he would have to start articling and eventually take his bar exams.

How lucky we are to know the exact time of our next date: 1:30 p.m. on Friday, June 5! We'll be together two weeks from today, she thought happily.

> Hotel Majestic
> Avenue Kléber
> Place de l'Etoile, Paris
> May 24th

Dearest Mother,

Just an hour before we leave for the station and we are all set, bags closed and locked and only our hats to put on. It is a perfectly lovely day and is going to be quite hot, I think, so we will leave Paris with a good impression after all. I'm really surprised to find how nice it is to be back. Sometimes last fall and winter, I felt as if I never wanted to see Paris again!

We had another fairly busy day yesterday. First an interview with the woman who has made our lingerie. She came here to bring one more slip Aunt Barbie had ordered, and of course brought a whole lot of other things to show us. Then we went down to the bank to close out my account and get some English money, which really feels quite solid after this flimsy French stuff. Then Win and I stopped to try our hats — mine is a brown, coarse, shiny straw, and hers a blue one she was having made over. They were not quite ready, so we walked around the block onto the Champs Elysées and had orangeades at a small table on the sidewalk, under a gay red umbrella. See how Parisian we have become!

In the afternoon, we went down to see Sainte Chapelle, Notre Dame, and another dear old wee church nearby. It was our first visit to S.C., as we'd always put off going hoping for a sunny day. It was certainly worth the wait. The glass does look so wonderful with the bright light outside. It was fearfully hot so we taxied home, cooled off a bit, and then went out to tea with Madame. It felt rather odd to ring the bell and be shown into the drawing room so formally. It was awfully nice to see everyone again.

Best love,

Betty

Betty was on the brink of changing her lodgings — moving cities (Paris to Montreal), countries (France to Canada), and continents (Europe to North America). Sitting in Le Gui's formal drawing room again brought up memories of her previous seven months — rushing off to lessons, dancing at parties, and going out with handsome men.

Betty reflected on how far she'd come since she left Montreal. *I was certainly very naïve last October when we first got here. I believed whatever I was told and went along with whatever was expected of me*, she thought as she waited for madame. *Talk about meek! I was completely spoiled and taken care of. How odd for a woman of twenty-four.*

Her private chat with Addie in Sicily had had a lasting effect. She now made a point of looking beyond facts as they were first presented to her. She realized, for example, that naturally all the people working in these expensive hotels and serving in these fancy restaurants were kind and helpful to them. They were angling for a good big tip, which Aunt Barbie always provided.

She forced herself to think critically and cautiously about Jack. *Is he really as perfect as he seems?* she wondered. She had no third-party opinions about his character. No one could vouch for his integrity. Roommate Klaus was the only associate of his she'd met, and that was only briefly at Christmastime. The two men both loved to drink and tease, sometimes to excess. *Trying to find out what Klaus thinks of Jack's moral fibre would be like trying to catch a firefly in a bottle*, Betty surmised.

Madame de Broin, Betty, and Win returned to Le Gui after going for tea. Mademoiselle Jeanne, the eldest daughter who ran the school, had heard they were briefly back in Paris, and she was waiting to bid them *au revoir*. Betty was delighted when Jeanne suggested the two of them take a private stroll around the neighbourhood. Win returned to the hotel.

It wasn't long before the topic of Mr. Jack Graham came up. It was the first time Jeanne had learned of his existence, so Betty summarized what had happened since their meeting at Christmas. The fact that Jeanne's English was very limited meant that the two spoke only in French. Betty was so pleased that she was able to hold a conversation in French about something as nuanced as romance and she rarely had to search for a word in her second language. When she couldn't make a direct English-to-French equivalence, she had no trouble finding alternative ways to get her meaning across.

"My problem is, Jeanne, that neither my parents nor my siblings have even met this man. Jack is really smart, good-looking, athletic, and charming, but how genuine are his motives?" She touched Jeanne's arm and looked her companion straight in the eye. "How do I know he's being honest with me? Maybe he's not even really studying at Cambridge. These are the questions that Ted and Eleanor would be asking if they were here. How I wish they were! In letters I've only described him as a platonic friend. Maybe it was a mistake to hide from them how crazy I've become about this man."

Jeanne motioned to a park bench where they could sit for this heart-to-heart conversation. "Does the fact that he's half-German matter to you?" she asked after they were seated.

"My feelings about the German people swing back and forth like a pendulum," Betty replied. "Positive attributes, like excellent manners, high intelligence, efficiency, and handsome physical appearance, all sit on one side; negative attributes, like military organization, sense of superiority, judgmentalism, and ruthlessness, are on the other. Jack is only half-German. He's said nothing about wanting to live in the *Vaterland*. It's his brother, Hans, who has embraced Deutschland, not Anglophile Jack."

Jeanne said, "Well, I recommend that you hold on to this uncertain feeling and proceed with caution — that's what your brother and sister would tell you to do. When you see Jack on English soil in a matter of days, let yourself be excited and happy but try to stay a little bit reserved. If you can, listen to his compliments and observe your interactions from a distance. Pretend your brother is sitting in the corner of the pub evaluating Jack. He's writing you a report!" They laughed at the image.

As the two women later hugged goodbye, Betty's heart overflowed with gratitude, and as she got into her taxi, she wept a little, finding it hard to believe she might never see her dear friend again.

Park Lane Hotel
Piccadilly
London, W.1
Monday, May 25th

Dearest Mother,

Such a lovely sunny morning and Win and I have just come in from our first ramble around London! We arrived at 7 o'clock last night, are comfily settled in this very nice hotel, and are so thrilled to be back after our nine months in "furrin parts." It sounds so queer to hear the taxi-men, police, etc. talking English and we still feel the urge to break out into French occasionally.

We were very lucky in having such a good day for travelling. It was quite rough coming across, but so lovely with the blue sky and water, fluffy white clouds, and shiny whitecaps. We came by the "Golden Arrow" — a quick and luxurious train on either side, and a good-sized boat, "The Canterbury" for the crossing. It seemed to be a long trip as we arrived at the station over an hour before train time, and by the time we started, felt as if we had been up for hours! Poor Aunt Barbie is so nervous and worried — strange when she has travelled so much.

We have accumulated several more pieces of luggage so have 11 in all: three large trunks, a small one, four suitcases, and three small bags! I went in one taxi with five large pieces, and Aunt Barbie and Win followed with the rest. It is really very easy. The porters just take the big things to be registered and then put the small ones in your carriage. It is terrible how they hold you up for tips. If you don't tip the man who weighs and registers your trunks, he is quite capable of letting them miss the train. Travelling by sleeper is exorbitantly expensive as you have to tip your porter 10% of the cost of your ticket, which means about $2 each, instead of the 25 or 50 cents we give at home.

This is really a lovely hotel and comparatively quiet. We are on the 7th floor, facing Piccadilly, but at the bend of the court. The hotel is U-shaped like this [sketch of floor plan], so our rooms are pie-shaped, very attractively decorated in cream and blue. This morning Aunt Barbie stayed in bed while we walked along to Regent Street, then cut across to the Marble Arch, and home along the Parks. Of course, being Whit-Monday everything is closed and the streets almost deserted. It is wonderful having two such fine days, as so many people are away for the weekend.

I wonder what sort of a May 24th you have had. We saw in the paper that a heavy rain had stopped the Davis Cup games in Montreal on the 23rd, but perhaps it did not continue. We are just going out to lunch and may see a movie this afternoon. It seems a shame on such a day, but Aunt Barbie says Kew, Richmond, etc. would be too crowded.

Best love,

Betty

Park Lane Hotel
Piccadilly
London, W.1
Tuesday, May 26th

Dearest Daddy,

Was so glad, on going to the Bank this morning, to find your letter of the 13th and Mum's note waiting for me. I was rather surprised to see you were still at Marlowe Ave as we have been picturing you at the Lake for the last couple of weeks. Our weather is continuing to be remarkably fine — really quite warm. Of course, one hears so much about excessive rain here. Perhaps it is risky even to mention the sunshine in case it changes.

This morning Addie came around to discuss some business with Aunt Barbie, then walked with us as far as Cooks. From there we went to the Bank and the C.P.R. office where we engaged cabins on the Duchess of Bedford; sailing from Liverpool on June 19th about 3:30, touching Belfast and Glasgow, and due to arrive Montreal on Saturday, the 27th. I trust you will see that the Montreal authorities will prepare a suitable welcome for the return of the distinguished travellers. We'll expect the Mayor and a band — at the very least! We still have not quite decided when I am going to Aunt Mary's.

After the C.P.R. we had lunch at a little Scotch restaurant on the Haymarket, and now are back at the hotel waiting for Addie to come and take us down to the temple. The poor man is rather at loose ends — says business at Cooks is frightfully slack and he has no definite prospects. Tonight we are going to the Drury Lane Theatre to see a musical show. Yesterday afternoon we saw a movie. Our first in over two months — George Arliss in "The Millionaire" — very good.

I'm hurrying to post this to go on the Empress of Britain on her maiden voyage. We saw pictures of her yesterday and she certainly looks like a marvellous boat.

I must run.

Very best love from your respectful and affectionate daughter

Betty

Park Lane Hotel
Piccadilly
London, W.1
May 30

Dearest Mother,

Another beautifully sunny morning! Win and Aunt B are looking at maps and discussing our doings for the day. I am sitting by the window watching Piccadilly and listening to the strains of music from the military band in the Park. Since my letter to Daddy on Tuesday, which should be nearly there if it went by the Empress, we have done a great many interesting things.

First theatres: Tuesday afternoon to see "Autumn Crocus" at the Lyric, a very clever play, the scene laid in the Austrian Tyrol; Thursday p.m. to the Garrick to see a farce "My Wife's Family," ridiculously amusing. Though not very well acted, seemed more like an awfully good amateur company than professionals. Yesterday afternoon it was raining so we went to see Charlie Chaplin in "City Sights." You may have seen it. We liked it very well, though it actually seems odd not to hear the talkies. There was a good English film, too, the story by John Galsworthy. Tonight we are going to a musical play, "Stand Up and Sing," very highly recommended. Our other two nights were employed by going to see Dr. & Mrs. Armstrong (Miss A's parents) who are staying nearby, and last night by writing letters and going to bed early!

Wednesday we went out to Richmond on a bus, had lunch, and walked up to the terrace to see the view. Then took another bus to Kew and Oh! The flowers are wonderful, masses and masses of rhododendrons and azaleas. We walked around the Queen's cottage to see the bluebells — lovely, though really almost over now. We must have seen 15 or 20 artists — both sexes and all ages — sitting about painting them. Some of their attempts were rather pathetic, though one elderly man had a good-sized water colour nearly finished, which was really splendid.

We sat for a long while and watched the ducks and geese by the pond. Two big brown geese with a family of five fluffy yellow babies were being fed breadcrusts and seemed so tame. About 4:30 p.m. we left the gardens and started to walk down the street beside the common — perhaps you remember it — lined with tea rooms, each with a very shabby old waiter outside touting for business. We allowed ourselves to be persuaded to enter, not by the old lad's eloquence, but by the glimpse of a very attractive garden running right down to the river. There we sat at ease in big canvas chairs and imbibed tea, bread and butter, and plum cake at a shilling each!

Since January, Betty had been determined to hide her feelings for Jack from Win, by reading his letters in private, then hiding them. They'd been sharing bedrooms since last August, and there were very few secrets between them. Win showed little interest in boys, never making any positive comments about anyone they'd met during their travels. Of course, Betty didn't talk about romance either. The age gap meant there was a huge discrepancy in sensitivities and experiences in that area.

Sitting in two enormous canvas chairs, the girls tucked into their tea alone in the garden. Win asked Betty point blank, "How do you feel about seeing Jack again?" Betty was caught off guard, blushed a little, and busied herself applying butter to her bread. "You really like him a lot, don't you?" Win continued. "Your eyes sparkle whenever you talk about having met him in Wengen or tell people about his coming all the way to Paris just to take you out to dinner. In fact," she speculated, "I'd say you're falling in love with this Aussie. The minute you see each other in person, you will dissolve into a puddle."

Betty continued blushing and looking away, but relief washed over her. Keeping up the pretense of Jack's friendship being platonic had been exhausting, so she relaxed, smiled broadly, and leaned over to give Win a long hug, pressing her cheek against her cousin's.

Then Betty grinned and said, "Please keep our romance from your mum and the others. Even Mother and Daddy have no idea." Win raised her eyebrows, disbelieving. "Unless they've been reading between the lines of my letters," Betty laughed, "which I imagine they have been pretty accurately."

"Your secret is safe with me, Bet. I won't say a word until you give me the go-ahead." Win's eyes twinkled in genuine delight for her lovely cousin. "I think he's gorgeous! You are one lucky girl — or should I say, lady."

(Letter continued)

Thursday we went downtown again, had lunch at Fuller's, then to the Academy. Some very good portraits and statuary. Much less of the ultramodern and futurist schools than usual. We came home in time to change for tea as we had invited Mr. and Mrs. McArthur who, however, had gone to their country house and did not get Aunt Barbie's letter in time.

Your letters sound as if dear "Aunt Helen" was rather a strenuous visitor — rather a job to entertain her and keep house at the same time. I do hope "Hilda" is a success. It would be a relief to have someone who can cook and put on meals without so much supervision and assistance.

I really must stop. We are hoping to go to Oxford on Tuesday so will probably write that night.

Very best love as always,

Betty

Park Lane Hotel
Piccadilly
London, W.1
Tuesday, June 2nd

Dearest Mother,

We didn't go to Oxford today after all as Win developed quite a nasty cold and was feeling rather miserable yesterday, so we'll go tomorrow instead. This morning Aunt Barbie stayed in bed for a rest and we went out to do some shopping but came home without accomplishing much.

Poor Win is a most unsatisfactory person. She doesn't like cheap shops, and yet is too "Scotch" to pay for the kind of things she wants. So, we walk in, look around, and out again! In spite of the fact that I say we've been "shopping" in almost every letter, we really haven't bought much. I am going to try and get a morning alone and see what I can do.

Sunday was lovely, sunny with a cool breeze. Aunt B and I went to the Abbey in the morning, taking a taxi down, then walking home through the Parks, simply crowded with people. We had lunch here, then went down to the National Gallery and walked home again. In Green Park a band concert was just starting, so we paid two pence halfpenny each and sat and listened for about half an hour. Yesterday we didn't do much but had Mrs. McArthur and Billy Ford to tea. Billy is still with the C.P.R., stays in Birmingham from Tues to Friday and comes down here for the end of the week. He happened to see our names in the Gazette so phoned us up. He seems just the same as ever — a little but stouter I think. I had asked Freda to come too but she didn't turn up. She phoned this a.m. to say she had moved so did not get my letter in time. She is in "digs" as they say, with a friend in St. Johns Wood.

I heard from Aunt Mary this a.m. and the 8th is quite convenient for her. Aunt B has practically decided to leave that day for a six days bus trip in Devon & Cornwall — getting back on Saturday.

Win's head cold had started on Sunday, so she spent the day in bed. As Betty and Aunt Barbie toured the National Gallery, Betty suggested they not spend much time looking at the Dutch, Flemish, and Spanish painters. They had visited this same gallery during the 1927 tour.

"I must admit I can't see any beauty in a great many of them," Betty told her aunt as they perused the gallery map. "Let's find the Turners, Gainsboroughs, and Romneys," she suggested. "Just follow me."

The two lingered to look at a gorgeous painting by John Constable of a stag standing in a bit of autumn woods. Betty was mesmerized by the piece, which was being illuminated by a shaft of sunlight coming through the gallery skylight. The light added a haunting and dazzling effect. For a long while, Betty stood transfixed, still as a statue.

Betty's aunt interrupted, "Can we head back now, please? I've just about had it with looking at galleries."

"Okay." But Betty was feeling resentful at being torn away from her moment with the painting and annoyed that her visit to the famous National Gallery was being cut short because her aunt was bored. *I'm so glad the trip is almost finished*, Betty thought.

(Letter continued)

This afternoon we are going to tea at the United Services Club with Mr. Archibald, tomorrow Oxford with Addie, Thursday St. Paul's in the a.m. and lunch with cousins Clive and Archie at "The Chesire Cheese," then to the Military Tournament at Olympia. Oh yes, and tonight to see "The Good Companions." So, you see we have lots to do. It's awfully hard to keep Aunt Barbie from overdoing it. She still insists on keeping on the go too much until she is absolutely worn out, and then we prevail upon her to take a morning off.

Very best love,

Betty

Only 17 days more — whoopee!!

Park Lane Hotel
Piccadilly
London, W.1
Thursday, 4th

Dearest Mother,

We have just come in from a very enjoyable afternoon spent at the Royal Military Tournament at Olympia — an awfully good display of riding and physical drill. We had tea at a little shop nearby. Very small and crowded, but with the most scrummy scones and cake — tasted more "homemade" than anything we've had for a long while. By the time we had finished the crowd had departed, so we took a bus as far as Kensington Gardens, got out by the Albert Memorial and walked through Hyde Park and along beside the Serpentine. It is certainly wonderful having these huge parks in the middle of this big city and the people do appreciate them and use them all the time. There were heaps of people boating and swimming, and others, with kiddies and dogs playing about.

This morning we walked across the Park, then past Buckingham Palace, and down Victoria Street to the Army and Navy store where we did some shopping. Then taxied to lunch with cousins at the "Chesire Cheese."

We had a lovely day at Oxford yesterday. We took the bus (2 ½ hours and so comfy and clean) — much nicer than the train. It's no wonder the buses are cutting into the railroads so heavily. We went there and back for seven shillings each and the train fare is 16 — third class! Of course, old Addie was in his element. We stopped first at the hotel for coffee, saw the gardens at St. John College, then took a taxi to New College — Addie's alma mater. After lunch we got another car and drove to Worcester, Merton, Ariel, Christ Church, Corpus Christi, Magdalen, and Wadham. In most colleges we just looked at the gardens with a peep into the chapel and Great Hall. But at Magdalen, we went down into the kitchen, a huge old place still used for preparing meals for about 350 boys (or men, I should say). We had tea and then took the 7 o'clock bus back, having dinner at 9:45 p.m. We were so lucky in having such a beautifully sunny day.

While viewing Christ Church college, Betty remembered that David McKay had studied there, but she decided not to share that information with her cousin or aunt. She had called him recently when she'd returned to Paris. His response to hearing her voice was one of pleasant surprise, with only muted enthusiasm. He didn't suggest getting together, saying that he was frightfully busy at the office. As she described her upcoming visit to England, he asked when she was sailing back to Montreal. Disappointed to sense that their friendship was evaporating, Betty recited only superficial details.

"Well, you have my mailing address," he said. "Let's keep in touch." She rang off, feeling let down and realizing she had to just let him go.

(Letter continued)

Of course, the Derby has been the subject of conversation the last few days. I felt like you did — it seemed a shame to be so near and not to go. I think you and I should come over here together. Wouldn't we have a great time?

Tuesday night we saw the "The Good Companions" — very well done. It was arranged in two parts with light scenes in each, with just about half a minute between them. One scene just on the front of the stage with a drop, while they arranged the next scene behind. I do hope it comes to Montreal next winter as I'm sure you and Daddy would enjoy it.

Tomorrow I am going out to Knightsbridge to buy a dress — something yellow I think, as I have nothing at all for warm weather on the boat. Then at 1:30 p.m. I'm going out with Jack Graham. He phoned me this morning, just back from writing his finals at Cambridge. He still has his car so we are going somewhere in the country — probably Henley or somewhere on the river. He suggested going for lunch, but I felt I really must shop in the morning, as we will be away most of Saturday at Burgh Heath.

There is a mail chute just outside the door, so I must get Win to take this out — as I am in my pajamas.

Best love,

Betty

It was finally June 5, 1931 — a day Betty had circled on her calendar weeks ago. As she finished breakfast, she realized her fingers were trembling a little. She had gotten her hair freshly styled at the hotel salon, and her nails were newly manicured with pale-pink nail polish. She planned to wear her blue-and-white flowered silk dress that afternoon, unless she found something more exciting during her morning shopping trip in Kensington.

Thankfully, Win was off doing something else so she could get ready without a dithering spectator. Returning from her very light lunch — she was too nervous to eat anything substantial —Betty brushed her teeth, donned the silk dress, and touched up her lipstick. Her Italian suntan was lasting so well that she didn't need any rouge or face powder.

The concierge telephoned at 1:23 p.m. — with every minute from 12:45 p.m. onward feeling excruciating — to announce, "Mr. Graham has arrived, madam, and is waiting for you in the lobby."

Betty carried a white scarf and a light sweater. *My heart is pounding*, she thought as she headed downstairs. *I might pass out!*

The elevator doors opened, and there he stood. Her handsome date wore a tan suit, white shirt, and dark-green tie, and in his left hand, he held a straw boater trimmed with Cambridge ribbon. He grinned and walked over to kiss her on both cheeks in the French style, followed by a quick hug. Betty noticed that his sandy-brown hair had been lightened a little by the summer sun. She didn't manage to say a single thing.

Jack led her out to the curb where his car was parked. *The Park Lane doorman is probably used to patrons owning such magnificent vehicles*, Betty thought, *so I suppose it makes sense he opened my door without saying "Nice car!"*

The vehicle was a 1929 Morris Cowley two-seater sports car with its convertible top folded down. As Jack settled into the driver's seat, he gently slipped his left hand onto her hair and leaned in to kiss her on the lips. This gesture was so smooth that she felt like an actress in a movie. In perfect gentlemanly style, he pulled away after just the right amount of time. It was hardly the right place for lengthy smooching.

She was pleased that she'd brought a scarf to keep her hair in place as they drove. The route took them through London to Marlow, Buckinghamshire, where he pulled into the car park at a picturesque pub beside the water.

The couple sat at a garden table under an enormous umbrella. The striking pair were served tea, scones with clotted cream and strawberry jam, and a lemon cake. Following the English habit, Betty "played Mother" and poured the tea for them both.

Just like the last time they were together in Paris, conversation was effortless. But now they were familiar with all kinds of intimate details about each other, having corresponded so regularly.

I can't stop staring, she thought. Nervous thoughts spun through her head while Jack talked: *I wonder if he's disappointed now that he's seeing me in the flesh. He knows so much about me after all those letters. Did I share too much? Focus on the conversation, Betty. Can he see me blushing? My God, he's handsome. How is he so calm about everything?*

It was sunny when they had first left the Park Lane, but at about 3:00 p.m. it began to pour, and by the time they had finished their high tea, the sky cleared. Betty declared, "Good heavens! Now the sun has come out again."

"This is just typically changeable English weather," said Jack. "There's a saying in England: If you don't like the weather, just wait five minutes."

Betty laughed, then asked, "Why do you think it's like that?"

"Oh, I don't know." Jack said. "It seems to me that it has something to do with the land mass of the British Isles. It is a relatively small place, and weather fronts just kind of scoot across it."

During the whole afternoon, she tried to notice the dynamics of the conversation, which wasn't easy as she was also trying to *participate* in the conversation. Thoughts whirled through her mind: *Is he being domineering and monopolizing what we talk about? Does he ask me about me and the people in my circle — my recent travel, Win, Aunt Barbie, or plans for the summer in Canada? Does he listen intently and follow up my answers? Does he care about people outside his social class? Is he a snob?*

All this analysis took incredible focus, but she was determined to stay in control. *It's so difficult to be objective the way Jeanne suggested,* she thought.

Jack did seem to be rather self-centred and a bit snobbish, and the fact that he ordered champagne to accompany the tea was mildly disconcerting. *Why do we need alcohol?* she wondered. But having anticipated this date for months, she tried to let that thought dissolve. *He really is so magnetic and charming.* But when she pretended wise sister Eleanor was sitting next to her, she found herself thinking, *He's a little too quick to flatter me — almost smarmy. He's used to getting his own way, I imagine. I wonder how he responds to confrontation.*

It rained again all the way back to London. Jack said, "I've managed to get us tickets to *The Barretts of Wimpole Street*. Would you like to go this evening? I'm sorry it's such short notice. I would pick you up at seven."

"That would be lovely! I'll just need a few minutes to change into something else." They held hands whenever he was not shifting gears.

She'd want her opera glasses to get a better look at the actors' faces onstage. She was glad she stored them permanently in her black evening bag so she'd never leave them behind when she went out in the evenings.

Park Lane Hotel
Piccadilly
London, W.1
June 7 10:30 p.m.

Dearest Mother,

We have just come up from listening to a really delightful program of music played by the hotel orchestra. They play every afternoon and evening and are really awfully good. Tonight the concert was being broadcast by the BBC, so they had a singer too. He sang several old English songs, then "Mary of Argyll" as one of his encores. A great many outsiders came in to listen, so the lounge was quite full. We have all been very lazy today. To begin with, we were pretty tired and overslept, so were too late to get to church. About 11:30 a.m. it started to rain and drizzled on and off the rest of the day. After tea we armed ourselves with umbrellas and went for an hour's walk in Hyde Park, quite full of people in spite of the weather.

Yesterday was gloriously sunny and so enjoyable. In the morning Aunt Barbie and I went out across the park and on the Mall saw the procession en route to the Trooping of the Colour. We saw the Queen, Duchess of York, Prince George, and Princess Elizabeth in one carriage and Princess Mary and her two cute little boys in another. The King, Prince of Wales, and Duke of York rode at the head of the soldiers. It was certainly a gorgeous sight with all the gay uniforms and the beautifully shiny horses. Then there was a huge mob so we did not attempt to see anything more, but went on to the Bank, then up to Bond Street where I got an adorable sports suit (dress and short coat) and beret in yellow and white. Really quite swish!

At 3 o'clock we left from Charing Cross Station and at 3:50 p.m. arrived at Burgh Heath where we were met by Mr. Archibald, and his daughter and dog. After tea he took us for a drive in his Baby Austin — it is such a lovely part of the country, so green and fresh. We had supper at 7 p.m. and talked and listened to the radio until 10:30 p.m. when we left to catch a train home. We were late getting to bed, so Aunt Barbie was still awake when the earthquake happened at 1:30 a.m. I was only half asleep, and though I felt the bed rock, I never thought it might be an earthquake. Thought it was merely imagination. It was apparently quite severe in the North, but of course you will have read all about it before you get this.

On Friday morning I went out to Kensington to shop, had a bite of lunch, and came back to change. At 1:30 p.m. Jack Graham arrived with his car — a bright yellow Morris-Cowley — quite small, but fast and comfy. We drove through Slough and Henley to Marlow where we had tea at "The Compleat Angler," a quaint old place right on the river. It was sunny when we left, but about 3 p.m. it started to pour, so we had to hurry out to put the car's top up. It cleared while we were having tea but rained again all the way home. Jack just came back on Wednesday from writing his law finals at Cambridge. He is going home to Australia, leaving the day after we do and flying as far as Kenya for the first leg of the journey.

That evening Jack took me to see "The Barretts of Wimpole Street" — so interesting and awfully well done. It portrays old Mr. Barrett, Elizabeth's father, as a perfect old beast. Everyone in the audience feels like getting up and doing something drastic to him.

I will probably only be writing once or twice more. I can hardly believe I will be seeing you all so soon. But when you've looked forward to a thing for so long, it's almost impossible to realize it has come.

Best love,

Betty

Their time together, before parting to return to Australia and Canada, was barely a fortnight, so Betty and Jack wanted to make the most of it. It took discreet wrangling for Betty to get away from Win and Aunt Barbie without being rude. Jack suggested a drive to the Surrey countryside, and Betty poured on the charm when explaining this plan to the others. She was proud to realize she'd finally mastered ignoring Aunt Barbie's famous look of disdain.

Two days after taking Betty to the play, Jack again appeared at the Park Lane in his yellow sports car. He drove on the A3 toward Woking, Surrey, took the Wisley exit, and then parked at the famous Royal Horticultural Society Wisley Garden. Before strolling among the magnificent flower beds and avenues of trees, Betty replaced the scarf tied over her dark hair with a wide-brimmed straw hat to protect her from the hot June sun.

"Stop!" Jack insisted. "I want to soak you in, Miss Elisabeth Harbert." He gazed at her and smiled. "You look stunning!" Betty blushed. She had worn a sweet pink sundress and sandals, with a string of pearls.

They slowly wandered hand in hand through the gardens. At lunchtime, Jack opened the boot of his car and produced a wicker picnic hamper. Its inside was lined with red-and-white-checked material. Glasses and white china plates were held in place by leather straps, and containers of sandwiches, plump strawberries, and petit fours were packed next to a thermos of cold water and a bottle of chilled white wine.

"How absolutely lovely!" Betty exclaimed. "Where on earth did you get this?" Jack didn't reveal his source, but Betty thought, *I bet it's from Harrods, everything there is such high quality*. He busied himself by spreading a plaid picnic blanket in the shade under an enormous oak tree, then pouring them drinks.

They ate while semi-reclining next to the hamper — sometimes lying down flat on their backs to stare up at the few cumulus clouds overhead. Newly mown grass nearby smelled of summer and the buzzing of bumblebees was the only sound. Betty wished they could stay there forever, enveloped by the effect of the wine and the peaceful surroundings.

Before heading back into the hectic centre of London, she convinced Jack to take another stroll through the early summer blooms. Her favourite peonies bent over under the weight of their enormous pink and burgundy blooms. They paused to watch black ants scramble over unopened buds.

Back at the car, Jack opened the boot to put in the picnic hamper. Betty noticed a folded newspaper lying inside. It was titled *Völkischer Beobachter*. She picked it up to examine it. Her German was not good enough to glean anything from the paper, so she dropped it back into the boot.

"You like reading German newspapers?" Betty asked. "Where do you get them?"

"Yes, I buy a copy every weekend from a London newsagent. It's the best way to find out what's happening in Germany these days."

"And what is happening in Germany these days?"

"Apparently Hitler has been giving confidential, in-depth interviews to journalists, and I want to keep tabs on him and the Nazi Party," he replied as he opened the car door for her. "Do you mind if we leave the convertible top folded down heading back?"

Thanks to the wind whistling past their ears as they drove to London, Betty couldn't have asked Jack anything even if she'd wanted to. She felt the knot of dismay in her stomach again. It seemed to hit her every time the topic of Hitler's Nazi Party came up.

Park Lane Hotel
Piccadilly
London, W.1
June 14th

Dearest Mother,

This will be a very hurried note as we are going out early, but I want to send it by the Empress as otherwise it might not arrive before we do.

I came back last night from Emsworth, after really a lovely visit with gorgeous weather the last few days. I wrote on Saturday a.m., I think.

That afternoon I went with Aunt Mary over to Warblington by bus, where we looked at and tidied up the graves. Then bussed back to Shadingfield to tea, tennis & talk, until 8 o'clock. The whole family and especially the boys seem much more "knowable" this time. Edward is rather a "stick" though not as shy as he was, but I liked the other three very much. Bob is so much like Dick it isn't even funny! When he was playing tennis, one could have sworn it was Dick about two years ago.

Sunday was really quite hot. Aunt Mary decided I was to visit Miss Green, i.e. Mrs. Parsons. So we went in and paid a call. She seems just the same — fatter if possible — and well settled in her snug little home. I did not meet Mr. Parsons but saw numerous photos. I don't know which would be the worst — to marry an old man for a home or to look after an old lady or old ladies all your life for one. The marrying seems pretty awful but I suppose she will inherit something at the end!

As our ship sails in only five days, I will simply say how very fortunate I have been to have spent all this time abroad. However, I've reached the end of my inquisitiveness and feel inclined to settle in one place and put down roots. Observing others' way of life has its appeal, but I'm impatient to get on with enjoying my own life.

See you very soon!

Best love,

Betty

On the evening of June 15, Jack picked Betty up at the Park Lane. The elevator doors opened to the lobby, and Betty stepped out wearing her dark-green dinner dress with silver art deco brooch.

"My, you look stunning as always," Jack said as he kissed her on both cheeks. "How do you do it?" She smiled and took his arm. Betty carried her black brolly on the other arm, ready for the inevitable weather change.

They walked to the Savoy Hotel where they enjoyed a sumptuous three-course dinner featuring roast chicken, which Betty loved because it reminded her of home. Betty drank only one small glass of wine but noticed that Jack drank the rest of the bottle. Just as they finished eating, Klaus and his brother, Johannes, arrived at their table. They were accompanied by a fashionable petite blond woman, who seemed to be Klaus's date.

"Betty, I'd like you to meet my girlfriend, Sarah Lewis." The two girls shook hands. "And this is our terrific, long-suffering host and my long-suffering brother, Johannes Fischer."

Smiling at Johannes, Betty said, "I'm delighted we finally meet, Johannes. Jack often says how much he enjoys staying in your flat. Tell me, does he ever make his bed, or is he a complete slob?" They all laughed.

To include the girls, the three men spoke English to each other, instead of German. The group ordered coffee and brandies and sat around trading stories and summer plans. Johannes peppered Betty with questions about Canada and followed every answer with another query.

Then Johannes suggested that everyone head to his nearby flat for a nightcap. Betty enjoyed the ten-minute walk to Johannes's famous London digs, strolling with Jack behind the others and holding hands. Traffic bustled by noisily, with plenty of honking horns. Headlights reflected off the wet asphalt, nearly blinding them as they prepared to cross a busy street.

When they reached Johannes's well-kept building, the gang climbed the two flights of stairs to his flat. Johannes unlocked the front door and stepped aside saying, "Ladies first." Betty and Sarah laughed and walked through.

Betty's smile quickly faded. Facing her on the wall just inside the front door hung a large framed photograph of Adolf Hitler in military uniform.

She watched in horror as each man entered the hallway, raised his straightened right arm, clicked his heels, and declared, "Heil Hitler!" to the photo. It seemed to be a type of greeting or homage. Betty detected no hint of laughter or fun in this deadly serious gesture. She felt nauseous. Sarah didn't seem bothered at all. *I suppose she's seen them do this plenty of times*, thought Betty. *But is she okay with this?*

Jack took Betty by the arm and offered her a tour of the flat, clearly unaware of her state of shock. In the living room, Betty noticed several more framed photos of Hitler; in these, he was making speeches to large gatherings. A flag about two feet by three feet was pinned on the wall in a place of honour. It was red with a white circle in the centre. A black hooked cross, what Betty had learned was called a *swastika*, sat prominently in the circle. Copies of *Mein Kampf* (volumes one and two) sat conspicuously — *Like the Bible*, Betty thought — on a table below the flag.

Johannes poured generous glasses of whiskey for everyone, but Betty asked for ice water instead. As the five young people sat around the dining table for about half an hour, the men lapsed into German for most of the conversation. The girls sat beside each other to chat more easily, and it turned out that Sarah was a secretary at Jesus College at the University of Cambridge, which is where she'd met Klaus.

Jack was clearly excited about some new development or demonstration Klaus and Johannes were describing and seemed to forget Betty was there. Although she tried to fully engage with Sarah, Betty was mortified to witness Jack's dark transformation. She longed to be safely back at the hotel, tucked up in her bed, and away from this ugliness.

"Jack, I'm really exhausted. Could you please take me back to the hotel now?" she interjected when there was a slight pause in the friends' conversation.

"Of course, darling." They bid the others goodbye and headed to the street. Walking on the outside of the sidewalk the way a true gentleman does, Jack Graham affectionately rested his arm across Betty Harbert's shoulders.

Overwhelmed with distress, she stopped walking and broke off all physical contact. "Jack, what's your honest opinion of Adolf Hitler? You've never actually told me," she said, her heart pounding.

"I think he's a brilliant man who will do great things for Germany," he answered directly. "Hitler will turn the German economy around when he takes power. The country has really suffered by having to pay so much money to other countries after the Great War. The Nazis surprised everyone by winning so many seats in the last election, so he'll soon be in charge."

Remembering what David McKay had told her about Hitler's writings, she asked, "Have you ever read *Mein Kampf*?"

"Yeah, I finished reading the second volume last autumn. Before I met you and became consumed with writing you long love letters," he teased, "I actually had time to read about things other than the practice of law."

"What do you think of Hitler's views about Jews?"

Jack said, "He's absolutely right. Disease can't be controlled unless you destroy the germs that cause it, and in Germany, Jews are like germs. They take all the best jobs, hoard their money, cheat people, and their influence must be stopped. One of the reasons Germany lost the war is because Jews refused to fight alongside their countrymen. They're parasites sucking up blood and making society sick."

"What should happen to them then?"

"They should be imprisoned or executed. Then Germany will be purified and able to reach its full potential." Jack's eyes glistened with fervour at this remark.

"Well then, it turns out the charming, athletic, handsome Australian I've been falling for is actually a bloodthirsty member of the so-called master race!" Betty's voice trembled. "My closest friend in Montreal is Jewish, and the fact that you think she should be exterminated makes me sick!" she yelled at him. "You're mesmerized by that ruthless bastard." She was shocked to hear herself use that word.

Her raised voice attracted the attention of passersby. Jack looked embarrassed, but he managed to retort, "There are plenty of well-educated people in high places who agree with me on this. As someone who's never studied political science or economics, you are in no position to judge me."

As though flipping a switch, he suddenly lowered his voice. "Betty darling, please just calm down," he said, raising his hand to gently stroke her hair. "Let's not ruin our precious time together by arguing."

Stepping farther away from him, she shook her head. "No, Jack. Learning about the real you has completely erased my affection for you." Betty crossed her arms across her chest. "Please just flag me a taxi."

As the black London taxicab pulled in at the curb, Jack leaned in to kiss her goodnight. She presented only her cheek to his lips, produced a fake smile, and spat out, "Thanks for a lovely dinner. Goodnight, Jack." She watched him through the car's back window. His cold, menacing expression cemented her resolve. *How could I have been so taken in by him?*

Once she was back in her hotel bed, she tossed and turned all night long. This man whom she had thought was too good to be true *was* too good to be true. *Did he hide his Nazi sympathies on purpose, or is this all my fault? Why didn't I dig deeper and ask him more about his politics weeks ago?* During all this travel, she'd heard over and over again about the havoc Germany had caused. *I should have known, since Jack is half-German. But then again, so is Win and she's not sympathetic to Nazism. Even still, why didn't I check to find out his political outlook?* Betty's old habit of just taking things at face value had let her down.

"How could I be so naïve!" she cried aloud in the dark, hoping Win wasn't awake enough to hear. She looked over at Win's bed. Her cousin slept soundly.

Finally, Betty joined her in dreamland, drifting off just before dawn.

Right after waking in the morning, Betty decided that Jack was a chameleon. *I daydreamed about marrying him, but it's clear we are poles apart,* she realized. *Maybe he'll join his brother, Hans, in Munich and work for Hitler, the rising star.*

After Betty and Win ate their breakfast from room-service trays, the telephone rang. Win answered, then turned to Betty. "It's Jack calling for you."

Betty said, "Please tell him I refuse to ever talk to him again. Our relationship is over, permanently." Win passed on the message in a neutral voice and quickly hung up.

Win then turned back to her cousin. "Betty, what happened?" she asked.

Betty explained the horrible saluting-Hitler scene in Johannes's flat. Win was mortified.

"I know how much you loved him, but you've done absolutely the right thing by ending it. Do you think he hid his politics on purpose? Or did he somehow think you agree with Nazism too?"

"Hard to say. We spent so little real time together, just brief meetings in Wengen, Paris, and here. In restaurants and pubs, there is no reason to talk about how Jews should be treated, and his political leanings didn't show up in any of his letters. Why should they have?"

The next day, Jack called again when Betty was out for a walk. Win recounted their exchange; "I just said to him, 'You're wasting your time. Betty will never speak to you again,' and slammed down the receiver dramatically. It felt really good!" Betty noticed a glint in her cousin's eyes and giggled at Win's glee.

She knew it would take time for her to forget the dashing Jack Graham with his handsome smile and hearty laugh. She had such high hopes for their future, and now she had to return home with no letters or visits to look forward to. No future dates. Just life as usual. Betty felt deflated.

On June 19, the cousins packed up their bags for the last time and took a taxi to the train station. Betty was distracted on the way to Liverpool. She quietly looked out the train window and relived her final date with Jack. *Oh well*, she sighed. *Now I have no one to miss, I suppose.* They arrived in Liverpool and stepped onto the beautiful SS *Duchess of Bedford*. Their European tour was officially over.

Once they'd all waved goodbye to the crowd on the Liverpool wharf, Betty began to mingle with other homeward-bound passengers, who were interspersed with people immigrating to Canada. The ship was about the same age and size as the SS *Duchess of York* she'd sailed over on and it felt almost familiar. But Betty felt different. She was still keen to play deck tennis and dress formally for dinner, but somehow the frivolity of youth had lost its appeal.

During her travels and studies in Europe, she'd witnessed beauty and decay, kindness and cruelty, sunshine and driving rain, luxury and poverty. She'd even felt an earthquake. Now her priorities had changed. She wanted to be more than just a passive observer, a social — *ignorant* — butterfly.

She was asking herself all sorts of questions: *What matters to me? What can I accept in other people and what must I walk away from? How can I make a positive contribution to the world? Should I concentrate on family, or should I start a career?* The soul-searching went on and on, as she sat on a deck chair mesmerized by ocean waves breaking over one another. Naturally, her aborted romance with Jack flashed through her mind too. She knew that her heart would take time to fully heal.

Betty even began writing notes to herself — something she'd never done before — using a blank exercise book for the purpose. She hoped that rereading them would help her figure out what is essential in life and what should be avoided. She fondly recalled Addie's wise words: "We all need to pay attention, Miss Betty."

During these contemplative moments, it occurred to Betty that, until very recently, her view of life had been constricted — rather like peering through her funny little Swiss opera glasses. *People, experiences, and opportunities are complicated. Never again will I jump to conclusions like that.*

Walking into the dining room on her second evening at sea, Betty headed toward their assigned table to join Aunt Barbie and Win. She wore her floor-length pale-blue silk dress, its narrow skirt flared with a few pleats. As she raised her water glass to her lips, she glanced across the room to survey the rest of the cabin-class passengers. Her gaze suddenly focused on a man a few tables over. Twenty-five feet away from her sat the handsome David McKay. He was watching her with a broad smile on his face.

She immediately excused herself from the others and walked over to him. Delighted to see her friend again, she cried, "What on earth are you doing here?" in a high-pitched squeal. He stood up to give her a brief but warm hug. "I'm heading to Montreal to start a new job," he said. "May I have the pleasure of buying you a drink after dinner? We could meet in the Starlight Bar." Waiters were beginning to serve the meal, so she couldn't linger.

"Absolutely! That would be fantastic. I'll meet you there at nine o'clock. Can't wait!" Betty blushed with joy as she returned to her table. After Win noticed where David was seated, she gave him a little wave hello.

After dinner, the two friends sat in a corner of the lounge getting caught up with what they'd been up to since having dinner together three months ago. As well as describing the itinerary on the continent, she gave a brief overview of her relationship with Jack. David described the process he'd had to endure in order to be transferred to the British Consulate in Montreal. His new job would start on July 2. She was curious why he'd decided to make this leap across the ocean, but she purposely avoided asking him, not wanting to jinx anything by putting him on the spot.

Their drinks in the Starlight Bar were followed by dancing, which led to a stroll, walking arm in arm, around the top deck. When David led her into an alcove behind a large lifeboat stored on the deck, Betty was caught off guard. He kissed her lips with a gentleness she'd never known before, and her body softly fell into his. *Isn't this a pleasant surprise*, she thought. *Please don't ever let go.*

A few days later, the new couple relaxed on adjacent deck chairs watching the horizon as they sipped lemonade. Betty summoned her courage and said, "David, I don't understand why you took so long to kiss me. In Paris I had decided that you were either secretly engaged or homosexual. Why were you so distant with me? We had such a romantic dinner together on Avenue Mozart, and then nothing."

"Oh dear," David laughed. "Betty, I fell for you the day we met, but I was petrified of scaring you off. You are such a remarkable woman that I'm sure all kinds of men have mauled you or been too forward right off the bat. I was determined to not be dismissed like those blokes." His comments made her feel genuinely cherished. She leaned over for another kiss.

Later, while basking in the afternoon sun, Betty contemplated her new life back in Montreal. In terms of social doings, she expected that she and David would spend masses of time together and he'd get to know her family and social circle. Having never been to Canada, he had lots to learn about its culture and geography.

The British consulate general had rented him a furnished apartment on Sherbrooke Street, but Betty wanted to help him get acclimatized without being overly accommodating — she knew that his fluency in French and his charming personality would simplify his getting settled. At that moment, she had no idea how deeply he cared about her. His feelings would become clearer as they became fully acquainted.

Wanting to eventually marry and have children, she was aware that rushing the process could lead to disaster. Personal independence was now essential to Betty, and she wanted time to develop her own opinions and lifestyle. She was happy that she could have David by her side in this process, believing that healthy relationships give each person space to breathe and grow.

Betty was keen to get a worthwhile job that paid a salary. *Now that I'm able to speak and write French pretty well,* she wrote in her journal, *I could easily apply for a teaching job, or at the very least, tutor private school pupils who need extra help. September is three months away. I must ask Eleanor what she thinks I should do next.*

Betty's heart began to pound at the first glimpse of Canadian soil, on the north side of the St. Lawrence River.

Author's Note

It was summer 2001, and the time had come to put our family home on the market. My father, P. Roy Wilson, had died on June 11 that year. My mother, Elisabeth Harbert Wilson, had died nine years earlier.

In 1951, Dad had designed and built our house in Beaconsfield, Quebec. He lived there until the last day of his life. The attic of any home continuously occupied for fifty years by a single family is bound to contain masses of holiday decorations, mementoes, packaging — "in case we have to return it" — old books and magazines and items that "might come in handy someday"— but somehow that day never came, or it came and went but the item remained in the attic, forgotten. Our attic was no different and it had to be emptied.

The day after Dad's funeral, my son Stephen went rummaging around in the attic and came across a cardboard box filled with a pile of handwritten letters. This label was on the top:

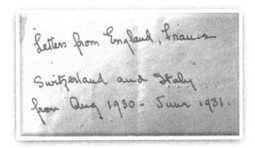

Being a responsible daughter and then sole executor, I was preoccupied with setting up an estate sale, distributing items to beneficiaries, and beginning the lengthy process of settling Dad's estate. Not surprisingly, when an architect and artist lives to be 101, he leaves plenty of detritus behind.

I only learned of the existence of Betty's letters once I'd returned to my Toronto home, and Stephen brought them over. To demonstrate the richness of his find, he read aloud an excerpt from September 3, 1930. Betty's ship is arriving in Liverpool:

The sun went down just like a ball of fire slipping into the water and leaving such a gorgeous pink glow which lasted until dark. There were numerous other boats coming and going from two big liners which steamed past us and dropped over the edge of the world, to several small freighters and fussy, smoky little tugs, puffing about. Then the big gulls soaring and darting about us — such strong graceful things — all rosy in the sunlight. Then, as it grew darker, though the pink still lingered in the sky, we could see the silver path of the moon on the water, first few tiny lights blinking and winking on the shore and then finally the lights of Liverpool itself, dominated by the city hall with its illuminated clock tower, whose chimes pealed out nine just as we bumped the dock.

I was hooked. My mother had written a total of seventy-eight letters between August 1930 and June 1931, and her family members had carefully saved them and presented them to her when she got home. With regard to her early life in Paris, Betty had previously told me only about the de Broins using napkin rings as place cards at Le Gui, never saying a word about any letters.

My childhood was spent in suburban Beaconsfield, and I can attest that during the 1950s and 1960s, it was no cultural hub. Any trips to art galleries, concerts, or theatrical and operatic performances required a twenty-mile drive into the centre of Montreal, so they occurred only once in a blue moon. What a stark contrast to young Betty's fancy-free life in Europe.

Imagine! My mother used to take her Swiss opera glasses in her clutch to performances in Paris and London. I remember these opera glasses from my childhood, when I loved playing with them. They're smooth and weighty to the touch and live in a little leather case. I treasure them, as Betty did, despite their inefficiency. And although they are currently in my care, I know that, like a piece of heirloom jewellery, they will continue to be passed down through the generations.

The performance skills Betty acquired in Paris served her well. After returning to Montreal, she landed acting roles in amateur productions. In fact, as she made her February 1932 entrance onstage in George Bernard Shaw's *Augustus Does His Bit*, a young architect in the audience fell for her. It was love at first sight, and my parents were engaged five months later.

As a wife and mother, Betty's only acting and singing performances were church based: writing and directing the annual Christmas pageant, singing in the choir, writing and acting in skits for a church variety show.

In 1980, at the age of seventy-four, Betty began showing signs of cognitive decline and was institutionalized with Alzheimer's disease from 1986 until her death in 1992. Anyone who has witnessed the toll taken by Alzheimer's can relate to my feeling of gradually losing the mother I adored. It was like watching her on a river, seated alone in a canoe without a paddle while a strong wind blew her just out of my reach, then farther and farther along the current, and finally down into the rapids. She was mute for her final two years.

The minute I began reading the letters she had written at the age of twenty-four, my heart skipped with excitement. I soon typed them up and shared this treasure with family members. Learning about her youthful travels, feelings, studies, friendships, talents, and romances brought her alive to me. I had no idea she'd ever smoked cigarettes or dated an Australian!

It was Stephen who recently encouraged me to find a way to make these letters public. Writing the fictionalized narrative has brought me pure joy. In attempting to view 1930s Europe from her perspective, I have met my mother anew.

Pat Butler
Toronto, Ontario
October 2021

Acknowledgements

Several years after finding the letters, my eldest son, Stephen Butler, came up with the concept of this book. He suggested, "Why not add a story to pull all the letters together?" And so, in January 2020 I began serious writing while on a month's holiday in New Zealand.

Thank you to Stephen for the spark that ignited this project, and thank you to my youngest son, Jeffrey Butler, for your hearty encouragement throughout. Both my sons have also shared the original letters with their children, who have been happy to get to know their great-grandmother in this small window of time. Thank you to all my family for helping me keep up the momentum of this project. It has meant a lot to me.

Thanks to my beta readers: Nancy Gillespie, Jennifer Harker, Juli Morrow, Rouvé Ritson, Sandy Russel, John Shaw, Susan Shaw, and Rae Tucker. Your willingness to read my manuscript — in most cases, twice — and give me frank feedback was invaluable.

Thanks to Meghan Behse at Iguana Books, who transformed my manuscript into this beautiful book. Thanks especially to my editor, Holly Warren, for your wisdom, gentle coaching, and attention to detail.

Thanks to my husband, Eric Hillmer, for scanning photographs, carefully listening to draft passages, and applauding my efforts.

Thanks to my darling Mum for having written such vivid, compelling letters in the first place.

Betty, Mother, Ted, Daddy, Eleanor & Dick
in Vermont in 1922

Elisabeth Harbert in 1927 (Betty, age 21)

Ted, Betty, Eleanor, Daddy, Mother & Dick
in Vermont in 1925

Winifred Munderloh in 1933 (Win, age 20)

Le Gui, 38 rue de l'Yvette, Paris 16e

Mrs. Henry Munderloh in 1933 (Aunt Barbie, age 60)

Win & Betty (on right) skiing in Wengen, Switzerland, 1930

Catching the train to Kleine Scheidegg (Win on far right)

Admiring the view from Kleine Scheidegg
(Win second from left, Aunt Barbie in dark coat)

Win & Betty viewing the Swiss Alps

Betty with family Hupmobile in Vermont, 1931

Family Tree

Omits seven other Martin children.

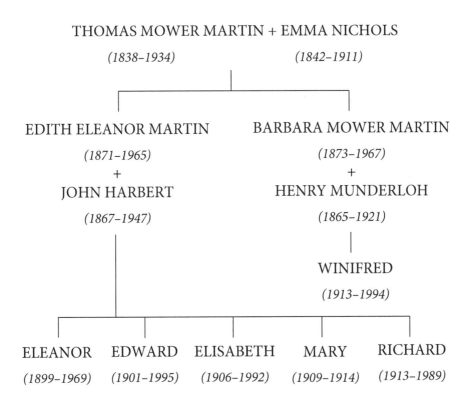

THOMAS MOWER MARTIN + EMMA NICHOLS

(1838–1934)   *(1842–1911)*

EDITH ELEANOR MARTIN   BARBARA MOWER MARTIN

(1871–1965)   *(1873–1967)*

+   +

JOHN HARBERT   HENRY MUNDERLOH

(1867–1947)   *(1865–1921)*

WINIFRED

(1913–1994)

ELEANOR   EDWARD   ELISABETH   MARY   RICHARD

(1899–1969)   *(1901–1995)*   *(1906–1992)*   *(1909–1914)*   *(1913–1989)*

Map of Betty's Travels

The numbers indicate the order in which she visited.